Growth Management
and Affordable Housing

JAMES A. JOHNSON METRO SERIES

JAMES A. JOHNSON
METRO SERIES

The Center on Urban and Metropolitan Policy at the Brookings Institution is integrating research and practical experience into a policy agenda for cities and metropolitan areas. By bringing fresh analyses and policy ideas to the public debate, the center hopes to inform key decisionmakers and civic leaders in ways that will spur meaningful change in our nation's communities.

As part of this effort, the Center on Urban and Metropolitan Policy has established the James A. Johnson Metro Series to introduce new perspectives and policy thinking on current issues and attempt to lay the foundation for longer-term policy reforms. The series examines traditional urban issues, such as neighborhood assets and central city competitiveness, as well as larger metropolitan concerns, such as regional growth, development, and employment patterns. The James A. Johnson Metro Series consists of concise studies and collections of essays designed to appeal to a broad audience. While these studies are formally reviewed, some are not verified like other research publications. As with all publications, the judgments, conclusions, and recommendations presented in the studies are solely those of the authors and should not be attributed to the trustees, officers, or other staff members of the Institution.

Also available in this series:

Edgeless Cities: Exploring the Elusive Metropolis
Robert E. Lang

Evaluating Gun Policy: Effects on Crime and Violence
Jens Ludwig and Philip J. Cook, editors

Growth and Convergence in Metropolitan America
Janet Rothenberg Pack

Laws of the Landscape: How Policies Shape Cities in Europe and America
Pietro S. Nivola

Low-Income Homeownership: Examining the Unexamined Goal
Nicolas P. Retsinas and Eric S. Belsky, editors

Redefining Urban and Suburban America: Evidence from Census 2000
Bruce Katz and Robert E. Lang, editors

Reflections on Regionalism
Bruce J. Katz, editor

Savings for the Poor: The Hidden Benefits of Electronic Banking
Michael A. Stegman

Still Stuck in Traffic: Coping with Peak-Hour Traffic Congestion
Anthony Downs

Growth Management and Affordable Housing

Do They Conflict?

Anthony Downs

Editor

BROOKINGS INSTITUTION PRESS
Washington, D.C.

Copyright © 2004
THE BROOKINGS INSTITUTION
1775 Massachusetts Avenue, N.W., Washington, D.C. 20036
www.brookings.edu

Library of Congress Cataloging-in-Publication Data
Growth management and affordable housing : do they conflict? /
Anthony Downs, editor.
    p.   cm.
Includes bibliographical references and index.
ISBN 0-8157-1932-9 (cloth : alk. paper) —
ISBN 0-8157-1933-7 (pbk. : alk. paper)
1. City planning.   2. Housing.   I. Downs, Anthony.   II. Title.
HT166.G74 2004
307.1'216—dc22   2004004191

9 8 7 6 5 4 3 2 1

The paper used in this publication meets minimum requirements of the
American National Standard for Information Sciences—Permanence of Paper
for Printed Library Materials: ANSI Z39.48-1992.

Typeset in Adobe Garamond

Composition by R. Lynn Rivenbark
Macon, Georgia

Printed by Edwards Brothers
Lillington, North Carolina

Contents

Foreword

STATE AND LOCAL governments are the gatekeepers to much of the affordable housing supply for America's working families. Although they do not directly construct affordable housing, those governments can influence the type and amount of housing that does get built, where it is built, the pace of its development, and the cost and type of infrastructure used to support it.

Local governments do this mainly through the many regulatory policies and practices used to influence the nature and pace of growth occurring within their boundaries. Such regulatory policies constitute local "growth management." For the most part, growth management policies seek to enhance and preserve the quality of life of the residents of local communities and to protect the environment. Regrettably, when these policies deliberately aim to limit the amount of local growth or make it hard for lower-income households to move into neighborhoods, such restrictive, or "growth control," policies also limit or may even prevent the development of housing, frequently called "workforce housing," to serve the needs of hard-working American families.

The outcome has been a seeming paradox. Many communities across the country are experiencing rapid growth, yet overwhelming evidence shows that most of these same communities also suffer from growing shortages of affordable, or workforce, housing. As a result, large numbers of lower-income families cannot afford to live in the communities where they work, or where they would like to live. The Advisory Commission on Regulatory Barriers to Affordable Housing, popularly known as the Kemp Commission, documented these barriers a dozen years ago in a groundbreaking report, *Not in My Backyard: Removing Barriers to Affordable Housing*. Regrettably, few barriers have fallen since that time; in fact, the situation has probably become worse.

Because of the growing urgency of this problem, the Department of Housing and Urban Development (HUD) has made removing regulatory barriers to affordable housing a top policy priority. And to begin to address the issues involved, the department, with the Fannie Mae Foundation and the National Association of Realtors, worked with Anthony Downs and the Brookings Institution to bring together researchers and practitioners in a symposium on the relationship between growth management and affordable housing. The symposium's goals were (1) to examine whether conflicts exist between communities' growth management efforts and the need to provide decent and safe affordable housing, and (2) to identify ways to reduce such conflicts.

The results of those proceedings are published in this volume. As usual, Brookings and Downs have achieved, with distinction, the purpose of this symposium. The research papers are stimulating and provocative, and Downs provides an insightful synthesis of the papers and discussions in his introduction, which summarizes the key issues that the public and private sectors must address in confronting the serious regulatory barriers that exist across the country.

This symposium is only one facet of the department's broader effort to improve the availability of affordable housing. HUD also has launched a new program, entitled America's Affordable Communities Initiative: Bringing Homes within Reach through Regulatory Reform. Through this initiative, the department seeks to address those federal, state, and local regulatory barriers that prevent the approval, construction, and availability of affordable housing. HUD Secretary Alphonso Jackson has announced a wide-ranging strategy to achieve the goals of this initiative—an increase in the supply of low-cost homes and apartments available to more of America's working families.

The department will work in partnership with state and local governments and community interests to identify and reduce barriers preventing the development of affordable housing or driving up costs. Many communities have already initiated efforts, including public-private partnerships. The department recognizes and respects that real estate development regulation is primarily a state and local government function. Yet HUD also believes it can play a constructive role in identifying regulatory barriers and providing solutions and incentives for their removal.

Clearly, addressing only these issues will not solve all affordable housing needs. Removing regulatory barriers must be viewed as a complement to, not a substitute for, other efforts to provide affordable housing. For many lower-income families, federal, state, and local subsidies are also fundamental tools for meeting these affordable housing needs. However, addressing regulatory barriers to housing affordability is a necessary component of any overall national housing policy.

The department expects that this publication will advance and illuminate the discussion on how state and local growth management policies, however well intentioned, can become regulatory barriers. Such knowledge can be the first step in overcoming them.

U.S. Department of Housing
and Urban Development

Growth Management
and Affordable Housing

1 ANTHONY DOWNS

Introduction

THE RAPID GROWTH of many American metropolitan areas over the past few decades has created several problems that have aroused widespread citizen dissatisfaction. These problems include rising traffic congestion in both cities and suburbs, the development of a great deal of open space and environmentally sensitive land, increased air pollution, the high cost to taxpayers of providing roads and other infrastructure to accommodate growth, some loss of the sense of community, and serious disinvestment in older inner-city neighborhoods. Citizens unhappy with these results attribute them primarily to the specific form that most U.S. metropolitan growth has taken for the past fifty years: urban sprawl.

Sprawl can be characterized as low-density peripheral growth that includes new subdivisions that leapfrog far beyond existing settled areas onto vacant or agricultural land. Sprawl also relies on the almost exclusive use of private automobiles for transportation; the control of land use by fragmented and relatively small local governments; and the lack of even moderately coordinated land use planning among communities.

Government officials and other citizens have reacted to sprawl by advocating several planning and policy responses. The most prominent strategies have been entitled *growth management, growth control,* or *smart growth*; however, all three have focused mainly on the specific growth-related problems mentioned above without strong regard for another major urban problem:

the high cost of housing for millions of American households, especially poor ones. Data from the 2001 American Housing Survey reveal that almost one-fourth of American households—including 85 percent of poor households—spent more than 30 percent of their incomes on housing. Most of these households suffer from what the U.S. Department of Housing and Urban Development (HUD) calls housing affordability problems, meaning that they cannot afford to occupy "decent quality" dwellings without devoting an "excessive" fraction of their income to housing.

Moreover, the highest-cost housing in most regions is in the suburbs, where the newest housing units have been built. Hence many people who work in the suburbs—or who would benefit from access to the new jobs being created there—cannot afford to live there. They are forced to drive long distances from neighborhoods where less costly housing is available, thereby aggravating traffic congestion, or are prevented altogether from gaining access to the jobs they need.

From the standpoint of rational planning, these two basic problems—sprawl and the lack of affordable housing—ought to be considered together and strategies to cope with each should deal with the other. But experience to date indicates that most growth management, growth control, and even smart growth efforts have not paid a lot of attention to providing more affordable housing in the U.S. suburbs where these strategies are being applied. The purpose of this book, which is based on papers presented at the Symposium on Growth Management and Affordable Housing held at the Brookings Institution on May 29, 2003, is to analyze why that is the case and to explore what can be done to change this disjunction. Is there some inherent conflict between trying to manage growth more rationally and providing more affordable housing? If not, why have those pursuing growth management, growth control, and smart growth not done more about making more affordable housing available?

Definitions of Key Terms

In the interest of clarity, all authors were asked to use the same definitions of key terms:

Growth management: specific regulatory policies aimed at influencing future growth so that it occurs in a more rational manner than it would without overall planning. Growth management policies affect density, availability of land, mix of land uses, and timing of development. It seeks to accommodate growth sensibly, not to limit or prevent it.

Growth control: specific regulatory practices aimed at deliberately slowing or halting growth within a locality or region. It encompasses building moratoriums, building permit caps, population growth caps, and severe downzoning of densities to prevent significant additional growth. It is much more restrictive in intent than growth management.

Smart growth: a set of broad goals and policies designed to counteract sprawl. Goals usually include limiting outward expansion; encouraging higher-density development; encouraging mixed-use zoning instead of fully segregating land uses; reducing travel by private automobiles; revitalizing older areas; and preserving open space. Promoting more affordable housing may or may not be an explicit smart growth goal.

Affordable housing: "decent quality" housing that low-income households (those whose income is below the poverty level or below 50 percent of the median income for their area) can afford to occupy without spending more than 30 percent of their income or that households with slightly higher incomes (50 to 80 percent of the median income) can similarly afford.

Most of the authors held strictly to these definitions, and those that did not usually indicated what other definitions they were using.

Does Growth Management Aid or Thwart the Provision of Affordable Housing?

In chapter 2, Daniel Carlson and Shishir Mathur tackle the subject of whether and to what extent growth management aids or thwarts the provision of affordable housing. They analyzed four fast-growing counties in states that had growth management policies—King County in Washington, Montgomery County in Maryland, and Somerset and Middlesex Counties in New Jersey—to examine the relationship between growth management and housing affordability. They also looked at one similarly fast-growing county—Fairfax County, Virginia—in a non–growth management state for comparison.

The authors devised three sets of measures for their analysis. The first looked at changes in housing affordability for low-income households in the metropolitan areas containing these counties during the 1990s. Changes were measured by comparing percent changes in home prices and gross rents during that decade with percent changes in median incomes; computing whether

the ability of low-income households to occupy median-price housing had
risen or fallen; and calculating changes in the percentage of such households
that spent more than 30 percent of their income for housing. The second set
of measures indicated whether each county made use of certain tactics that
favor the creation of affordable housing, such as allowing small "cottage"
units, allowing accessory apartments, waiving impact fees for affordable units,
adopting inclusionary housing programs that grant bonuses to developers who
built affordable units, encouraging transit-oriented development, and others.
The third set of measures contained data on how many additional affordable
housing units had been built in each county during the 1990s, both in absolute numbers and as a share of total housing construction.

Their findings are more suggestive than conclusive, given the complexity
of the environments that they analyzed and the questions that they probed.
The authors find that the affordability of homeownership for low- and
moderate-income households worsened during the 1990s for all four counties with growth management programs, although the affordability of rental
units varied among them. Montgomery County, Maryland, had the best
record in improving affordability for both low- and moderate-income residents, and it had the second-best record in producing the highest share of affordable units among its additional units. Montgomery County also had the
most complete repertoire of tactics to improve affordability. King County,
Washington, had a wide range of affordability tactics and the second-best
overall record. The authors therefore conclude that employing a full panoply
of instruments to encourage affordable housing and exhibiting a strong political desire to do so were the two key factors in aiding the provision of affordable housing under a growth management program.

COMMENT BY GERRIT KNAAP. Knaap expresses considerable skepticism
of Carlson and Mathur's analysis. He points out that their list of growth
management tactics that might affect affordability did not include growth
boundaries, minimum-lot zoning, and agricultural reserve areas, which he
thinks are much more significant than the tactics they included. He is surprised at the finding that overall the affordability of owner-occupied housing
increased in four counties even though housing prices rose notably. The reason given was that incomes rose even faster, which Knaap argues might have
occurred because poor people could not afford to live there. His third criticism was that causality is unclear: perhaps the counties with the most growth
management programs had them because their housing was less affordable
instead of their housing being less affordable because they had the most programs. In short, he says, the authors do not present enough evidence to

answer the basic question that they pose about whether growth management aids or thwarts affordable housing.

COMMENT BY SAM STALEY. Staley raises two other criticisms of the Carlson and Mathur analysis. First, he notes that they did not take into account the complexities of the private housing market and the fact that most housing for low- and moderate-income households was provided by filtering in the existing inventory. Hence they did not pay enough attention to the market's ability to meet housing needs through different kinds of housing. Second, they ignored the political reality that often a huge difference exists between the stated goals of regulatory policies and the actual motives of the localities that adopt them. Some areas, like Ventura County, California, adopt many tactics seemingly well-suited to achieving smart growth goals, but they apply those tactics in ways that deliberately thwart achievement. That an area has formally adopted certain tactics—which is what Carlson and Mathur measured—does not in itself mean that the area actually uses those tactics effectively in practice. More realistic data about actual practices are needed to test the question they analyzed.

Is There an Inherent Conflict between Smart Growth and Affordable Housing?

Richard Voith and David Crawford explore in chapter 3 the issue of whether adopting smart growth policies makes providing affordable housing more difficult. They start by declaring that they analyze how smart growth *could* affect affordable housing in theory, not how it does, will, or is likely to affect it in practice.

Their fundamental argument has two main points. First, smart growth policies encourage high-density housing and discourage low-density, land-intensive housing. This effect tends to make high-density housing less expensive and low-density housing more expensive than under other land use policies. The net effects on housing affordability are ambiguous. However, since higher-density housing—especially multifamily rental housing—has traditionally been a major source of shelter for low-income households, smart growth policies can improve housing affordability for such households. The restriction of land available for housing called for by smart growth therefore need not always generate higher housing prices for the poor.

The second point is that smart growth policies, at least in theory, encompass many nonhousing aspects that can affect housing affordability. For example, smart growth policies call for concentrating more people in smaller areas and redeveloping older inner-city areas. If those goals are achieved, such policies can bring more jobs closer to low-income households. The authors did not explore whether such effects actually occur on any significant scale or are likely to occur in the future. However, they cited the "Costs of Sprawl: 2000" by Burchell and others to show that if a significant amount of future sprawl were replaced by more compact settlements, the savings over the next two decades could be significant.

Smart growth policies are not likely to benefit everyone. There are almost certain to be some gainers and some losers—including some low-income households. But the disparity could be offset if certain now-dominant institutional arrangements are changed to compensate those who would lose from smart growth policies. For example, permitting construction of low-cost housing within a locality may cause property taxes to increase if many new families with school-age children move in. Such an increase would violate local zoning principles aimed at minimizing property taxes, and because of that local governments often resist creating such housing. Their resistance could be mitigated if tax base inequalities among communities within a metropolitan area were reduced by adopting some type of regionwide tax-sharing agreement, as in the Twin Cities area of Minnesota. Or the state government might increase its funding for total public education costs, thereby reducing local property taxes.

In summary, the authors conclude that there is no theoretical reason why adopting smart growth policies should negatively affect housing affordability, even for poor households, if all the appropriate smart growth policies are in fact implemented.

COMMENT BY MICHAEL SCHILL. Schill argues that it is politically unrealistic to expect either suburbs or central cities to encourage affordable housing. Suburbs are unlikely to do so because they are politically dominated by homeowners, most of whom want to protect the value of their homes by excluding lower-value single-family units or multifamily units—in other words, affordable housing. And each suburb's officials are concerned only with the welfare of their own voters, not the region's overall need for affordable housing. As a result, many suburban governments accept those aspects of smart growth that limit the availability of land for housing but not those that encourage the development of affordable housing.

So proponents of more affordable housing have to try to place it mainly in denser communities like central cities. But many city residents also are opposed to increasing the density of their neighborhoods; furthermore, construction costs typically are much higher in central cities. Complex city regulations also add to costs because ensuring compliance with them delays completion of projects. Moreover, putting more low-income households in central cities is not socially desirable in view of the heavy concentration of the poor already there.

Schill therefore fears that adopting smart growth policies in a region would result in successful implementation of land use restrictions that raise housing prices, but not of policies that increase production of units affordable to the poor. He believes that affordable housing is best encouraged by *reducing* existing land use regulations that block it, not by creating more regulations.

COMMENT BY BURCHELL AND MUKHERJI. Burchell and Mukherji essentially ignore the Voith and Crawford analysis except for one aspect: they regard the author's definition of "affordable" housing as highly unrealistic. The chapter states that households can be considered to "need" affordable units if they meet two conditions: they have an income of below 80 percent of the regional median income and they spend more than 30 percent of their income on housing. But this definition encompasses about 24 percent of all the households in a typical American region, according to recent housing survey data. The U.S. housing supply typically has expanded by about 1.5 percent per year, including all new units, affordable or not.[1] If one-tenth of all new units were made affordable through an inclusionary zoning program, then the annual addition to the supply of affordable units would be only 0.15 percent. At that rate, it would take 160 years to create enough new affordable units to provide 24 percent of all *existing* households—as of the first year—with units. Therefore using the definition of affordable housing needs proposed by Voith and Crawford creates insurmountable obstacles to meeting those needs within a reasonable time period, at least through a land use mechanism like inclusionary zoning. Only massive housing subsidies could meet needs defined in this way within a reasonable period.

Burchell and Mukherji therefore propose an alternative definition of the need for affordable housing based on how many poor households occupy deteriorated units. If an inclusionary zoning program were to set aside 20 percent of all new units as affordable housing and if new housing equaled 1.5 percent additional units each year, then the initial need for affordable

1. The actual compound annual growth rate of the U.S. year-round housing inventory from 1970 to 2000 was 1.80 percent. U.S. Department of Housing and Urban Development, *U.S. Housing Market Conditions* (August 2003), p. 81. From 1970 to 2000, the average percentage of new housing starts, including manufactured housing, as a fraction of the prior year's total housing inventory was 2.37 percent.

housing calculated by using their definition could be met within ten years. Burchell and Mukherji believe that this definition is much more realistic than the one proposed by Voith and Crawford, which is the same definition used by the U.S. Department of Housing and Urban Development.

Burchell and Mukherji also describe a method of analyzing how large the density bonus provided to developers under inclusionary zoning programs should be.

The Link between Growth Management and Housing Affordability: The Academic Evidence

In chapter 4, Arthur Nelson and his colleagues carry out a comprehensive review of the academic literature on the relationship of growth management and affordable housing. They seek to evaluate the common assumption that by limiting the supply of developable land, all growth management policies reduce the supply of housing, thereby increasing housing prices and decreasing housing affordability.

While this reasoning may seem logical, the authors conclude that it is far too simplistic. Housing prices are actually determined by many interacting factors, including the price of land, the supply and types of housing, the demand for housing, and the amount of residential choice and mobility in the area. Moreover, growth management policies vary widely by state and region and are unevenly enforced and implemented. The authors arrive at the following main conclusions.

The strength of market demand is the primary determinant of housing prices, not regulatory constraints on land supplies. The effects of growth management policies on housing prices are hard to isolate because of variations in policies and their implementation; the structure of local housing markets; patterns of land ownership; and the stringency of other local regulations. True, research on the effects of urban growth boundaries (UGBs), largely in Portland, Oregon, suggests that UGBs can affect land values. But the effects of UGBs on housing affordability remain in dispute.

Both traditional land use regulations and growth management policies can raise the price of housing, but they do so in different ways. Traditional zoning and other planning and land use controls limit the supply and accessibility of affordable housing, thereby raising home prices; certain growth control and land use policies also reduce a jurisdiction's housing supply. Such policies include requirements for low density or minimum housing size and bans against attached or cluster homes, and they frequently are intended to make housing more expensive and thereby exclude lower-income families, which often belong to racial and ethnic minorities. This "chain of exclusion" surely limits the affordability of housing in certain jurisdictions.

In contrast, many growth management policies improve the supply and location of affordable housing and accommodate other development needs, thereby increasing the desirability of the communities concerned. This raises the demand for housing in those communities and thus increases housing prices. When crafted properly, growth management programs can break the chain of exclusion by increasing housing densities, mandating a mix of housing types, and promoting regional fair share housing or other inclusionary housing provisions. Studies have found that growth boundaries and adequate public facilities ordinances often were associated with shifts toward multi-family housing. Growth management programs also can make housing more affordable by lowering public infrastructure costs and minimizing regulatory delays. Finally, properly designed growth management programs also plan for all development needs, such as more open space, greater access to public transportation, and more walkable neighborhoods. In communities with such programs, residents are not necessarily worse off if housing prices increase. Instead, higher housing prices may be offset by lower transportation and energy costs and better access to jobs, services, and amenities.

Housing prices may increase because of either restricted land supply (bad) or rising demand stimulated by improved environments (good) or by some combination of both. Therefore the key decision for policymakers is not how to avoid increases in housing prices; it is to determine what type of regulation will best expand the range of housing choices for all income groups. In other words, which type of regulation—traditional land use practices or growth management programs—will best increase the distribution of housing types in a metropolitan area? Traditional land use practices tend either to be laissez-faire in their approach to affordable housing or to deliberately zone for low-density, expensive homes to exclude low-income households. Properly designed growth management programs, on the other hand, aim to overcome exclusionary effects. Portland, for instance, has a growth management policy that draws a growth boundary to protect farmland but that also increases densities inside the boundary. Moreover, Portland's policies mandate the development of a mix of housing types, including affordable housing.

However, even well-intentioned growth management programs can be poorly designed. They can accommodate too much growth and thereby allow sprawl or accommodate too little growth and thereby increase housing prices. This is arguably what happened in parts of California where growth boundaries were drawn so tightly—without accommodating housing needs—that housing supply fell relative to demand. Housing prices therefore rose dramatically, and poor residents were priced out or forced to live in over-crowded conditions.

Properly designed growth management programs mitigate both the adverse effects of urban growth and the adverse price effects on lower-income households, as noted in the preceding paragraphs.

COMMENT BY ROBERT LANG. Lang disputes the likelihood that many suburban communities would adopt the balanced set of growth management policies, including strong support for affordable housing, that Nelson and his colleagues say are at least theoretically possible. Lang notes that even liberals like himself would probably oppose affordable housing in their own neigh-borhood because of the fear that when they try to sell their homes, more conservative homebuyers would refuse to buy if low-income households live there. That would reduce the number of potential buyers for their homes, reducing competition and probably sale prices. Even though they had no personal objection to having affordable housing near their homes, home-owners would oppose it because they might suffer serious depreciation of their most valuable asset.

COMMENT BY WILLIAM FISCHEL. Fischel also expresses strong skepti-cism about the realism of the authors' arguments. He notes that smart growth advocates were thrilled by the conclusion that smart growth's key policies did not make housing less affordable but says that the conclusion goes far beyond the evidence presented. In fact, most of the studies reviewed in the chapter conclude that growth management policies raised housing prices signifi-cantly. Fischel says the authors are politically naïve when they claim that if growth management proponents merely say that they intend to create afford-able housing, they actually want to and will do so.

Fischel agrees with the authors that growth management policies at the regional level are more likely to produce affordable housing than those at the local level. However, he points out, some regional policies of this type are "double veto" arrangements in which both the region and the locality can block affordable housing. Fischel then analyzes the case of Portland, Ore-gon—the poster child of smart growth proponents. Portland has several advantages: it has the longest-established UGB, it has the one with the most "bite," it is run by a regionally elected board chosen at large, and it has the power to alter local land use policies. Yet home prices in Portland have risen just as fast as those in other Western regions, except in some California communities. If growth management does not succeed in making housing more affordable in Portland, with all its unique powers, than it is elsewhere, it is not likely to do so anywhere.

Fischel further points out that two other recent comprehensive studies of housing prices—one in the United States and one in the United Kingdom—conclude that regulatory barriers to affordable housing were the main cause of high housing prices, not strong housing demand. That directly contradicts the conclusion reached by Nelson and others, which Fischel strongly rejects.

Review of the Literature on the Impact of Affordable and Multifamily Housing on the Market Value of Nearby Single-Family Homes

In chapter 5, George Galster reviews the voluminous statistical literature on the impact of affordable and multifamily housing on the prices of nearby single-family homes, categorizing impacts according to building type (single-family or multifamily), tenure (owner- or renter-occupied), clientele (market-rate, low-income, or special needs buyers/renters), and development technique (new construction or rehabilitation). Galster argues that the vast majority of previous studies suffer from serious methodological weaknesses and that many do not plausibly establish that affordable or multifamily housing has any measured effect on the prices of nearby homes. Instead, such types of housing might have been systematically placed in neighborhoods with preexisting price idiosyncrasies—such as low or falling prices—that would attract affordable housing. In those cases, causality would be reversed.

Several recent studies have overcome these weaknesses by employing a "difference in differences" methodology. Home price levels and trends were measured in two neighborhoods, one containing housing very near the affordable or multifamily housing concerned and another neighborhood similar in nature but far enough away that it was unlikely to be affected by the affordable/multifamily units. The studies were conducted in both neighborhoods in two periods—before and after the subject housing was created—to overcome the methodological weaknesses of earlier studies.

These studies reveal that the direction and magnitude of apparent home price impacts were contingent on the concentration, context, and type of new development. In regard to concentration, higher amounts of new construction or rehabilitation in a given area involving either single- or multifamily affordable units seemed to have larger positive price impacts on nearby homes. However, this effect had a diminishing marginal positive impact. In fact, at least in the case of affordable, multifamily rental complexes, the effect can become negative after concentrations exceed a certain threshold. This potentially negative "overconcentration" effect seems particularly strong with respect to tenant-based subsidy programs. Affordable housing seemed least likely to generate negative impacts when inserted into high-value, low-poverty, stable neighborhoods.

Neighborhood context also affected the magnitude and even direction of concentration effects. There is growing evidence that neighborhoods with modest values, nontrivial poverty rates, and homeowner perceptions of vulnerability experience smaller positive price impacts—and a greater risk of negative ones—at lower concentrations of affordable multifamily housing. That was the case for tenant-based programs, scattered-site public housing developed through rehabilitation, or newly constructed low-income housing tax credit (LIHTC) developments. In depopulated, highly distressed neighborhoods, however, the effects of such new or improved units may be more positive.

Finally, the particular type of affordable or multifamily development influenced its impacts. Owner-occupied affordable developments apparently generated more positive impacts than those occupied by renters. Developments that removed a preexisting source of negative externalities (either through rehabilitation or construction) were likely to generate more positive impacts than those developed on vacant land.

The author shows that developing affordable and multifamily housing in a metropolitan area clearly can be done in ways that enhance nearby property values. But, just as clearly, it can be done in ways that, because of inappropriate concentrations and neighborhood contexts, erode those values.

COMMENT BY INGRID GOULD ELLEN. Ellen begins by praising Galster's methodological analysis and innovations but argues that he did not pay enough attention to the differences in the types of neighborhood in which he analyzed the impacts of affordable housing. In particular, when new units were placed in older, high-density, distressed neighborhoods, the new units often generated positive price impacts because the developers first removed negative features such as dilapidated structures—something that did not happen in typical suburban single-family areas. Therefore, conclusions derived from older, distressed inner-city areas should not be transferred to newer suburban areas. In fact, Ellen thinks Galster should remove the term "single-family homes" from the chapter title and more clearly differentiate between the impacts of new affordable units in low-density, stable suburban neighborhoods and those in high-density, distressed inner-city neighborhoods.

Ellen also points out that in practice affordable housing is not often a key part of growth management programs. She believes that Galster's conclusion that such housing *could* have a positive impact on nearby housing if properly included in growth management programs overestimates the probability that it actually will be included.

COMMENT BY JILL KHADDURI. Khadduri also praises Galster's methodological analysis, but she points out that most of the studies Galster considered valid involved subsidized housing. In contrast, the affordable housing most relevant to most growth management programs involves non-subsidized multifamily and other higher-density units in suburban areas. Two exceptions involve low-income housing tax credit units and Section 8 vouchers, both of which can be used in low-density neighborhoods. These are the two biggest subsidized housing programs, and in neither does low-income housing have to look as if it is occupied by low-income households.

Khadduri argues further that Galster did not place enough emphasis on his finding that both positive and negative impacts of subsidized housing on nearby home prices were quite small. Because even negative impacts were small, neighbors of affordable units need not fear having such units located near them. She believes that this conclusion should be very widely broadcast.

Two other criticisms were that conclusions based on studies made in New York City may not have taken sufficient account of the unique traits of the city's housing policies and that some other studies from which Galster drew conclusions do not consider important variables such as the quality of property management. Khadduri also makes several suggestions concerning additional research that should be done, including studies of the impacts of the Section 8 voucher program, the administration of housing in suburban areas, density around transit stops, different types of LIHTC tenant mixes, and different shapes and styles of subdivisions at the metropolitan periphery.

The Promise and Practice of Inclusionary Zoning

Inclusionary zoning refers to regulatory programs that pressure housing developers to include in their projects a certain percentage of units to be sold or rented at below-market prices to relatively low-income households. These programs can be either voluntary or mandatory. Most are adopted by cities, counties, or states. In nearly all such programs, the developers are given density bonuses or other incentives to compensate for having to market units at prices that are lower than those the market would bear.

In chapter 6, Douglas Porter presents a remarkably thorough treatment of this subject. He begins with a historical review of how and why this form of regulation came into being, then covers the legal and economic issues involved. He finds the two most important conditions for adoption of inclusionary zoning by a local government to be having a prosperous, relatively affluent local or regional housing market and a strong political will to expand the supply of affordable housing.

In the past two decades, inclusionary zoning and housing programs have been adopted by several major states and dozens of counties and communities. Their specific terms vary considerably on many dimensions, and Porter describes these and other variables in detail. The "big three" states using the device most widely are New Jersey, Massachusetts, and California, although the longest-established program is in Montgomery County, Maryland. In all big-three states, only a minority of localities have actually adopted and implemented inclusionary zoning regulations, even if state law requires them to do so. Porter estimates that

> the total of units known or estimated to have been produced across the nation [through inclusionary programs] reaches a range of 80,000 to 90,000 units—about 65,000 units in states that mandate production of affordable housing and perhaps 15,000 to 25,000 units from individual jurisdictions in other states. Admittedly, without a nationwide survey, this is a rough estimate. . . . The range of affordable units created by inclusionary programs over a thirty-year period amounts to a fraction of units produced under HUD subsidy programs.

Porter believes that as a result the overall effectiveness of inclusionary programs in meeting the nation's need for affordable housing has not been very great:

> To date the contributions of inclusionary zoning have been far less dramatic than originators of the concept had hoped. Except in a few communities, inclusionary programs have produced only a small proportion of needed units. Most programs have served existing community residents rather than increasing housing opportunities for

poor and/or minority residents from central cities and declining suburbs. . . . Experience with state mandates demonstrates the fallibility
of expectations that reluctant local governments can be coaxed or
coerced to do the right thing, and few states even try.

Porter concludes with four pieces of advice for potential future users of
inclusionary zoning: governments must be sure to combine inclusionary zoning regulations with many other tools and programs in a broader package of
policies; inclusionary zoning works best if state laws require every community to attend to the local need for affordable housing; inclusionary zoning
does not work in weak housing markets or even in strong markets during
periods of general housing market weakness; and inclusionary zoning cannot
by itself meet *all* of any region's need for affordable housing—other tools
and programs, including government subsidies, also are necessary.

COMMENT BY KAREN DESTOREL BROWN. Brown thinks that Porter
provides a very useful summary of inclusionary zoning programs but that he
greatly underestimates both their present importance and their potential for
helping to create affordable housing. Porter points out that such programs
have contributed only a small fraction of total housing production where
they were used, but Brown believes that the relevant measure is the proportion of *total affordable housing production* they have been responsible for. By
that measure, the best inclusionary zoning programs—such as the one in
Montgomery County, Maryland—have done very well, probably better than
any other approaches to creating affordable housing.

Brown also thinks that the author did not focus enough on how effectively
inclusionary zoning could be used to meet such smart growth goals as creating affordable housing, distributing it throughout a community, raising
housing densities, stimulating infill development, and encouraging collaborative efforts between the public and private sectors. She points out that
although Porter criticizes the failure of inclusionary zoning to help achieve
racial integration of low-income minority households in the suburbs, that
was not one of its key goals. The main goal was to create mixed-income communities to ensure that local residents could continue to live throughout
their jurisdictions.

Brown also points out that inclusionary zoning programs can be only as
successful as their framers design them to be. If the framers exempt many
types of new construction projects—as most ordinances do—or otherwise
limit the applicability or scope of the programs, the programs will not provide a lot of affordable housing. If the framers maximize the potential

impact of the basic concept of inclusionary zoning, the programs can be very effective.

COMMENT BY MICHAEL PYATOK. Pyatok is a practicing architect who has designed and helped build thousands of affordable housing units, mainly in cooperation with community development organizations in low-income neighborhoods; his comment therefore reflects his unique view of inclusionary zoning. Essentially, he believes that inclusionary zoning is appropriate only in relatively well-off suburban communities where there is an acute shortage of housing affordable to low- and moderate-income households and no local community development organizations exist.

Pyatok argues that in central cities and older suburbs containing neighborhoods where many low- and moderate-income households already live—especially members of minority groups—inclusionary zoning should not be used. Instead, efforts to create affordable housing should focus on operating through indigenous nonprofit community development organizations, which provide more socially beneficial results than the profit-oriented commercial residential developers involved in most inclusionary zoning programs because of the following five factors:

—The term of affordability is usually much longer, since there is no intention to cash out or refinance in the future.

—Unlike market-rate housing, in which all residents are expected to blend in with the majority population even if they have special needs, community development housing often is "service-enriched," providing child care, counseling, and other social services that meet the particular needs of lower-income households.

—The housing is managed by nonprofit corporations or for-profit corporations with special experience in serving the needs of lower-income households.

—The process of designing the housing often is inclusive and participatory and therefore provides a community-organizing opportunity. In contrast, market-rate housing often is designed behind closed doors, restricting community input to the minimum number of public hearings required by environmental impact reviews.

—The housing often is designed to express the culture and pride of the people it is intended to serve, unlike market-rate housing, which often must project a bland homogeneous image to lure the broadest population.

Pyatok describes five housing projects in neighborhoods in which local community development organizations serving ethnic communities designed and built affordable housing appropriate to their needs. The housing was much better suited to the local residents than it would have been if it had been built by a profit-oriented developer using "normal" inclusionary zoning methods. Pyatok therefore concludes that, wherever possible,

> the financial fuel for self-determination and capacity building in the nonprofit sector, whether from local or state sources, should not be siphoned off to assist the for-profit sector. *If there is to be inclusionary zoning, private developers should pay for such housing primarily from their own profits or pay in-lieu fees to local affordable housing trust funds and at sufficient levels to accomplish the task* [emphasis added]. Such funding pools are an important assistance to the local nonprofit sector, which is far more capable of meeting the needs of lower incomes in a comprehensive way.

Growth Management, Smart Growth, and Affordable Housing

In chapter 7, Anthony Downs focuses first on the "affordability gap" between what poor households can pay for housing and what it costs to occupy a "decent" unit. That gap can be closed only by raising household incomes or reducing occupancy costs. The former requires subsidies; the latter can be done in four basic ways: reducing financing costs; decreasing development and construction costs; changing quality and amenity standards, as by using manufactured homes or accessory apartments; or building so many new units that the overall price of existing housing goes down. Most poor households live in existing units, so cutting the price of those units would be effective. But reducing the price of existing housing threatens the economic interests of all the nation's homeowners, lenders, real estate agents, mortgage bankers, homebuilders, and local governments—a politically insuperable group whose members all benefit from increasing the prices of existing homes or at least from preventing those prices from falling. That path to greater affordability, therefore, is blocked.

In fact, because homeowners want to protect the market value of their homes from any downward movements and because they politically dominate suburban governments, most suburban governments oppose creating affordable housing or accepting low-income residents. As long as control over land use is left solely with local governments, it is unlikely that any significant amount of affordable housing will be created outside of central cities and older suburbs. Other parties that could exercise more authority over where housing is located within a region include developers, state governments, regional agencies, and public-private partnerships. But persuading state governments to transfer any significant authority over housing location from local governments would be extraordinarily difficult. Even in the one state with a statewide housing policy—New Jersey—more than half of all localities have refused to go along with state policy.

Most smart growth advocates realize that trying to promote affordable housing as well as key smart growth goals arouses hostility in the suburbs; hence not many put creating affordable housing high on their list of priorities. But many aspects of smart growth involve reducing the supply of land available for housing—such as limiting outward growth, emphasizing infill development, and increasing densities. Without specific countervailing actions to promote affordable housing, smart growth policies tend to raise housing prices.

Only strong leadership—especially by state governments—can overcome this impasse. The few states that have done so have been responding to some type of crisis, such as pressure from the state courts in New Jersey. In California, housing prices have become so high that many thousands of households have had to double and triple up in overcrowded units—in short, in slums. In fact, many working-class and even middle-class households cannot afford to live anywhere near their jobs, so they have long commutes that aggravate traffic congestion.

Smart growth goals would be furthered by much more widespread creation of affordable housing. Because the most affordable housing consists of multifamily or attached units, it would lead to higher densities; reduce traffic congestion, since low-wage workers would have to travel less to reach their jobs; promote more mixed-use development; and require a shift of some land use regulations away from local governments. From this standpoint, smart growth proponents should make alliances with promoters of affordable housing in the suburbs so that both groups can increase their net influence on attaining basically unpopular objectives. Such coalitions could include churches and nonprofits interested in social justice, businesses seeking housing for their employees, and developers who want to build low-cost housing.

There is no guarantee that such combined forces will prevail, but the chances of attaining either effective smart growth or more affordable housing without forming coalitions are nil. Regions will wind up instead with more purely local growth management policies that push growth out farther, worsening sprawl and increasing housing prices more than ever.

Conclusion

This summary reveals three major themes. First, even though most growth management programs contain provisions that limit the land available for development and therefore normally place upward pressure on housing prices, it is theoretically possible for growth management to coexist with, and even promote, affordable housing. This can happen in the suburbs as well as in cities. But such a desirable outcome will occur only if the growth management programs involved contain provisions specifically designed to create affordable housing by offsetting those aspects of growth management that inherently limit the land available for development *and* if there is a strong political will in the communities concerned to actually implement those pro-affordability provisions.

Second, deeply entrenched political forces reduce the likelihood that either of those necessary conditions will be met on any broad scale, especially in the suburbs. A great many homeowners believe that their economic interest in their home must be protected by preventing or limiting the construction of lower-cost housing in their community, and homeowners dominate suburban politics. True, several studies showed that existing home values in high-value, low-poverty, stable suburban neighborhoods are not likely to be adversely affected by relatively small numbers of affordable housing units built nearby and that clusters of new or rehabilitated units in lower-value, deteriorated neighborhoods can have a positive impact on the value of nearby homes. If those facts become better known, resistance to placing affordable housing in such neighborhoods can perhaps be overcome.

Third, programs encouraging growth management will in fact promote affordable housing only if advocates of both goals work closely together to overcome entrenched resistance to affordable housing. Various forms of growth management have widespread political support, including the support of suburban residents, but proponents of growth management will have to greatly increase their focus on affordable housing—and their efforts to promote it—to avoid having growth management thwart rather than encourage affordable housing.

2

DANIEL CARLSON
SHISHIR MATHUR

Does Growth Management Aid or Thwart the Provision of Affordable Housing?

AT FIRST GLANCE, growth management policies that confine development to limited areas can be viewed as making housing more costly and
in effect discriminating against moderate- and low-income households. According to Nelson and others, "the common assumption is that by limiting the
supply of developable land, all growth management policies reduce the supply
of housing. Basic economic theory suggests that if housing supply is low relative to demand, then the price for it will be high, reducing its affordability."
However, they point out that "while this reasoning may seem logical, it is far
too simplistic. Housing prices are actually determined by a host of interacting
factors, such as the price of land, the supply and types of housing, the demand
for housing and the amount of residential choice and mobility in the area."[1]

In fact, growth management programs and policies attempt to do many
things: limit urban sprawl, improve transportation options, create more compact development, and provide housing that a wide range of residents can
afford. Nelson and others contrast laissez-faire land use practices with what
growth management could achieve:

The authors are indebted to Tony Downs, the review panel of the sponsors of the Symposium
on Growth Management and Affordable Housing, and discussants Gerrit Knaap and Samuel Staley for their insights and constructive suggestions.
    1. Nelson and others (2002).

Traditional land use practices tend to be "laissez-faire" in their approach to affordable housing, or they deliberately zone for low-density, expensive homes to exclude low-income households or communities of color. Properly designed growth management programs, on the other hand, aim to overcome these exclusionary effects. Portland, for instance, has a growth management policy that draws a growth boundary to protect farmland but also increases densities inside the boundary and mandates the development of a mix of housing types including affordable housing.[2]

This chapter examines whether and to what extent growth management aids or thwarts the provision of affordable housing. In the attempt to answer this question, we studied several metropolitan counties that have growth management policies to see whether moderate- and low-income residents can afford housing in those counties and whether they have programs and policies to influence the creation and preservation of affordable housing.

Growth Management

Growth management is "the utilization by government of a variety of traditional and evolving techniques, tools, plans, and activities to purposefully guide local patterns of land use, including the manner, location, rate, and nature of development."[3] Calling growth management "active and dynamic," Benjamin Chinitz writes that

> it seeks to maintain an ongoing equilibrium between development and conservation, between various forms of development and concurrent provisions of infrastructure, between the demands for public services generated by growth and the supply of revenues to finance those demands, and between progress and equity.[4]

Growth management is a policy response to the rapid, unbridled outward growth of U.S. metropolitan areas that occurred after World War II, which has eaten up farmland and sensitive environments while outpacing the provision of

2. Nelson and others (2002).
3. Randall W. Scott, ed., *Management and Control of Growth*, quoted in Porter (1997, p. 10).
4. Benjamin Chinitz, "Growth Management: Good for the Town, Bad for the Nation?" in Porter (1997, p.10).

government services, including utilities, schools, and roads. Growth management represents a set of comprehensive planning and investment policies that tie planning to the financing of public infrastructure. It also is a political response to the local no-growth or antigrowth movements that emerged in the 1970s that forced citizens to strike an appropriate balance between protecting natural areas and permitting urban development and between defending private and upholding public rights.

A dozen states have adopted comprehensive growth management laws to guide the process of defining the long-term future, creating plans, and devising tools to manage the interrelationships among development, land use, transportation, and the environment.[5] In general terms, each state establishes a process to protect natural resources and critical and agricultural lands, to create urban growth areas, to relate local plans and activities to regional and statewide efforts, and to link concurrent public investments.

Smart Growth

Growth management, Douglas Porter notes, "is a dynamic process . . . an ever-changing program of activities, a continuous process of evaluating current trends and management results and updating both objectives and methods."[6] This chapter views smart growth as part of that dynamic, ever-changing process. Smart growth draws on important concepts and tools from the past thirty years of growth management, such as sustainability, neotraditional development, transit-oriented development, and mixed-use development that provides access to housing, services, and jobs. It represents finer-grained and more prescriptive growth management implementation strategies. For example, smart growth promotes specific kinds of high-density developments like those advocated by new urbanists such as Andres Duany and Peter Calthorpe. These developments are pedestrian oriented, constructed on a tight grid, and connected to high-capacity public transit; they also contain a mix of uses, and they are built at high densities. But smart growth is not about high density alone. As Danielsen, Lang, and Fulton point out, metropolitan Los Angeles has the highest gross population density of the nation's twenty largest metropolitan areas, demonstrating that

5. Johnson, Salkin, and Jordan (2002).
6. Porter (1997, p. 11).

it is possible to have both high density and spreading, auto-oriented development that does not achieve smart growth goals. Smart growth development represents certain kinds of carefully nuanced development that create or reinforce community.[7]

Smart growth makes the relationship between public investment and promoting desirable land uses and community building projects explicit. In Maryland, for example, the state will consider funding projects only in preferred development areas where existing infrastructure can support development and where projects contribute to existing communities first. Smart growth calls for providing choices in housing type, location, and cost and for offering alternative means of transportation so that the automobile is not the sole option. Many of smart growth's goals can be accomplished through providing urban and suburban infill housing.[8]

Just as the term "growth management," first used in the 1960s, had political dimensions, so does the term "smart growth," which was coined in the 1990s. In contrast to the more radical no-growth movement, growth management presented a rational, businesslike alternative to accommodating future growth, enabling various stakeholders to embrace the concept and pass growth management legislation. Today, smart growth places proponents on the high ground in political debate—who, after all, who wants to be seen as favoring "dumb growth"?

In this chapter we generally use the term "growth management" to refer to the concepts and laws regarding the coordination, timing, and location of growth, of which smart growth is a part. We use the term "smart growth" to refer to evolving principles and practices that encourage the development of compact, pedestrian-oriented, livable communities within urban growth areas.

Affordable Housing

With great effectiveness, the U.S. private housing and mortgage markets provide housing to the majority of American households. After all, the United States is a nation of homeowners—two-thirds of American households own

---

7. Danielsen, Lang, and Fulton (1999, p. 516–17).
8. Smart Growth America and the Smart Growth Network provide Internet access to smart growth principles and information (www.smartgrowthamerica.org [December 10, 2003]).

their own homes. Generally speaking, mortgage lenders prefer that housing costs represent one-third or less of total income, making the housing payment affordable. HUD traditionally has used an affordability guideline of 30 percent of income for housing costs, and we also use that guideline as our working definition of affordability, although a higher percentage is sometimes used. A fuller picture of affordability is provided by combining housing and transportation costs, a subject that is worthy of further investigation.

This study focuses on the availability of affordable housing for moderate-, low-, and very-low-income residents earning less than 80 percent of the median income in counties in urban metropolitan areas. Such residents are not likely to be able to buy or rent at prevailing market rates without spending an "excessive" fraction of their income on housing. There are several reasons to focus on housing for these income groups.

First, growth management principles emphasize equity in the development and availability of housing for residents at all income levels. In states where growth management laws exist, jurisdictions are asked to plan for affordable housing. For example, under Washington state's Growth Management Act, counties and cities must include a housing element in their comprehensive plan and show how they will accommodate state twenty-year population projections. At least two states, New Jersey and Massachusetts, have fair share housing laws that go further. In New Jersey, the state supreme court has ruled that every municipality in a growth area has a constitutional obligation to provide, through its land use regulations, a realistic opportunity for creation of a fair share of its region's present and prospective needs for housing for low- and moderate-income families.[9] Second, a variety of policymakers and stakeholders believe that "healthy communities means having a mix of housing styles and prices without detracting from the attractiveness of overall development."[10] Third, jurisdictions have a practical interest in making sure that public servants—including teachers, firefighters, police officers, and service providers—are able to live in the community in which they serve. For the fast-growing, desirable metropolitan counties that are the subject of this chapter, median household income ranged between $53,157 and $76,933, making it very difficult indeed for many kinds of wage earners to compete in the housing market.[11]

9. New Jersey Permanent Statutes 52:27D-301 referencing Mount Laurel N.J. Supreme Court ruling 92 NJ 158 (1983) (www.njleg.state.nj.us/ [December 10, 2003] and www.state.nj.us/dca/coah/about.htm [February 16, 2003]).

10. Kleit (1998).

11. Median household income for King, Montgomery, Somerset, and Middlesex counties as reported in the 2000 census.

Purpose of This Study

The purpose of this study is threefold:

—to analyze the affordability of housing for moderate- and low-income households in several metropolitan counties that have growth management laws

—to understand the growth management and smart growth laws and tools in place and determine whether they aid or thwart the development and preservation of affordable housing

—to offer an approach to monitoring efforts to provide affordable housing that jurisdictions can tailor to meet their own needs.

According to Danielsen, Lang, and Fulton, "the literature on the link between smart growth and housing remains underdeveloped."[12] This chapter aims to make a modest addition to the literature by looking at affordable housing in four metropolitan counties in growth management/smart growth states. To what extent do the growth management policies in four counties in New Jersey, Maryland, and Washington offset the potential exclusionary effects of limiting land for development? Is it possible to tell whether they have a mix of policies, programs, and market forces that can provide a range of housing types in similar large, growing, affluent urban counties?

Research Approach

In order to show the relationships between growth management and housing affordability, we needed to define and apply criteria for choosing the metropolitan counties to be studied and for choosing indicators of housing affordability and growth management policies and practices.

Selecting Cases

Because growth management policies can be applied to areas of new growth at the urban periphery as well as to infill sites in established communities, we looked for metropolitan counties that had both developed and undeveloped land. Our approach required excluding urban counties that are largely built-out, like Bergen County in New Jersey, so that we could look at policies and tools affecting new development as well as old. We sought counties in states

12. Danielsen, Lang, and Fulton (1999, p. 513).

that have adopted or counties that themselves have adopted the following core growth management principles:

—Limit outward growth

—Reduce dependency on automobiles

—Promote compact, higher-density development

—Preserve open space and sensitive and resource lands

—Redevelop core areas and infill sites

—Create more affordable housing

—Create a greater sense of community through new urbanist, pedestrian-friendly, mixed-use villages.

Because there are only a dozen growth management states, our search centered on Delaware, Florida, Georgia, Maryland, New Jersey, Oregon, Pennsylvania, Rhode Island, Tennessee, Vermont, Washington, and Wisconsin. We wanted both East and West Coast examples. Portland, Oregon, is often studied and cited, so we decided to eliminate that area, selecting instead King County, Washington, as the West Coast case. King County is a large urban county that includes Seattle, other cities, suburbs, and rural areas and has a comprehensive plan and urban growth boundary consistent with the state's Growth Management Act. On the East Coast, we turned to New Jersey, in part because it has twin statewide laws adopted in 1985 that require state comprehensive planning and fair housing. We selected the adjacent counties of Somerset and Middlesex, which include both established cities and some of the state's fastest-growing boroughs and townships at the periphery of the metropolitan area. Maryland was of interest because it was the first state to name and adopt smart growth legislation. We selected Montgomery County, a large, affluent county bordering Washington, D.C., that had developed its own pioneering growth management and inclusionary housing laws in the late 1960s and early 1970s respectively. That may explain why it has both an extensive job market and housing centers as well as remaining open space and farmland. At the suggestion of the sponsors of the Symposium on Growth Management and Affordable Housing, we then compared these counties with Fairfax County, Virginia, an urban county in the Washington, D.C., metropolitan region that has an inclusionary housing law similar to Montgomery County's but does not have a similar growth management framework.

Certainly a case could be made to include more counties, to substitute others, or to examine the impact of growth management policies on housing affordability in communities of different sizes altogether. However, given the time and funding limitations of this inquiry, we elected to look at these four counties, which have populations of a million or more (Somerset and Middlesex combined). We were able to use census data from 1990 and 2000, reference state and local legislation, and contact key officials of public agencies and nonprofit organizations as well as other observers and experts in each county.

Our research approach was fourfold:

—derive a profile of housing affordability from 1990 and 2000 census data

—identify selected programs and policies that could aid or thwart the provision of affordable housing

—document the number of affordable housing units developed

—identify, when possible, links between affordable housing provision and growth management programs and policies.

As previously noted, the provision of affordable housing is very complex, and it is greatly affected by the prevailing real estate market. Attributing the adequacy of affordable housing in metropolitan counties to growth management policies and techniques alone may never be possible.

Selecting Housing Affordability Indicators

We used census data from 1990 and 2000 to show the portion of income that moderate- and low-income households spent on housing costs in that ten-year period. We also looked at the value of owner-occupied housing and the cost of renting a house to determine whether either was changing relative to median household income.[13] While we were interested in the degree of change in housing affordability over time, it was essential to show whether housing was affordable for low- and modest-income households. To do that we compared the median home and rental costs for each county with the amount that the metropolitan region's low- and modest-income households could afford to spend on housing.[14] That comparison is important because housing may have remained unaffordable for most of these households in real terms even if it became incrementally more affordable during the 1990–2000 period.

We used three groups of indicators to estimate the changes in housing affordability in the last decade for the counties under consideration. The first group assesses the absolute and percent changes in the prices of median-value

13. Value is the respondent's estimate of how much the property (house and lot, mobile home and lot, or condominium unit) would sell for if it were for sale.

14. The metropolitan region of the county is the Consolidated Metropolitan Statistical Area (CMSA) in which the county is situated, as demarcated in the 2000 census.

owner-occupied and rental housing and compares them with the changes in the median household income of the metropolitan area. The metropolitan area data give a more complete picture of households that may seek housing than that provided by the wealthiest counties. It also recognizes that metropolitan regions are dynamic, with residents making location decisions among many cities and counties.

The change in affordability of renter- and owner-occupied housing for median-income households was assessed by creating two data relationships: a "rent-to-income ratio'" and a "house-value-to-income ratio." The rent-to-income ratio is the ratio of percent change in median gross rent to the percent change in median household income. A ratio above 1 indicates reduced affordability; a ratio below 1 indicates increased affordability. For example, if from 1990 to 2000 the median gross rent increased from $500 to $1,000 (a 100 percent increase) and the median household income increased from $50,000 to $75,000 (a 50 percent increase), then the rent-to-income ratio would be 100/50, or 2. This means that median gross rent rose twice as much as median household income, reducing the affordability of housing. Similarly, the house-value-to-income ratio is the ratio of percent change in the median value of owner-occupied housing to the percent change in median household income. For example, if the median house value increased from $100,000 to $170,000 (a 70 percent increase) and median income increased from $50,000 to $75,000 (a 50 percent increase), then the house-value-to-income ratio is 70/50 or 1.4, also an indication that housing became less affordable.

The second group of indicators assesses the housing affordability gap by showing first the additional annual income required by families in the metropolitan region earning median and 80 percent of median household income to be able to afford median-price owner-occupied housing and second the additional annual income required by families earning 80 percent of median and 50 percent of median household income to be able to afford median-price rental housing.

The third group of indicators assesses the change in affordability of owner- and renter-occupied housing costs for modest- and low-income households earning below 80 percent of median income.[15] Here, the percentage of households in each income category paying more than 30 percent of income

15. Another way to estimate housing affordability is to examine the affordability of houses in different price ranges for various income groups by looking at the house sale price. That approach could not be used in this study because of the lack of reliable and consistent housing sales data for the whole study period across all the counties examined here.

for housing was compared for the years 1989 (1990 census data) and 1999 (2000 census data). The census tables provide renter and owner housing cost data for various income categories in terms of the percentage of income spent on housing. We transformed the income groups used in the census tables into income groups based on the percentage of median income that each group earned, using the median household income of the county. It was assumed that the distribution of households within each income group was linear with respect to income and housing costs.[16]

The housing affordability indicators listed below are arrayed graphically in tables or charts, with accompanying explanatory text, later in this chapter:

—absolute changes in the median price of owner-occupied and rental housing

—rent-to-income ratio

—house-value-to-income ratio

—affordability gap in median-value owner-occupied housing

—affordability gap in median-price rental housing

—proportion of owner-occupied households paying more than 30 percent of income for housing costs

—proportion of renter-occupied households paying more than 30 percent of income for housing costs.

Selecting Growth Management Policy and Program Indicators

If the right combination of growth management policies and smart growth regulations is in place, jurisdictions are at least capable of enabling and encouraging the development of affordable housing. Whether the funding or political will to do so exists is a different matter. What policies and programs might aid or thwart affordable housing?[17] We looked at three key issues that we believe must be addressed in order to enable affordable housing to be created in urban growth areas: incentives for high-density and infill development; development costs; and permanent affordability of housing. Within these broad areas we sought to learn whether the metropolitan

16. We would like to acknowledge that Chandler Felt, chief demographer in King County and author of the county's annual growth report, developed this methodology, which was adopted by the county (King County 2002).

17. The indicators are taken in part from the *2002 King County Growth Management Planning Council Housing Survey*, produced by the King County Housing and Community Development Program. The county and twenty-eight municipalities representing all the urban growth centers responded to questions about actions taken or under way to meet housing affordability and production targets in the comprehensive plans.

counties studied employed any or all of the following eleven indicator policies and programs.[18]

Incentives for higher-density and infill development

Cottage housing: allows for small (1,000-square-foot), single-family detached homes at densities of from ten to twenty-five dwelling units per acre in urban growth areas.

Transit-oriented development: enables jurisdictions to plan for dense mixed-use developments located with or adjacent to transit stations and park-and-ride lots.

Accessory dwelling units: permit detached mother-in-law or granny flat apartments in single-family residential areas, which can increase density with minimal change in neighborhood character.

Flexible/reduced parking requirements: allow off-street parking requirements to be shared, reduced, or eliminated to reduce the cost of housing.

Design standards: require designing multifamily and affordable housing units so that they blend in with existing development, reducing the stigma associated with living in subsidized housing.

Incentive programs: create density bonuses through inclusionary zoning and tax exemptions for infill and affordable housing projects to increase the supply of housing.

Transfer of development rights: protects agricultural and resource lands in rural areas while offering density bonuses in urban and infill areas.

Factors Affecting the Cost of Developing New Affordable Housing Units

Five-story wood-frame construction: allows greater height and densities at lower cost to developers.

Impact fees: charge for infrastructure and services for new development, including parks, transportation, fire protection, and schools

Fee waivers: exempt affordable housing from impact fees.

Making Affordability Permanent

Preservation of affordable housing: makes housing permanently affordable through rent restrictions or outright ownership by a nonprofit or public entity.

18. Are these the right indicators? We selected ours in part on the progressiveness of the policy or program. Bogdon (2001) suggests that urban growth boundaries, minimum lot zoning, or agricultural reserve areas have a more direct and intrusive effect on housing affordability. These

A corollary to protecting open space and natural resources is concentrating housing within urban growth areas, which invariably results in housing densities that are far greater than in most suburban residential developments and in an entirely different form of housing and community development. Urban and suburban residents often oppose increasing affordable housing densities through infill development because higher densities threaten the existing neighborhood scale and character and raise fears of reduced property values and racial succession.[19] Providing affordable housing requires providing incentives to both developers and local residents. For this reason we inquired whether the counties offered density bonuses through inclusionary zoning or tax exemptions for infill and affordable housing projects. Transfer of development rights (TDR) programs also provide density bonuses in urban growth areas while protecting farmland and open space outside growth boundaries, which is used and enjoyed by urban residents.

Higher density alone is not the answer to providing affordable housing. New urbanists advocate building accessory dwelling units (ADUs), or "mother-in-law apartments," as a way to reinforce traditional neighborhood character while providing affordable housing and increasing density without high-rise construction. An appealing aspect of ADUs to single-family residential areas is that they are developed by private homeowners who may receive new income from renting out an apartment—over a detached garage facing an alley, for example. ADU ordinances enable the private market to provide affordable housing stock without the intervention of nonprofit developers or public housing authorities, institutions that may be anathema to many urban and suburban private homeowners. A major stumbling block to increasing densities or implementing ADU programs is parking. Standard suburban off-street parking requirements significantly increase development costs for multifamily housing, and neighbors' fear of losing on-street parking stands in the way of using ADUs. Flexible and reduced parking standards can go a long way toward addressing these problems.

Transit-oriented development (TOD) zones and enabling regulations further reduce dependence on cars and enhance the compactness of urban form. Originally conceived of as pedestrian-oriented, mixed-use developments within a quarter-mile of light-rail or train stations, TODs also can be adapted

---

and other indicators could be incorporated in future efforts to monitor the relationship between growth management and affordable housing.

19. Danielsen, Lang, and Fulton (1999, p. 516).

to bus systems at transit centers and hubs. Residents and workers can use high-occupancy transit, thus reducing roadway and parking costs and space use. TODs also free up more of residents' incomes for housing, a concept recognized in the "location efficient mortgages" now being piloted by banks in selected regions.

One growth management feature that accounts for a major cost of many developments is the use of impact fees, which are aimed at ensuring that new development pays its share of the roads, parks, schools, and other infrastructure and services that its residents use. In this way, existing residents do not subsidize new peripheral development. Impact fees charged on a per-unit basis add to the cost of a house, and they also may give developers an incentive to build higher-priced housing. Hence such fees could thwart construction of affordable housing and other socially beneficial facilities in new development areas unless they are waived. For this reason we are interested in both whether impact fees exist and whether they are waived for affordable housing, since one policy could thwart and the other assist affordable housing development. Design standards for affordable housing could be another additional cost. Design standards help affordable units blend into new development and reduce the stigma associated with living in cheaper-looking housing. Some affluent communities employ design standards to encourage affordable units to fit in; some waive the standards to reduce construction costs.

Building code adjustments can reduce construction costs without compromising safety, and the savings can make housing more affordable. Some jurisdictions are allowing wood construction of multifamily developments over four stories in height.

Growth Management Counties

The population, geography, and income of the counties studied along with information on housing affordability, growth management policies and programs, and housing production are summarized below.

King County, Washington

King County has a population of 1.8 million, including the city of Seattle (570,000), in an area approximately the size of Rhode Island. It is the state's most populous and affluent county, with a median income for a family of four of $72,000. About three-quarters of its residents live in incorporated municipalities and about one-quarter live in unincorporated, often rural areas of the county. In the late 1980s King County and the three other central Puget Sound counties began to develop a regional plan called Vision 2020. It called for the designation of twenty-one urban centers to accommodate future population and job growth within the metropolitan growth area. Shortly thereafter Washington state enacted the Growth Management Act (GMA) of 1991.

The GMA requires counties and cities to prepare twenty-year comprehensive plans to identify where and how growth should occur. The plans also must show how the area will accommodate the increase in population projected by the state Office of Financial Management for the twenty-year period. All incorporated jurisdictions within the county must prepare a comprehensive plan that is consistent with the county plan; they also must update their comprehensive plan every five years. If cities and counties do not meet the update deadlines, they automatically lose their eligibility for assistance from the Public Works Trust Fund and for Centennial Clean Water Act funds; they also lose their right to collect impact fees.

County plans must cover at least six topics: land use, housing, capital facilities, utilities, transportation, and rural areas, and they may include seven more.[20] Under the GMA, the state can use a combination of incentives and sanctions to ensure compliance. The most notable sanction is the withdrawal of state funds from counties that do not comply with the GMA.

HOUSING AFFORDABILITY INDICATORS. Between 1990 and 2000, the median value of owner-occupied housing in King County increased by $95,800 (67.9 percent). Similarly, the median gross rent increased by $248 (48.63 percent). Meanwhile the median household income of the region increased by $15,686 (44.76 percent) (tables 2-1 and 2-2). Thus the rent-to-income ratio and house-value-to-income ratio were 1.09 and 1.52 respectively. The increase in gross rent was only 9 percent more than the increase in median household income for the period 1990–2000, while the increase in the value of owner-occupied housing was 52 percent more than the increase in the median household income for the same period. This indicates a significant rise in the price of owner-occupied housing over the ten-year period.

20. The GMA sets goals in thirteen areas, which can become elements of the comprehensive plan: urban growth, sprawl reduction, transportation, housing, economic development, property rights, permits, natural resource lands, open space and recreation, environment, citizen participation, public facilities/services, and historic preservation.

Table 2-1. *Changes in Median Value of Owner-Occupied Housing Related to Income, King County, 1990 and 2000*

Dollars, except as indicated

Year	1990	2000
Median value (county)	141,100	236,900
Absolute change in median value (county)	. . .	95,800
Percent change in median value (county)	. . .	67.90
Median household income (county)	36,179	53,157
Median household income (metropolitan region)	35,047	50,733
Absolute change in median household income (metropolitan region)	. . .	15,686
Percent change in median household income (metropolitan region)	. . .	44.76
House value-to-income ratio (metropolitan region)	. . .	1.52

In 2000, households earning median and 80 percent below median income could not afford median-value owner-occupied housing. The affordability gap was approximately $5,000 for a median-income household and $15,000 for a household earning 80 percent below median income.[21] Households earning 80 percent of median household income could afford median-

Table 2-2. *Changes in Median Gross Rent Related to Income, King County, 1990 and 2000*

Dollars, except as indicated

Year	1990	2000
Median gross rent (county)	510	758
Absolute change in median gross rent (county)	. . .	248
Percent change in median gross rent (county)	. . .	48.63
Median household income (county)	36,179	53,157
Median household income (metropolitan region)	35,047	50,733
Absolute change in median household income (metropolitan region)	. . .	15,686
Percent change in median household income (metropolitan region)	. . .	44.76
Rent-to-income ratio (metropolitan region)	. . .	1.09

21. "Affordability gap" has been defined as the additional annual income needed to afford the desired housing.

Figure 2-1. *King County: Percent of Owner-Occupied Households Paying More than 30 Percent of Income for Housing*

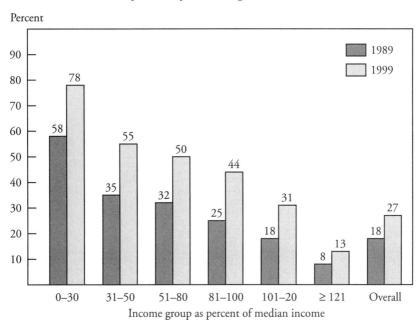

Percent

Income group as percent of median income

price rental housing, but households earning 50 percent of median income could not; the affordability gap in this income category was approximately $5,000. Figures 2-1 and 2-2 show changes in housing affordability for moderate- and low-income households by income group, as follows:

—The affordability of homeownership decreased for all income groups.

—The percentage of households paying more than 30 percent of their income for housing costs increased by approximately 20 percent for households earning below 100 percent of median income.

—In 1999, overall 9 percent more households paid more than 30 percent of their income for housing costs than in 1989.

In summary, in 2000 in King County, even households earning median household income could not afford owner-occupied housing and households earning 50 percent of the median household income could not afford rental housing. Analysis of the trends between 1990 and 2000 shows that the affordability of rental housing at the median rent and household income levels stayed the same, while the affordability of median-value owner-occupied housing decreased. The affordability of homeownership for households earning below

Figure 2-2. *King County: Percent of Renter Households Paying More than 30 Percent of Income for Housing*

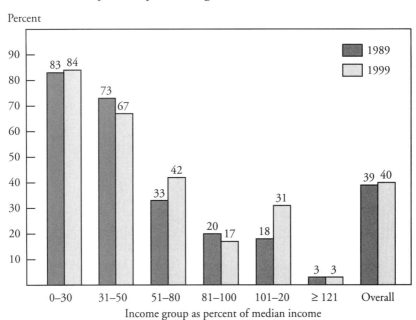

Percent

Income group as percent of median income

80 percent of median income decreased over the last decade. The affordability of rental housing did not decrease by the same magnitude; it has stayed about the same for households earning below 80 percent of median income, except those in the 51 to 80 percent below median income group, for whom the affordability of both owner-occupied and rental housing decreased.

PROGRAM AND POLICY INDICATORS. Several of the larger municipalities in King County have adopted cottage housing provisions in their zoning codes that limit the size of detached single-family cottage units to less than 1,000 square feet. Typical density is twice that of standard single-family houses; in Seattle the density is 1 cottage per 1,600 square feet of lot size, or about twenty-five units per acre. TOD zoning is in place in many jurisdictions on commuter rail lines and anticipated light-rail lines; two affordable housing developments have been integrated with county park-and-ride bus transit centers. From 2000 to 2002, six cities in the county have approved five-story wood-frame construction, and another seven are considering approval. Most cities allow ADUs if attached to a home, while several cities permit detached ADUs in single-family neighborhoods.

Table 2-3. *Program and Policy Indicators, King County*

Indicator	Use by jurisdiction
Cottage housing	Used by some
Transit-oriented development	Used by many
Five-story wood-frame	Used by some
Accessory dwelling units	Used by some
Flex parking	Used by many
Impact fees	Used by some
Impact fee waiver	Used by some
Transfer of development rights	Used by some
Incentives	Used by some
Design standards	Used by many
Preservation	Used by many

Almost all jurisdictions allow for shared parking, many reduce parking requirements for affordable and senior housing, and Seattle waives parking requirements for affordable housing projects serving very-low-income (below 30 percent of median income) residents. Impact fees are used fairly extensively in King County, but some or all of the fees are waived for affordable and infill housing projects in many jurisdictions. TDR programs are in place in King County and several cities to protect agricultural and resource lands and to provide density bonuses in urban receiving areas. Most jurisdictions offer density bonuses for affordable housing and mixed-use projects in downtown areas; several jurisdictions have inclusionary zoning requirements as well. Most cities have design standards and plan reviews that apply to multifamily and mixed-use developments. One affluent city exempts affordable housing projects from design review. Most cities work through a county consortium to use block grant funds for affordable housing preservation through repair, rehab, weatherization, and financing programs. (See table 2-3 for policies and programs in use in King County.)

AFFORDABLE HOUSING PRODUCTION. During the 1990–2000 decade, 94,894 new residential units were built in King County. Based on figures from a coalition of nonprofit housing providers, we estimated that 13,000—nearly 14 percent of the total—were affordable housing units.[22]

22. The Housing Development Consortium of Seattle-King County, which represents twenty-nine nonprofit housing development organizations, reports that it has produced 14,000 affordable housing units since 1988. We are estimating that this represents 70 percent of the total production of affordable housing when units developed through the Seattle housing levy

King County estimates that the gap between demand for and supply of affordable housing in 2000 was 29,690 housing units.[23]

Montgomery County, Maryland

Montgomery County, the nation's sixth-richest county, is located immediately north and northwest of Washington, D.C. With more than 800,000 residents, it is the most populous county in Maryland. During the 1970s and 1980s, it grew from a bedroom community to the region's second-largest employment center. Now more than 60 percent of residents work and live in the county. Montgomery County has been at the forefront of both fair housing policy and land use planning.[24]

In 1969 Montgomery County adopted a master plan entitled "On Wedges and Corridors," which directed development along two major transportation corridors, the I-270 and Highway 29 corridors, while preserving low-density development and open space between the corridors.[25] The county implements the plan through zoning and regulatory mechanisms. Porter identifies four initiatives that characterize this pioneering growth management effort:

—the use of adequate public facilities measures as a core concept for year-to-year management of development

—the agricultural land preservation program

---

and various public housing authorities are included. We have prorated the production figure for 1990–2000. Several agencies provide or assist in providing affordable housing, including the King County Housing and Community Development Program, the King County Housing Authority, the Washington State Housing Finance Commission, the Washington Housing Trust Fund, and the other city-level housing agencies like the City of Seattle Office of Housing, the Seattle Housing Authority, the Renton Housing Authority, and the Muckleshoot Housing Authority. At present, there is no comprehensive inventory of units created through affordable housing grants or incentive programs.

23. King County (2002).

24. The state of Maryland adopted a set of laws collectively known as Smart Growth in 1997, which built on a line of previous state planning legislation that began in 1974 with the state intervention policy and the 1992 planning act requiring all jurisdictions to address resource protection and sprawl reduction in their comprehensive plans. Because Montgomery County's growth management plan predates these efforts and includes an affordable housing law, our study focuses on the county. More information on smart growth and its predecessors can be obtained from the Maryland Department of Planning (www.mdp.state.md.us [December 10, 2003]).

25. The plan was prepared by the Maryland-National Capital Park and Planning Commission for Montgomery and Prince George's counties. Today Montgomery County has its own planning board, which updates and administers the plan. A case study of the plan, its history, and its attributes appears in Porter (1997, pp. 33–43).

—the inclusionary housing program

—the encouragement of development around Metrorail subway stations.[26]
In 1974 the county adopted the Moderately Priced Housing law, the country's first mandatory, inclusionary zoning law. It also established the Moderately Priced Dwelling Unit program (MPDU), which requires 12.5 to 15 percent of the total units in every new subdivision or high-rise building of fifty units or more to be sold or rented at specified affordable prices. Developers are granted density bonuses of up to 22 percent, which allow them to build more units on a particular parcel of land than zoning normally permits. Households with an income at or below 65 percent of the area median qualify for the program. Since 1974 more than 11,000 units of affordable housing have been built. More than 1,600 of these units are owned and managed by the Housing Opportunities Commission, the county's public housing agency.

HOUSING AFFORDABILITY INDICATORS.   Between 1990 and 2000, the median value of owner-occupied housing in Montgomery County increased by $21,000 (10.46 percent); the median gross rent increased by $174 (23.51 percent). Meanwhile, the median household income of the region increased by $10,407 (22.20 percent) (tables 2-4 and 2-5). Thus the rent-to-income ratio and the house-value-to-income ratio were 1.06 and 0.47, respectively. The increase in gross rent exceeded the increase in median household income for the period 1990–2000, while the increase in the value of owner-occupied housing was only half of the increase in median household income for the same period. These data indicate an increase in the affordability of owner-occupied housing and a decrease in the affordability of rental housing for county residents at the median-income level.

In 2000, households earning area median income could afford median-value, owner-occupied housing, but those with incomes below 80 percent of the median could not. The affordability gap was approximately $6,000. Households earning 80 percent of median household income could afford median-price rental housing, but those earning 50 percent of the median could not. The affordability gap in this income category was approximately $8,000. Figures 2-3 and 2-4 indicate the change in housing affordability for the various income groups, as follows:

—Overall, the affordability of owner-occupied housing remained almost unchanged between 1989 and 1999, in spite of the fact that income increased more rapidly than rents or house prices.

26. Porter (1997, p. 35).

Table 2-4. *Changes in Median Value of Owner-Occupied Housing Related to Income, Montgomery County, 1990 and 2000*
Dollars, except as indicated

Year	1990	2000
Median value (county)	200,800	221,800
Absolute change in median value (county)	. . .	21,000
Percent change in median value (county)	. . .	10.46
Median household income (county)	54,089	71,551
Median household income (metropolitan region)	46,884	57,291
Absolute change in median household income (metropolitan region)	. . .	10,407
Percent change in median household income (metropolitan region)	. . .	22.20
House-value-to-income ratio (metropolitan region)	. . .	0.47

—The affordability of owner-occupied housing decreased for all groups earning less than 80 percent of median income.

—Overall, the affordability of renter-occupied housing increased between 1989 and 1999.

—Among groups earning less than 80 percent of median income, the affordability of rental housing decreased for those in the 31 to 50 percent

Table 2-5. *Changes in Median Gross Rent Related to Income, Montgomery County, 1990 and 2000*
Dollars, except as indicated

Year	1990	2000
Median gross rent (county)	740	914
Absolute change in median gross rent (county)	. . .	174
Percent change in median gross rent (county)	. . .	23.51
Median household income (county)	54,089	71,551
Median household income (metropolitan region)	46,884	57,291
Absolute change in median household income (metropolitan region)	. . .	10,407
Percent change in median household income (metropolitan region)	. . .	22.20
Rent-to-income ratio (metropolitan region)	. . .	1.06

Figure 2-3. *Montgomery County: Percent of Owner-Occupied Households Paying More than 30 Percent of Income for Housing*

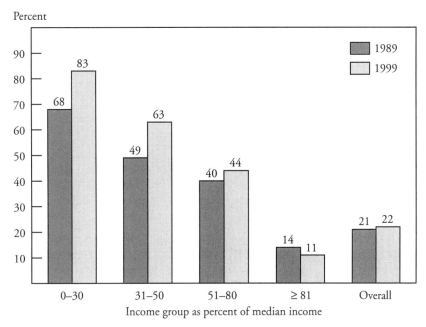

Percent

Income group as percent of median income

below median income group while it increased for those in the below 30 percent and in the 51 to 80 percent of median income groups.

In summary, in 2000 in Montgomery County, households earning 80 percent of median household income could not afford owner-occupied housing. Households earning 50 percent of median household income could not afford rental housing. Analysis of the trends between the years 1990 and 2000 shows that the affordability of both median rental and owner-occupied housing increased. Affordability of homeownership for households with incomes of below 80 percent of the median income decreased over the last decade. Affordability of rental housing in general increased, except for the 31 to 50 percent below median income group.

POLICY AND PROGRAM INDICATORS. Montgomery County does not have cottage housing zoning but does have mixed-use, high-density zoning and development in the areas around the Bethesda subway station. It does not allow five-story wood-frame construction or accessory dwelling units (except by special exception). Parking credits are awarded for residential development that is close to transit, and parking requirements are

Figure 2-4. *Montgomery County: Percent of Renter Households Paying More than 30 Percent of Income for Housing*

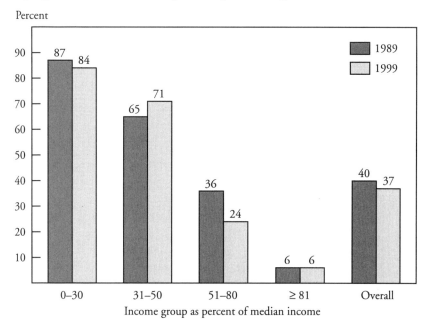

Percent

Income group as percent of median income

reduced by half for moderately priced dwelling units in multifamily developments. Impact fees for MPDUs are waived. The county's TDR program allows one additional dwelling unit above existing zoning requirements in infill receiving areas for every five acres of agricultural development rights purchased.

The MPDU law combines density bonuses with preservation measures. When developers build fifty housing units or more in a single development, they must set aside 12 to 15 percent as moderately priced dwelling units. In return, the developer receives a density bonus; the more MPDUs, the larger the bonus. The bonus is only 1 percent if 12.6 percent of the housing units are MPDUs, but it increases to 22 percent if 15 percent of the housing units are moderately priced. For a period of ten years, the developer must price three-fifths of the MPDUs so that households with incomes at or below 63 percent of area median income can afford them.[27]

27. Kleit (1998).

The remaining two-fifths of the units are made available for long-term preservation as affordable housing. The Housing Opportunities Commission has the option of buying 75 percent of the long-term units; local non-profit organizations can purchase the remaining 25 percent. Design standards enable MPDU townhouses to be constructed in single-family zones with reduced setbacks. Also, compatibility and façade allowances are given to the developer; they can be passed along as an additional cost to the buyer.[28]

AFFORDABLE HOUSING PRODUCTION. Under the MPDU program, Montgomery County has seen the production of 11,210 units of affordable housing. Approximately 8,000 were for-sale units and 3,000 were rental units. Affordable housing production hit its peak from 1980 through 1987, when as many as 1,200 units per year went on the market. Since 1997, production has steadily tapered down, to an average of 220 units per year.[29] During the period 1976–2002, 120,000 housing units were built in Montgomery County. Thus approximately 11 percent of the housing produced during the period was affordable. However, under the MPDU program, price controls expire after fifteen to twenty years. By 2000, the prices of 6,767 units no longer were controlled. Montgomery County conducted a survey in 2000 that found that approximately two-thirds of the units whose prices no longer were controlled remained affordable to the target households. "Only the best-built MPDUs in the most desirable areas" showed major price increases.[30] The extent to which growth management policies and programs are used in Montgomery County is shown in table 2-6.

Somerset and Middlesex Counties, New Jersey

Somerset and Middlesex counties are among New Jersey's fastest-growing counties. They contain a mix of established communities, some dating back to the American Revolution; new land-intensive suburban development; and open space at the periphery of the New York City metropolitan area. Middlesex County's population is 750,000 and Somerset's is 298,000; each

28. Telephone interview with Sally Roman, research division of Maryland-National Capital Parks and Planning Commission, December 2002.
29. Montgomery County (2003).
30. Correspondence with Sally Roman, MPDU planner, Maryland-National Capital Parks and Planning Commission, April 2003.

Table 2-6. *Program and Policy Indicators, Montgomery County*

Indicator	Use by jurisdiction
Cottage housing	Unavailable/unused
Transit-oriented development	Used by many
Five-story wood-frame	Unavailable/unused
Accessory dwelling units	Unavailable/unused
Flex parking	Used by many
Impact fees	Used by many
Impact fee waiver	Used by many
Transfer of development rights	Used by many
Incentives	Used by many
Design standards	Used by many
Preservation	Used by many

county comprises just over 300 square miles. Median household incomes are $72,000 and $77,000 respectively.[31] Along with Hunterdon County, these counties constitute the Council on Affordable Housing's region 3, an area in the middle of the state that sometimes is called the "wealth belt." Under guidelines established by the council, a state agency, a family of four with an income of $72,000 or below qualifies for affordable housing. Middlesex County is home to one large city, New Brunswick, and several older suburban cities like Metuchen and Carlstadt. These communities are served by one of three commuter rail lines, including the main Northeast corridor line serving Washington, Philadelphia, and New York.

In 1985, the New Jersey legislature passed the State Planning Act, which affirmed that the state needed sound and integrated statewide planning in order to "conserve its natural resources, revitalize its urban centers, protect the quality of its environment, and provide needed housing and adequate public services at a reasonable cost while promoting beneficial economic growth, development and renewal." New Jersey employs a cross-acceptance process in which the state presents its preliminary plan to its twenty-one counties for review and comparison with their plans.

Both the cross-acceptance process and the State Redevelopment and Development Plan adopted in 1992 and revised in 2001 are voluntary. The plans call for locating new development in designated centers, for infill development, and for protection of agricultural land; they also define the state's

31. 2000 census.

dollar savings from smart growth initiatives: $1.3 billion in capital infra-
structure costs over twenty years and up to $400 million annually in operat-
ing costs. This approach has proven weak primarily because it is voluntary
and leaves most land use decisions and activity to the state's 566 municipalities. Governor James E. McGreevey has proposed adopting a new smart
growth Big Map for the state, which would show where development is per-
missible, questionable, or prohibited.

However, New Jersey is a leader in the fair share approach to the provision
of affordable housing.[32] This is an outgrowth of the New Jersey supreme
court's Mt. Laurel decisions of 1975 and 1983, in which the court ruled that
every municipality in a growth area has a constitutional obligation to provide
through its land use regulations a realistic opportunity for low- and moderate-income families to receive a fair share of its region's current and prospective housing.[33]

The Fair Housing Act of 1985 was a companion to the State Planning Act
of the same year. It established the Council on Affordable Housing (COAH),
with which any municipality can file a housing component to its comprehensive plan to show how its fair share goals for low- and moderate-income
housing will be met. COAH certifies the plan and thereby protects the city
from lawsuits as long as the municipality is contributing to its allocated share
of affordable housing units. Common approaches include rehabilitation and
repair of existing affordable housing, regional contribution agreements, and
inclusionary housing requirements. Under a regional contribution agreement, up to half of a community's allocation of affordable units can be transferred to a receiving city in its "housing region," along with a commensurate
payment to the receiving city.

A little less than half the state's municipalities participate in the COAH
process. They have provided approximately 44,000 affordable units since
1985, mostly in areas zoned for housing and infill consistent with smart
growth policies. The remaining majority of cities are vulnerable to lawsuits
brought by developers seeking to build new housing and to having to accept
the "remedies" proposed by developers to provide their fair share of low- and
moderate-income housing. Such remedies, which have been upheld by the
courts in about ten cases, often are large developments built in greenfields,
yet the lawsuit-losing communities must accept them. For this reason, there

32. Interviews with David Listokin and Steve O'Connor at the Center for Urban Policy
Research, Rutgers University, and other knowledgeable land use and housing officials.
33. Mount Laurel, 92 NJ 158 (1983).

Table 2-7. *Changes in Median Value of Owner-Occupied Housing Related to Income, Somerset and Middlesex Counties, 1990 and 2000*
Dollars, except as indicated

Year	Somerset		Middlesex	
	1990	2000	1990	2000
Median value (county)	194,800	222,400	164,100	168,500
Absolute change in median value (county)	. . .	27,600	. . .	4,400
Percent change in median value (county)	. . .	14.17	. . .	2.68
Median household income (county)	55,519	76,933	45,623	61,446
Median household income (metropolitan region)	38,445	50,795	38,445	50,795
Absolute change in median household income (metropolitan region)	. . .	12,350	. . .	12,350
Percent change in median household income (metropolitan region)	. . .	32.12	. . .	32.12
House value-to-income ratio (metropolitan region)	. . .	0.44	. . .	0.08

is a widespread public perception that the state's affordable housing policy is a cause of urban sprawl.[34]

HOUSING AFFORDABILITY INDICATORS. Between 1990 and 2000 the median value of owner-occupied housing in Somerset County increased by $27,600 (14.17 percent), and the median gross rent increased by $179 (24.90 percent). In Middlesex County over the same period, the median value of owner-occupied housing increased by $4,400 (2.68 percent), and the median gross rent increased by $178 (26.69 percent). Meanwhile the region's median household income increased by $12,350 (32.12 percent) (tables 2-7 and 2-8). Thus the rent-to-income ratio was 0.77 and 0.83 and the house-value-to-income ratio was 0.44 and 0.08 for Somerset and Middlesex County respectively. This means that for Somerset County, the increase in gross rent was only approximately three-fourths of the increase in median regional household income for the period, and the increase in the value of owner-occupied housing was only about half of the increase in median income. These data indicate an increase in the affordability of housing for median-income house-

34. Interviews with Dan Hoffman, executive director, New Jersey Coalition for Affordable Housing and the Environment.

Table 2-8. *Changes in Median Gross Rent Related to Income,*
Somerset and Middlesex Counties, 1990 and 2000

Dollars, except as indicated

	Somerset		Middlesex	
Year	1990	2000	1990	2000
Median gross rent (county)	719	898	667	845
Absolute change in median gross rent (county)	. . .	179		178
Percent change in median gross rent (county)	. . .	24.90		26.69
Median household income (county)	55,519	76,933	45,623	61,446
Median household income (metropolitan region)	38,445	50,795	38,445	50,795
Absolute change in median household income (metropolitan region)	. . .	12,350	. . .	12,350
Percent change in median household income (metropolitan region)	. . .	32.12	. . .	32.12
Rent-to-income ratio (metropolitan region)	. . .	0.77	. . .	0.83

holds. The situation is similar for Middlesex County, where the increase in median gross rent was about four-fifths of the increase in median regional household income, while the increase in the median value of owner-occupied housing was less than one-tenth of the increase in median income.

In 2000, Somerset County households earning median and 80 percent below median income could not afford median-value owner-occupied housing. The affordability gap was approximately $1,500 for median-income households and $12,000 for households earning 80 percent of median. In Middlesex County, median-income households could afford the same housing but households earning 80 percent of median could not, an affordability gap of approximately $1,000.

In 2000, households earning 80 percent of the median household income could afford median-price rental housing in both counties, but households earning 50 percent of the median could not. The affordability gaps for this income category were approximately $10,000 and $8,500 for Somerset and Middlesex County respectively.

Figures 2-5 through 2-8 indicate the change in housing affordability for the various income groups for the two counties, as follows:

Figure 2-5. *Somerset County: Percent of Owner-Occupied Households Paying More than 30 Percent of Income for Housing*

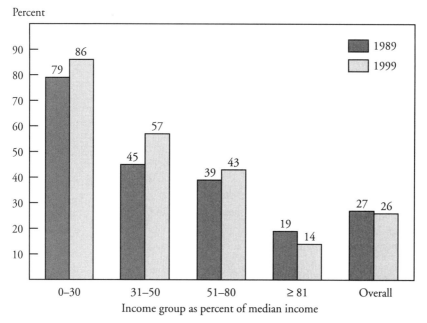

Percent

Income group as percent of median income

Somerset County

—Overall, the affordability of owner-occupied housing in Somerset County showed a slight increase from 1989 to 1999.

—Affordability owner-occupied housing decreased for all groups with incomes below 80 percent of median income.

—Overall, the affordability of renter-occupied housing increased slightly between 1989 and 1999.

—Among the groups with incomes below 80 percent of median, affordability of rental housing decreased for those earning 31 to 50 percent below median; it remained unchanged for those earning below 30 percent of median; and it increased for those earning 51 to 80 percent of median.

Middlesex County

—Overall, the affordability of owner-occupied housing in Middlesex County did not change between 1989 and 1999.

Figure 2-6. *Somerset County: Percent of Renter Households Paying More than 30 Percent of Income for Housing*

Percent

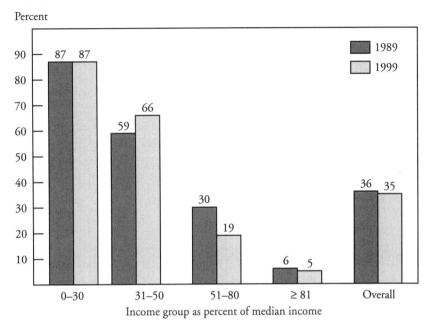

Income group as percent of median income

—Affordability of owner-occupied housing decreased for all groups earning below 80 percent of median income.

—Overall, the affordability of renter-occupied housing increased slightly between 1989 and 1999.

—Among the groups with incomes below 80 percent of median, affordability of rental housing decreased slightly for those earning 31 to 50 percent below median; it increased for those earning 51 to 80 percent of median.

In summary, for the year 2000, households earning median household income in Somerset County could not afford median-value owner-occupied housing. Households earning 50 percent of median household income could not afford rental housing. In Middlesex County, households earning 80 percent of median household income could afford median-value owner-occupied housing, while households earning 50 percent of median income could not afford rental housing. Analyzing the trends in both Somerset and Middlesex counties shows that between 1990 and 2000, the affordability of

Figure 2-7. *Middlesex County: Percent of Owner-Occupied Households Paying More than 30 Percent of Income for Housing*

Percent

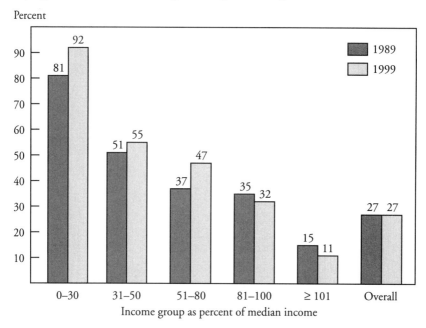

Income group as percent of median income

median renter- and owner-occupied housing increased. Examining the affordability of housing for households with incomes below 80 percent of median income shows that owner-occupied housing became less affordable over the last decade, while overall the affordability of rental housing remained largely unchanged.

PROGRAM AND POLICY INDICATORS. The strongest affordable housing tool that New Jersey boroughs and townships have is the inclusionary zoning mandate that comes with plan certification through COAH. Developers typically provide one unit of affordable housing for every four market-rate units; hence 20 percent of their new units are affordable. In addition, in Somerset County fees associated with transportation improvement districts are waived for such units. Impact fees to cover the costs of schools, parks, and other facilities are not imposed in New Jersey. Design standards are used by some municipalities to help affordable units blend in with the prevailing market-rate housing. Apparently no systematic way of tracking the duration and expiration of deed restrictions on COAH affordable hous-

Figure 2-8. *Middlesex County: Percent of Renter Households Paying More than 30 Percent of Income for Housing*

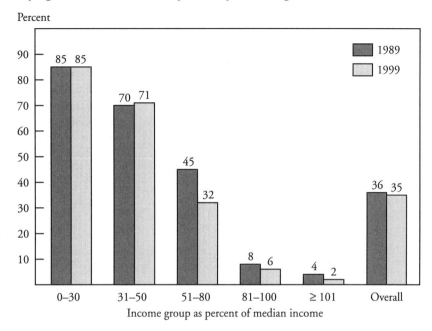

Percent

Income group as percent of median income

ing exists in the state; some jurisdictions track this information, but others are caught off guard when formerly affordable units are suddenly placed on the market at market prices. Preserving their affordability is problematic once that occurs. Both counties and multiple jurisdictions fund home reha-bilitation and weatherization programs to maintain the stock of units occu-pied by moderate- and low-income households. Flexible parking standards are employed by some jurisdictions. Cottage housing and five-story wood-frame housing do not exist, although some housing units restricted to senior residents are smaller than the prevailing new homes and sited on smaller lots; however, they are not as small as cottages. Accessory dwelling units generally are not permitted. While the state plan and the counties have advocated mixed-use and pedestrian-oriented TODs, those tactics have not been adopted yet by any Somerset County municipality and they are being explored by only two or three municipalities in Middlesex County. (See table 2-9 for the programs and policies in use in Middlesex and Somerset counties.)

Table 2-9. *Program and Policy Indicators, Somerset and Middlesex Counties*

	Use by jurisdiction	
Indicator	*Somerset*	*Middlesex*
Cottage housing	Unavailable/unused	Unavailable/unused
Transit-oriented development	Unavailable/unused	Used by some
Five-story wood-frame	Unavailable/unused	Unavailable/unused
Accessory dwelling units	Used by some	Unavailable/unused
Flex parking	Used by some	Unavailable/unused
Impact fees	Used by some	Unavailable/unused
Impact fee waiver	Used by some	Unavailable/unused
Transfer of development rights	Unavailable/unused	Unavailable/unused
Incentives	Used by many	Used by many
Design standards	Used by some	Used by some
Preservation	Used by some	Used by some

AFFORDABLE HOUSING PRODUCTION.   According to the COAH, since 1985 approximately 44,000 affordable housing units have been built or rehabilitated statewide. This represents approximately 8 percent of the 567,000 housing units that were issued permits in the state during the 1985–2002 period. In Somerset County, 3,550 affordable housing units were added from 1980 through 2000, representing approximately 8 percent of the 42,350 housing units added during the twenty-year period. In Middlesex County, 6,900 new and rehabilitated affordable housing units were added from 1985 to 2002, representing approximately 10 percent of the 70,000 housing units added during the 1980–2000 period.[35] COAH does not track how long units remain affordable, and jurisdictions often do not know when affordability restricitons expire.

Under New Jersey's Fair Housing Law, up to half of a community's affordable housing obligation can be met through a regional contribution agreement (RCA), under which approximately $25,000 per unit is paid to a "receiving" city within the housing region. Somerset and Middlesex Counties are in region 3, in which a total of 1,437 RCA units have been transferred (of 7,882 transfers statewide). About 80 percent of the RCA units in the two counties were sent to New Brunswick and Perth Amboy, two larger, older

35. These totals do not include tax credit, HOPE VI, or other affordable housing units not tracked by COAH.

cities in Middlesex County. Somerset and Middlesex counties' RCA units have added approximately 1,000 affordable units to Middlesex County's affordable housing stock since 1985.

Interviews with affordable housing experts and county planners indicate that most new development during the last twenty years of rapid growth has occurred in boroughs with available open space, not in already established cities or inner-ring suburbs.[36] Over the past twenty years, 21,000 acres of open space and farmland has been converted to residential building lots in Somerset County. In Middlesex County during the period 1974–1995, residential acreage grew by 10,000. Interestingly, the 25,000-acre decline of farmland and vacant land was partly offset by a 14,000-acre increase in public open space. Neither county has an urban growth boundary or TDR program to protect farmland or open space.[37]

Comparison with a Non–Growth Management County

Montgomery County, Maryland, and Fairfax County, Virginia, are the two largest urban counties in the Washington, D.C., metropolitan area. Fairfax County does not have Montgomery County's forty-year history of growth management planning, and Virginia does not have a statewide growth management law. Fairfax County adopted an inclusionary zoning law in 1991 that is similar to although lesser in scope than the one in Montgomery County. Here we apply the same analytic approach to Fairfax County, followed by a discussion of our findings.

Fairfax County, Virginia

Fairfax County covers an area of 395 square miles and had a population of 969,749 in 2000. It is the state's most populous and most affluent county; median household income was $81,050 in 1999. The county adopted its first inclusionary zoning law in 1971. However, that law was challenged and then overturned by the courts, which ruled that as a Dillon Rule state, Virginia had to explicitly empower counties with the authority to adopt such

36. Interviews with Somerset County principal planner, Laurette Kratina; Somerset County Affordable Housing Coalition executive director, Sharon Clark; and Middlesex County assistant planning director, Bill Kruse.

37. Somerset data were obtained from Smart Growth Somerset County, a private organization; Middlesex data were obtained from the Middlesex County Planning Board.

Table 2-10. *Changes in Median Value of Owner-Occupied Housing Related to Income, Fairfax County, 1990 and 2000*
Dollars, except as indicated

Year	1990	2000
Median value (county)	213,100	233,300
Absolute change in median value (county)	. . .	20,000
Percent change in median value (county)	. . .	9.48
Median household income (county)	59,284	81,050
Median household income (metropolitan region)	46,884	57,291
Absolute change in median household income (metropolitan region)	. . .	10,407
Percent change in median household income (metropolitan region)	. . .	22.20
House value-to-income ratio (metropolitan region)	. . .	0.43

laws. Fairfax County adopted its new inclusionary zoning law, called the Affordable Dwelling Unit Program, in 1991 after authority was granted by the state legislature. Like Montgomery County's MPDU, it offers residential developers density bonuses for projects of more than fifty units when affordable housing units are included. Unlike Montgomery County, which requires a minimum of 12.5 percent of the units to be affordable, Fairfax County uses a sliding scale, adjusting the density bonus to the number of proposed affordable units. Hence, the incentive principle is the same, but its requirements are less robust.

HOUSING AFFORDABILITY INDICATORS. In Fairfax County between 1990 and 2000, the median value of owner- occupied housing increased by $20,200 (9.48 percent), and the median gross rent increased by $164 (19.66 percent). Meanwhile the region's median household income increased by $10,407 (22.20 percent) (tables 2-10 and 2-11). Thus the rent-to-income ratio and house-value-to-income ratio were 0.89 and 0.43 respectively. The increase in median gross rent was nine-tenths of the increase in median household income for the period, while the increase in the median value of owner-occupied housing was only approximately half of the increase in median income. These data indicate a significant increase in the affordability of renter- and owner-occupied housing for median-income households over the ten-year period.

In 2000, households earning median household income could afford median-value owner-occupied housing, but households earning below

Table 2-11. *Changes in Median Gross Rent Related to Income,*
Fairfax County, 1990 and 2000

Dollars, except as indicated

Year	1990	2000
Median gross rent (county)	834	998
Absolute change in median gross rent (county)	. . .	164
Percent change in median gross rent (county)	. . .	19.66
Median household income (county)	59,284	81,050
Median household income (metropolitan region)	46,884	57,291
Absolute change in median household income (metropolitan region)	. . .	10,407
Percent change in median household income (metropolitan region)	. . .	22.20
Rent-to-income ratio (metropolitan region)	. . .	0.89

80 percent of median could not; the affordability gap was approximately $9,000. In 2000, households earning 80 percent of median household income could afford median-price rental housing, but households earning 50 percent of median could not; the affordability gap in this income category was approximately $11,000.

Figures 2-9 and 2-10 show the changes in housing affordability for various income groups, as follows:

—Overall, owner-occupied housing became more affordable in Fairfax County.

—Affordability of owner-occupied housing did not decrease for households earning below 80 percent of median income.

—The increase in the affordability of housing can be attributed to a large extent to the rapid increase in income.

—Overall, renter-occupied housing became more affordable in Fairfax County.

—Affordability of rental housing also increased for households earning below 80 percent of median income.

In summary, in 2000 Fairfax County households earning 80 percent of median household income could not afford owner-occupied housing and households earning 50 percent of median could not afford rental housing. Analysis of the trends between 1990 and 2000 shows that the affordability of both median renter- and owner-occupied housing increased. For households earning below 80 percent of median income, owner-occupied housing

Figure 2-9. *Fairfax County: Percent of Owner-Occupied Households Paying More than 30 Percent of Income for Housing*

Percent

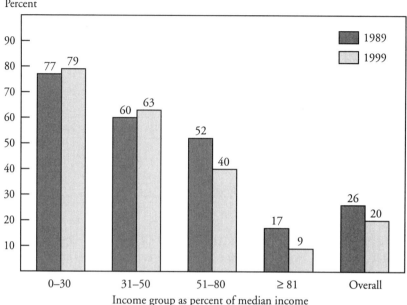

Income group as percent of median income

became marginally more affordable and the affordability of rental housing in general increased significantly.

PROGRAM AND POLICY INDICATORS. The one program commonly used in Fairfax County is the Affordable Dwelling Unit program, which offers a density bonus to qualifying developers. Impact fees are employed, but not universally, and they are not waived for affordable housing. A modest amount of affordable housing is preserved through purchase by the housing authority, and accessory dwelling units are permitted but only for elderly residents. Cottage housing, TOD zoning, five-story wood-frame construction, flexible parking, and TDR programs are not available. (See table 2-12 for policies and programs in use in Fairfax County.)

AFFORDABLE HOUSING PRODUCTION. Since 1991, when the Affordable Dwelling Unit program went into effect, 759 rental and 971 for-sale units have been completed, for a total of 1,730 units. As of 2003, an additional 500 units had been approved for construction but not yet built. Under the law, the affordability of rental units is controlled for twenty years and that

Figure 2-10. *Fairfax County: Percent of Renter Households Paying More than 30 Percent of Income for Housing*

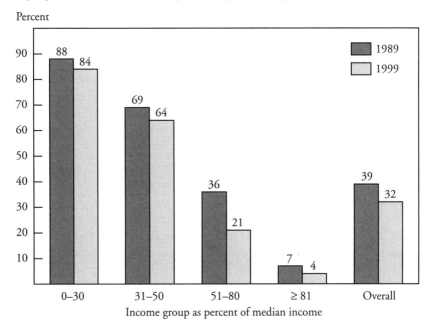

Percent

Income group as percent of median income

Table 2-12. *Program and Policy Indicators, Fairfax County*

Indicator	Use by jurisdiction
Cottage housing	Unavailable/unused
Transit-oriented development	Unavailable/unused
Five-story wood-frame	Unavailable/unused
Accessory dwelling units	Used by some
Flex parking	Used by some
Impact fees	Used by some
Impact fee waiver	Used by some
Transfer of development rights	Used by some
Incentives	Used by many
Design standards	Unavailable/unused
Preservation	Used by some

of for-sale units for fifteen years. The Redevelopment and Housing Authority may purchase up to 30 percent of the units produced under the program as permanent affordable housing stock, and it has bought forty-one units to date. From 1990 to 2002, 73,000 residential dwellings were built in Fairfax County; housing built under the inclusionary housing law represents 2.4 percent of that total. Affordable housing was produced through other means as well, mainly through developer proffers (negotiated developer agreements or contract zoning) and by the housing authority itself. These additional units are estimated at 750 altogether. The total number of affordable housing units developed since 1991 equals an estimated 3.4 percent of the total housing added during that period.[38]

Discussion

What have we learned from our efforts to collect and analyze data on growth management and affordable housing? Our findings merit discussion within the group of growth management counties and comparison with conditions in all urban counties that have not adopted a growth management framework.

The Growth Management Counties

Our analysis of 1990 and 2000 census data in the Washington, Maryland, and New Jersey metropolitan counties studied shows that the affordability of owner-occupied housing decreased for moderate- and low-income households in each of the counties during the 1990s. The affordability of rental housing varied, staying the same in King County, increasing in Montgomery County, and decreasing in Somerset and Middlesex counties. In fast-growing affluent areas, rental housing and multifamily rental housing in particular provide the only real options for moderate- and low-income households to live in the community.

We speculate that Montgomery County's relative success in providing an adequate supply of affordable rental housing is attributable to its full palette of growth management programs, policies, and laws, applied over time. The MPDU program has resulted in a high percentage of new affordable housing—11 percent of all new units built in the county since its inception.

---

38. Interview with Gordon Goodlett, development officer, Fairfax County Redevelopment and Housing Authority, May 6, 2003.

Under the law, results are tracked and documented. The mandatory inclusionary zoning law does not stand alone, but operates in concert with long-standing growth management policies that concentrate new development in centers and serve the centers with high-capacity rail service. As shown in table 2-13, more than any of the other counties, Montgomery County uses a full complement of tools to promote affordable housing, including TOD zoning, TDRs, impact fee waivers, and affordable housing preservation programs and incentives. The MPDU program experienced peak production in the 1980s during rapid suburban-type expansion. Its density bonus incentive is proving more difficult to implement in high rise–type TOD developments surrounding Metro subway stations, as in Bethesda.

King County, Washington, also employs a robust variety of growth management tools. While the county does not have a mandatory fair share housing or inclusionary zoning law, residents of Seattle have supported affordable housing bond and levy measures every six years for the past twenty years. Political support for moderate- and low-income housing extends statewide as well. The state's Housing Trust Fund has dedicated a real estate transfer tax as a permanent source of financing for affordable housing. King County's comprehensive plan sets targets for moderate- and low-income housing production, although the targets are not required by state law. A result of this political and financial support, coupled with aggressive activity by the city and county housing authorities, has been the addition of approximately 13,000 new affordable housing units, which constituted 14 percent of all new housing for the 1990–2000 decade. Even with this production record, the affordability of housing for the county's moderate- and low-income renter households has stayed the same.

Somerset and Middlesex counties have the fewest growth management tools—no urban growth boundary, no ADU or cottage housing zoning. These counties rely on the Council on Affordable Housing to monitor compliance with affordable housing regulations and goals. In New Jersey, the emphasis on local jurisdictions capturing "ratables" (taxable properties), the absence of impact fees to pay for new development, and fears of racial and economic integration have blunted political support for affordable housing. Most observers note that senior housing is the only type of new affordable housing tolerated in many communities; its impact on schools and other public facilities is perceived to be less than that of housing for lower-income families with children. Contrary to the intent of state planning and housing laws that attempt to reward communities for reinforcing established centers through compact new development, COAH and affordable housing are perceived in

Table 2-13. Program and Policy Indicators, All Counties

Indicator	King	Montgomery	Somerset	Middlesex	Fairfax
Cottage housing	Used by some	Unavailable/unused	Unavailable/unused	Unavailable/unused	Unavailable/unused
Transit-oriented development	Used by many	Used by many	Unavailable/unused	Used by some	Unavailable/unused
Five-story wood-frame	Used by some	Unavailable/unused	Unavailable/unused	Unavailable/unused	Unavailable/unused
Accessory dwelling units	Used by some	Unavailable/unused	Used by some	Unavailable/unused	Used by some
Flex parking	Used by many	Used by many	Used by some	Unavailable/unused	Used by some
Impact fees	Used by some	Used by many	Used by some	Unavailable/unused	Used by some
Impact fee waiver	Used by some	Used by many	Used by some	Unavailable/unused	Used by some
Transfer of development rights	Used by some	Used by many	Unavailable/unused	Unavailable/unused	Unavailable/unused
Incentives	Used by some	Used by many	Used by many	Used by many	Used by many
Design standards	Used by many	Used by many	Used by some	Used by some	Unavailable/unused
Preservation	Used by many	Used by many	Used by some	Used by some	Used by some

Table 2-14. *How the Counties Compare*

Rank	Rental housing affordability (50 percent of median income)	Trends in rental housing affordability (<80 percent of median income)	Range of policies and programs in use	Production of affordable housing as percent of total housing
1	King	Fairfax	Montgomery	King
2	Montgomery	Montgomery	King	Montgomery
3	Middlesex	King	Somerset	Middlesex
4	Somerset	Somerset/Middlesex	Middlesex	Somerset
5	Fairfax	Somerset/Middlesex	Fairfax	Fairfax

New Jersey to be a *cause* of urban sprawl. An explanation for this perversion of the original intent is that half of the state's municipalities have refused to develop plans for affordable housing, thus opening themselves to the "builder's remedy" clause of the Fair Housing Act, under which housing developers, with court support, determine how affordable units will be added to the housing stock. Such "remedies" have resulted in several high-profile cases in which large new subdivisions including affordable housing were built against the wishes of local municipalities.

Our observation is that in the growth management counties, three factors—the force of law regarding fair share and inclusionary zoning, a full range of policies and programs, and the political will and support necessary to implement them in various combinations—make a difference in increasing the affordability and production of housing. Table 2-14 ranks the five counties studied in the following four key areas:

—affordability of median-price rental housing for households earning 50 percent of median household income[39]

—trends in the affordability of housing for households earning below 80 percent of median income[40]

—the use of growth management policies and the types of policies and programs used

—the production of affordable housing as a percentage of total new housing.

39. In calculating the housing affordability gap, the median household income of the metropolitan region and the median gross rent of the county are taken into account.

40. In calculating the trends in housing affordability, both the income and rents are county specific.

Comparison with Fairfax County

Comparing the growth management counties with Fairfax County, a metropolitan county that has fewer growth management programs and policies
and no statewide growth management framework, yields paradoxical results.
On one hand, the affordability of housing during the 1990s for moderate-
and low-income homeowners and renters in Fairfax County improved the
most. On the other hand, as of 2000, the housing affordability gap in Fairfax County remained the worst among the counties considered.[41]

There are several possible explanations for this paradox: the housing market is softer in Fairfax County than in Montgomery County; the supply of
new market-rate housing is greater; residents' incomes rose faster than in
other parts of the region; and more land is available for residential development in Fairfax County than in the other counties. The absolute and relative
increases in housing stock from 1990 to 2000 in the five counties analyzed
are shown in table 2-15.

Fairfax County had a higher percent increase in its housing stock than any
other county studied except Somerset County, the smallest county analyzed.
Fairfax County's median household income of $81,050 in 2000 was higher
than median income in any of the other counties in this study. Last, less land
is restricted from residential development in Fairfax County than in Montgomery or King counties.

We speculate that rapid growth in a region's housing supply is related to
the absence of growth management efforts to concentrate urban and suburban development and to balance development with farmland and open
space. If growth management is viewed solely through the lens of housing
affordability, one could conclude from our comparisons that growth management thwarts the provision of affordable housing. However, this conclusion does not factor in the benefits to residents' quality of life and to the
environment itself that come from maintaining a mix of land uses.

A hallmark feature of growth management is that it seeks to balance land
use and community objectives. We observed that regular reporting and monitoring keeps the political focus on achieving growth management objectives.
Both Montgomery and King counties prepare annual growth reports that

---

41. The affordability gap is measured by the additional income required by the households
earning 50 percent of the median household income to afford median-price rental housing. The
affordability gap for Fairfax County—$9,918 in 1990 and $11,275 in 2000—was highest
among all the counties considered.

Table 2-15. *Absolute and Relative Increases in Housing, Five Counties*
Dollars, except as indicated

County	Housing units (1990)	Housing units (2000)	Absolute change	Percent change
King	647,343	742,237	94,894	14.65
Montgomery	295,723	334,632	38,909	13.16
Middlesex	250,174	273,637	23,463	9.37
Somerset	92,653	112,023	19,370	20.91
Fairfax	307,966	359,411	51,445	16.71

document and benchmark progress toward county goals, including affordable housing. We also believe that the census-based affordable housing indicators developed in this study are valuable in answering the question of whether an area is providing enough and the right kind of affordable housing options. Knowing that an affordability gap exists in the low- to moderate-income household range but not in the low- to very-low-income range, for example, informs public policymakers about which types of affordable housing programs to emphasize and to fund. The same is true for periodic testing of new growth management tools, such as cottage zoning, so that local officials can evaluate their utility in providing infill housing in suburban and urban environments.

Suburban environments are where smart growth principles will be tried in the heat of political battle. While cottage zoning has been accepted in several communities in the Puget Sound area, density increases and multifamily housing for all but the elderly are vigorously fought in most of the townships and boroughs of Somerset and Middlesex counties. Which smart growth tools will work in the suburban infill environment? Implementing and monitoring a variety of pilot programs is essential to answering this study's primary and secondary research questions. A multifaceted approach that assesses new tools and monitors housing affordability and production would be useful for many types of communities and jurisdictions.

The Right Definition of Affordability?

We define housing that costs 30 percent of household income as affordable. Arthur Nelson suggests that a better definition includes the average household transportation cost, which, on the basis of survey data, he estimates to be 12 percent of household income.[42] Traditional metropolitan development patterns locate less expensive housing stock at the periphery, where commute distances and time and travel costs are greatest. A study conducted by Kara Kockelman showed that in San Francisco, the price of a house decreases by $7,502 for each mile of distance from the central business district.[43] Similarly, a study conducted by Denise DiPasquale and Matthew E. Kahn estimated that a one-mile increase in distance from the Los Angeles central business district reduced the price of a house by 4 to 6 percent.[44] Another Los Angeles Study showed that to compensate for the extra cost of commuting, the price of a house needs to decrease by at least 1.69 percent per mile of distance from the urban center.[45] A Washington, D.C., metropolitan area study estimated that the price of a house decreased by 1.23 to 1.43 percent for every mile from downtown Washington.[46]

The evidence from all these studies suggests that housing prices decline with distance from the center of the city or region. However, moderate- and low-income households are caught in a dilemma: it is difficult for them to absorb either increased automobile transportation costs or housing costs. Except in relatively high-cost housing markets, lower housing costs at the metropolitan fringe may not be low enough to compensate for the higher costs of commuting. We know that lower-income households already practice trip reduction and that additional travel costs will impose more of a burden.[47] Intentionally planning to provide affordable housing through continued outward expansion is, of course, antithetical to growth management principles. If affordable housing options were available in a more compact urban form, closer to work and services, or if high-capacity public transportation were available, reduced transportation costs could be expected. If such were the case, it would be reasonable to assign 40 percent or perhaps even more of household income to housing.

The concept of the location efficient mortgage (LEM) combines the same factors; namely, crediting a homeowner for good access to transit or for walking to work by servicing a larger mortgage because auto-related costs decrease. Holtzclaw also found that neighborhood residential density and the

42. In discussion with Dan Carlson, November 14, 2002.
43. Kara Kockelman (1996).
44. DiPasquale and Kahn (1999).
45. Burchell (2002).
46. Burchell (2002).
47. Murakami and Young (1997).

availability of public transit influence auto ownership and use. Residents of denser neighborhoods owned fewer cars and used them less.[48] The LEM approach merits broader piloting and evaluation as a tool for increasing housing affordability and implementing growth management.

Future Research

The research questions themselves, the approach we have taken in answering them, and our findings lead to several areas of further research that could inform and improve efforts to implement growth management and achieve a desirable balance of affordable housing goals, other community objectives, and protection of the natural environment.

The first concerns suburban infill development. Which smart growth tools and approaches to compact development have greater political acceptance and the potential to increase densities? New zoning tools such as TOD overlays and cottage zoning need to be monitored and evaluated in order to understand what works, what does not work, and what can be done to capitalize on existing commuter rail lines in established cities.

The second concerns the permanence of affordable housing. Under federal and local laws, the tenure of affordable housing is between fifteen and twenty years. In some cases provisions exist for public and nonprofit entities to purchase units on expiration of the affordability restrictions, but the percentage is limited and expiration dates are not always anticipated. What can be done to increase not only the production of affordable housing but also its permanence?

The third concerns inclusionary zoning. Montgomery County is finding that the density bonuses developed thirty years ago for suburban attached and multifamily housing do not provide the same incentives for developers of high-rise projects near transit stations in a more mature urban environment. Can inclusionary zoning continue to work in TOD environments when construction becomes more expensive and height limits are in place?

The fourth concerns the housing-transportation nexus and the right definition of "affordable housing." Should a more dynamic definition of affordable housing be employed to show the relationship between access to jobs and services and relative dependence on travel by automobile?

The fifth concerns the relationship over time of the variety of policies and programs introduced here to housing affordability. What is the impact of

48. Holtzclaw and others (2002).

any given tool on the price of a house? To answer this question, it might be possible to design an econometric model to estimate the effect of an individual growth management policy or tool—or of a group of them—on the price of a house. Estimation of the effect of various factors on the price of a house has long been theoretically and empirically discussed within the hedonic analysis framework pioneered by Rosen.[49] Here the price of the house is the sum of the implicit prices of the components of the bundle of services rendered by a housing unit. Thus the price of the house depends on structural attributes (lot size, square feet of living space, number of bathrooms and bedrooms, topography, and so forth), locational attributes (access to employment centers, traffic noise, and so forth), neighborhood and jurisdictional attributes (level of infrastructure and services, tax rates, crime rates, and other quality of life factors), regional demand and supply factors (including population growth, income growth, new permits issued), and other policies, including growth management policies and tools.[50] Some of these growth management policies and tools may be operationalized as continuous variables, some as categorical variables, and others as dummy variables, depending on the variable of interest and the availability of data. For example, one such variable may be the number of permits issued per year for accessory dwelling units; thus the effect that provision of accessory dwelling units may have on the price of the house can be estimated. A set of such studies could yield a fairly accurate estimate of the effect that various growth management policies and tools have on the affordability of housing.

COMMENT BY

Gerrit J. Knaap

Daniel Carlson and Shishir Mathur have written an interesting and ambitious chapter that provides an inventory of growth management policies in King County, Washington; Montgomery County, Maryland; Somerset County and Middlesex County, New Jersey; and Fairfax County, Virginia. It also presents indexes of housing affordability for the same set of counties, and it attempts to identify whether "growth management aids or thwarts the provision of affordable housing." As the authors concede, this is a dicey propo-

---

49. Rosen (1974).
50. Mathur, Waddell, and Blanco (2003).

sition, since it is difficult to generalize from the experience of five counties and housing affordability is influenced by many disparate factors. As a result, the study comes to no definitive conclusion. Still, it is thought provoking and offers useful insights for additional work.

To characterize the growth management regimes of the various jurisdictions, Carlson and Mathur determine whether some or all of them have programs that include specific features, such as cottage housing, transportation-oriented development, five-story wood-frame construction, design standards, and more. Table 2-13 reveals that King and Montgomery counties have many more such programs than Fairfax County. So Carlson and Mathur characterize King and Montgomery as growth management counties and Fairfax as a non–growth management county.

The authors use two approaches to measure housing affordability. The first involves determining the ratios of median rent and the median price of owner-occupied housing to median income; the second involves determining the percent of income spent on housing. Changes between 1990 and 2000 are reported for both measures. The results of the first measure, which are summarized in table 2-16, suggest that housing affordability has improved for residents of each of the jurisdictions, except for homeowners and renters in King County and renters in Montgomery County. The results of the second measure are summarized in table 2-17. They suggest that housing affordability decreased in King County for homeowners, increased in Fairfax County for both homeowners and renters, and increased in Montgomery County for homeowners.

By observing that King and Montgomery counties have the most extensive growth management programs and that housing affordability increased most in Fairfax County, Carlson and Mathur conclude that "growth management thwarts the provision of affordable housing."

While their conclusions have some empirical support, there are many reasons to be skeptical. First, table 2-13 demonstrates that local governments in King and Montgomery counties have more growth management programs, but the programs inventoried are an odd set. Absent from the inventory are perhaps the most intrusive growth management tools—urban growth boundaries, minimum-lot zoning, and agricultural reserve areas. Included in the inventory are many programs explicitly designed to improve housing affordability—for example, cottage housing, impact fee waivers, and affordable housing preservation programs. If the results are taken at face value, they suggest that the affordable housing elements of growth management programs make housing less affordable.

Table 2-16. *Relative Change in Housing Prices, Rents, and Incomes,*
1990–2000

County	Rent/income (percent change)	Price/income (percent change)
King	1.09	1.52
Montgomery	1.06	.47
Middlesex	.83	.08
Somerset	.77	.44
Fairfax	.89	.43

Second, Carlson and Mathur's measures of housing affordability are suspect. The weaknesses of measures that rely on percentages of income spent on
housing are well known.[51] Perhaps the most interesting result of the study is
that housing affordability—measured by the changes in median rent and
median owner-occupied housing price relative to median income—increased
in four of the five counties in the 1990s, including for homeowners in Montgomery County! Since house prices rose substantially in Montgomery County
over this period, most observers and residents of Montgomery County would
be surprised by this result. Apparently, housing affordability rose in Montgomery County because median income rose faster than median housing
prices. But it is possible—perhaps even likely—that median income in Montgomery County rose faster than housing prices because fewer poor people
could afford to live there. In metropolitan areas where residents are mobile,
changes in median housing price and income reflect a complex web of intra-
urban commuting and relocation patterns. It is possible that greater insight
into changes in housing affordability can be gained by examining absolute
changes in incomes, prices, and rents, as well as the ratios among the three.

Third, the analysis begs the question of causation. King and Montgomery
counties might have less affordable housing because they have more growth
management programs; they also might have more growth management programs because housing is less affordable. The lack of information about when
growth management programs were adopted by the local governments further complicates the question of causation. Exactly when should growth
management programs begin to affect housing affordability?

51. Bogdon (2001).

Table 2-17. *Percent of Households Paying More Than 30 Percent on Housing, 1989–99*

Household	1989	1999
Renters		
King County	39	40
Montgomery County	40	37
Middlesex County	36	35
Somerset County	36	35
Fairfax County	39	32
Owners		
King County	18	27
Montgomery County	21	22
Middlesex County	27	27
Somerset County	27	27
Fairfax County	26	20

In sum, Carlson and Mathur provide new information about the relationship between growth management and affordable housing. But can we tell whether growth management aids or thwarts affordable housing? Not from the evidence presented here.

COMMENT BY
Samuel R. Staley

Housing affordability has emerged as a crucial concern for growth management advocates. More and more policymakers are worried that growth management policies may create upward pressure on housing costs, reduce affordability, and create significant obstacles to accessing quality housing for low- and moderate-income families. The U.S. experience with growth controls suggests that this concern has an empirical foundation: in practice, growth management reforms often restrict the supply of housing, contributing to rising regional housing costs.[52] The most recent wave of growth management

52. Mayer and Somerville (2000); Staley and Gilroy (2001); and Jud and Winkler (2002).

reforms, sometimes called "smart growth," promises to minimize these effects on housing affordability. That is the core premise of this chapter by Daniel Carlson and Shishir Mathur.

Whether smart growth reduces housing affordability or limits the ability of the housing market to provide housing for low- and moderate-income families (affordable housing) is both a theoretical and empirical question. Carlson and Mathur's approach is primarily empirical. It attempts to

—analyze housing affordability for moderate- and low-income households in several metropolitan counties with growth management laws to determine whether smart growth encourages or discourages affordable housing

—determine whether these counties use growth management and smart growth tools to promote affordable housing goals

—monitor efforts to provide affordable housing through growth management or smart growth or both.

Their study is only partially successful in achieving these goals. Conceptually, the study seems to falter in three primary areas: its distinction between smart growth and growth management and how that distinction is applied in assessing affordable housing goals; adequately capturing the nature of housing demand; and adequately characterizing the nuts and bolts, or "black box," of growth management.

Admittedly, achieving the stated goals would be a difficult task for any researcher. One of the issues this study correctly highlights is the dearth of good data and research with which to answer these questions. Unfortunately, even though more than a dozen states have statewide growth management laws in place and affordable housing is a key goal in almost all of them, none is actively engaged in identifying the right data and systematically assessing the ability of their laws to achieve statewide growth management goals— particularly housing affordability.[53]

Smart Growth and Housing Affordability

A more appropriate title for Carlson and Mathur's chapter might be "Can We Tell Whether *Smart Growth* Aids or Thwarts Affordable Housing?" This

---

53. When Reason Public Policy Institute, for example, embarked on a project to assess the effects of statewide growth management laws on housing affordability in California, Oregon, Florida, and Washington State, only two states (Florida and Washington) had sufficient data to

change is not just semantic. On the contrary, smart growth and growth management are conceptually distinct. *Growth management* is now defined as a set of policies that attempt to guide or direct growth in more efficient ways but not to limit it. *Smart growth* is a particular kind of growth management tool that focuses specifically on policies intended to preserve open space, encourage higher densities, reduce reliance on automobiles, and allow more mixing of residential and commercial development. In contrast, some communities are "managing" growth by imposing permit caps, temporary growth moratoriums, and large-lot zoning to preserve rural character and by adopting prescriptive design criteria. In the Symposium on Growth Management and Affordable Housing, attempts clearly designed to *limit* growth were referred to as *growth control*. In many cases, such actions would not be considered consistent with smart growth.

Understanding the difference between these three concepts is necessary in order to understand the public policy debate over the new wave of growth management tools and their relationship to the affordability of housing. For example, growth controls like effective permit caps would limit the housing supply to below-market levels. That supply constraint would likely result in higher housing prices and create a significant obstacle to providing affordable housing through the spontaneous, unsubsidized private market. The practical implications of this, discussed below, are evident in King County, Washington.

Drawing these distinctions clearly also would be consistent with the spirit of the authors' intent, since they specifically identify smart growth as a growth management paradigm that attempts to achieve certain urban design objectives—higher density, mixed uses, transit-oriented development.

Carlson and Mathur's focus is smart growth, not growth management per se. For example, a community of 50,000 adjacent to my hometown proudly proclaims itself to be an "open space community." The community mandates "large lots" (one acre or more) to preserve its "open" character and a rural aesthetic while nearby cities are developed at urban densities. The community is also one of the more sophisticated jurisdictions with respect to its use of planning tools, techniques, and processes. Yet it is not a smart growth community as defined by the authors. On the contrary, an "open space community" like this could not exist under a growth management regime

---

analyze housing affordability on a countywide level (Staley and Gilroy 2001). Even in Florida, data on housing prices, income, and household size were available only for metropolitan counties.

bounded by smart growth principles, and it would not be embraced by entities such as the Smart Growth Network, Portland Metro, Montgomery
County, or the U.S. Environmental Protection Agency.

Another important distinction the authors make is between *affordable
housing*—housing that targets specific low-income populations—and *housing
affordability*—the ability of all income groups to purchase housing of the
type and quality they want. Carlson and Mathur choose to focus primarily
on low- and moderate-income populations. But this approach is problematic:
the distinction may be more conceptual that real when housing market
dynamics are considered.

First, the thresholds and definitions of housing affordability and affordable housing actually used in practice vary. In Somerset and Middlesex counties, for example, a family of four making under $72,000 qualifies for "afford-
able housing." Put another way, any family whose income does not allow it
to "afford" a house costing $280,000 or more qualifies for "affordable hous-
ing" under New Jersey's affordable housing guidelines for these counties.
Many professional and technical workers and households with one income
would easily qualify under those criteria. Therefore in New Jersey, "affordable
housing" is not restricted to housing for low- and moderate-income households. On the contrary, most northern New Jersey families are likely to qualify. In fact, defined in this way the "affordable" housing market represents a
substantial portion of the overall housing market in these counties. The literature thus discusses two fundamentally different types of "affordable housing," often without clearly distinguishing between them: units—including
subsidized units—that low-income households can afford to occupy without
spending more than some upper limit of their incomes on housing (usually
30 percent); and units that non–low-income households can qualify for
under various government rules because their income is below area-defined
thresholds—which may be quite high because the area has a high overall
income. However, in the remainder of this comment, unless otherwise specified, the term "affordable housing" will refer to the first type: units—including subsidized units—that low-income households can afford to occupy.

Growth management policies have impacts on the broader housing market, particularly in higher-growth areas such as mid-state New Jersey, suburban Washington, D.C., and Seattle. The wrong kinds of growth management policies could quickly move entire groups and classes of families into
the second "affordable housing" category simply because of the way local
governments choose to regulate the mainstream housing market. Assessing
the impact of growth management and smart growth policies in particular

requires a broader view of the housing market than Carlson and Mathur acknowledge in their study.

Affordable Housing and Housing Market Dynamics

Real world housing dynamics, however, are too complex for standard empirical measures to track accurately. While the study attempts to use case studies as a way to more fully understand the character of smart growth policies implemented at the local level, the empirical analysis used by the authors is at the regional level, not the neighborhood level. This is understandable: data are easier to obtain and manipulate and conclusions are more readily drawn at the former level and recommendations are clearer. But this approach often underestimates and trivializes the complexity of the housing market. The implications for growth management are fairly significant.

The purpose of the housing market is not simply to add units, although often this is the metric used. Housing markets should add the *right kind of units* at the *right time* and in the *right places*. If the type, quality, or timing is off, shortages and surpluses are likely to emerge for certain kinds of housing. This effect has implications for housing prices. Shortages in some kinds of housing, such as ranch homes, arising from constraints on their production will create upward pressure on prices for that kind of housing. If the mismatch between supply and demand is significant enough, price effects will arise across housing-type categories. While overall housing prices may be stable, certain segments of the housing market will experience dramatic spikes. In many suburban communities, these spikes occur in the multifamily housing market because demand exceeds supply in that segment. In higher-density urban settings, low-density housing often experiences such spikes.

In short, housing prices within a region distinguish what consumers want from what they will buy because it is available. If a certain housing type is not available, demand does not decline or disappear—after all, everyone needs shelter. Demand is simply rechanneled into another part of the housing market. But the demand for the scarce types of unit will result in higher prices for them.

Herein lies the peril and promise of smart growth. Smart growth, to the extent that it highlights meeting housing demand where a shortage exists, may well moderate housing prices or at least not contribute to price increases. Many communities face a shortage of higher-density housing choices but rising demand for town homes, apartments, and detached housing on smaller lots. This is particularly true in the newer suburbs, where zoning often has reinforced the one-type-fits-all approach to housing. Yet local codes prevent the development of such types of housing, and the local regulatory process creates significant obstacles to making them more available, thereby increasing their cost. To the extent that smart growth can remove the obstacles or mitigate the costs, land use planning reform can improve housing affordability and improve access to affordable housing.

But smart growth is about more than housing choices, as Carlson and Mathur make clear. Smart growth promotes *certain types* of housing. Among the indicator policies that the authors use to evaluate whether communities are encouraging affordable housing is whether they allow for cottage housing (units of 1,000 square feet or less) in densities of ten to twenty-five units per acre, five-story wood-frame multifamily housing, accessory dwelling units, or transit-oriented development. In the more aggressive jurisdictions, such as Portland, there is also an explicit attempt to ban certain types of housing. Portland has prohibited the construction of "snout" houses—houses whose garage sits on the front setback—and adopted a maximum lot size of 8,500 square feet. Whether in the more benign sense evaluated by Carlson and Mathur (whereby certain uses are allowed) or the more restrictive sense employed by the Portland region, smart growth is about promoting a certain form of land use. Here is where the danger lies.

If smart growth's regulations provide realistic, practical options that consumers desire but cannot obtain in the housing market, smart growth policies are unlikely to have a significant negative impact on housing affordability. Moreover, to the extent that smart growth policies increase the total housing supply relative to demand, they could promote broad-based, market-driven affordable housing. If, on the other hand, they create a supply of less desirable housing, housing affordability can erode and the number of affordable housing units could drop significantly.

The effects on affordable housing are not obvious. To the extent that the supply of market-rate housing is restricted, demand will increase for ordinarily less desirable units. Higher housing prices push more families over the affordable housing threshold by raising the share of their income that they must pay for shelter. This increases the number of households that qualify for the second type of affordable housing defined earlier, because of the unintended consequences of restricting market-rate housing. The key is the quality of housing and whether it matches the desires of consumers.

While an implicit assumption of smart growth is that households will be better off as the benefits of more choices are apparent, that effect may apply only to certain housing segments. Consumers who prefer urban lifestyles may have been poorly served in the housing market, and they will clearly benefit from higher densities, mixed uses, and wider access to public transit. But, generally applied, smart growth rules might exacerbate the mismatch between what consumers want and what they can get if the market for the types of units smart growth encourages is not broad. The pendulum may swing in the opposite direction.

Unfortunately, Carlson and Mathur do not address these possible effects or draw implications from the data they present on housing options and prices. Their methodology arrays a series of self-described smart growth programs and policies against general trends in housing affordability for different income groups. They do not provide evidence that the programs and policies they associate with smart growth are in fact used by the private market or widely desired by consumers. Thus their methodology does not provide an effective way to measure whether supply and demand are in sync, on either the macro or the micro level. Nor does the methodology allow the analysts to determine whether the policies they have selected as indicators of smart growth are the correct ones. For example, perhaps the permissiveness of the local zoning code or the administrative efficiency of the planned unit development process provides a more effective avenue for increasing the supply of affordable housing or encouraging mixed uses. A methodology that allows for more precise evaluation of the tools available through smart growth would substantially increase the value of the research and allow researchers to assess smart growth's effects on the broader housing market as well as affordable housing.

Income certainly constrains the range of housing choices available to households. This economic constraint, however, does not necessarily imply a different preference for housing. In fact, many low-income households may well desire the proverbial single-family home on a private lot with an attached garage. They, in fact, may be willing to trade a lower-quality housing unit for the amenities of more privacy or immediately accessible open space. In fact, recent research suggesting that "sprawling" metropolitan areas are associated with higher levels of housing consumption and ownership may be confirming this.[54] In the United States, housing preferences seem to be very stable and do not seem to favor small housing units in very dense urban environments. Therefore growth management policies that establish incentives to build one type of housing—apartments—over other types may reduce overall housing

54. Kahn (2001).

options for low- and moderate-income households and reduce the overall quality of the housing stock relative to the preferences of the population.

However, if that is the case, it will be reflected in relative price movements of different types of units: prices of the oversupplied types will fall relative to prices of the undersupplied types. Housing turns out to be a fairly heterogeneous product for low-, moderate-, and high-income households. Income—not necessarily the supply of certain types of units—determines the extent to which households can maximize their housing preferences.

The "Black Box" of Growth Management

These criticisms aside, one of the primary advantages of the new wave of growth management (in the form of smart growth) appears to be a broad-based acceptance of the fact that fundamentally housing is provided in a market context. Therefore public planners recognize that their decisions about land use and the regulatory process will have an impact on decisions in the private market about the type, quality, and volume of housing provided. This is implicit in the framework used by Carlson and Mathur.

Nevertheless, more thought needs to go into how the regulatory process influences the private housing market. Historically, most affordable housing—that is, units that low-income households can afford—has been provided by the private market. Indeed, the era that produced the most affordable housing may have been the late nineteenth and early twentieth centuries, when the private sector created hundreds of thousands of housing units for low- and moderate-income factory workers in cities.[55] These tenement houses became the bottom rung of the "housing ladder." New generations of higher-income households created a market for higher-priced housing, including mass-produced subdivisions such as Levittown in the post–World War II era.

In more recent times, the private market has produced less housing that specifically targets low- and moderate-income households. While most of the *new* affordable housing units have been produced through public subsidy, most low-income households live in units made available primarily in the existing housing stock by means of market filtering—as homes depreciate, they become more affordable. As incomes in a community increase, private investors respond to the demand for different and often higher-quality

55. Husock (1996, pp. 20–25).

homes; the existing housing stock then is used to meet the needs of most less-well-off homeowners and renters.

The data provided by Carlson and Mathur seem to confirm this. In King County, for example, the authors note that 94,894 new housing units were built between 1990 and 2000. About 13,000 were "affordable." The gap between "need" and the actual number of units produced was 29,690 in 2000. But the families represented by the gap are not homeless; they reside in existing homes or apartments in King County. These data are a general indicator of the housing ladder in action. That may be true in Montgomery, Middlesex, and Somerset counties as well, but the authors do not report the estimated number of units needed. These data, however, are crucial for assessing whether affordable housing policies such as those described in this study are going to match actual needs. Unfortunately, the data do not allow for a finer-grained analysis of the interaction between new and existing housing units and their relationship to different income groups.

If smart growth embraces the provision of affordable housing as a core goal or principle and hopes to improve access to affordable housing, its tools must be commensurate with the scope of the problem. If the primary mechanism for meeting affordable housing goals is public intervention, then it must be able to offset other more constraining aspects of growth management. The techniques employed must have the conceptual and actual potential to meet the need, however defined.

For example, suppose a community has a need for 100,000 housing units, including a "need" for 14,000 affordable units. Absent growth management policies—either mandates or incentives—these units are provided by the private market. The need is met through adjustments on either the *demand* side (doubling up, paying a higher amount of income, and so forth) or the *supply* side (new units, conversions).

If growth management policies have the effect of shifting private suppliers to a higher-end market, overall housing production could fall. Tools such as inclusionary zoning or density bonuses may simply be incapable of providing the kinds of incentives necessary to generate a sufficient number of units for low-income households. Indeed, with the wrong kinds of policies, the problem could become worse because the private sector would be less capable of providing affordable housing units, and that effect could be exacerbated if smart growth policies tended to increase housing prices.

This concern is not just theoretical. On the contrary, a Reason Public Policy Institute (RPPI) analysis of the effects of statewide growth management laws in Washington state and Florida found that about one-fifth of the housing price increase in those states could be attributed to the state growth management laws.[56] Both laws could be described as smart growth since they explicitly attempt to achieve the land use outcomes described by Carlson and Mathur.[57]

Unfortunately, any study of this subject must get "inside the planning box" to really investigate the effects of growth management policies on the decisions of local developers to supply certain types and quantities of housing. To the extent that Carlson and Mathur provide a better glimpse of what is happening inside the box, that may be their most important contribution. For example, buried in the methodological framework of this study is the presumption that the formal, adopted policies of a community are a true representation of broader community interests and concerns. Often, however, policies are justified in public discussion for reasons that bear little relation to actual intent or practice.

Ventura County, California, illustrates this paradox. The county has adopted growth management policies consistent in intent and form with smart growth principles for more than three decades. New growth-related policies intended to preserve open space, increase densities, and promote mixed uses were adopted throughout the county and by its cities in the late 1990s with the explicit purpose of managing (not stopping) future growth. Yet cities in Ventura County consistently approved housing developments at densities significantly below the levels necessary to meet housing demand.[58] Whether this outcome was intentional is unclear. Project approval is a political process, and local politics plays an important role in local deliberations. Even if the intent was to accommodate higher-density development, the process of approving development applications tends to protect the status of existing neighborhoods and often favors lower density. Now reliable projections indicate that Ventura County cities will literally run out of land for new

56. Staley and Gilroy (2001).
57. The study also examined housing prices over a decade, using multiple regression analysis to control for factors such as density, household income, household size, and geography. More important, the analysis included variables that captured the effect of planning under the statewide growth management law on housing prices. While not definitive, the results were able to capture between 30 percent and 40 percent of the variation in housing prices. In both cases, the number of years in which the county had been actively planning under the statewide growth management law had a statistically significant, positive impact on housing prices.
58. Fulton and others (2001; 2003).

housing by the middle of this decade—well before the technical twenty-year planning horizon for the growth management initiatives.[59]

This has implications for how researchers frame their research questions, select assessment methods, and develop recommendations. If communities adopt formal affordable housing policies whose goals do not truly represent their broader values or goals, then researchers may have asked the wrong research question. In fact, much of the inconsistency in the research results may reflect underlying political and social realities that are fundamentally at odds with formal program goals and design.

Inconsistencies such as these will have various impacts on outcomes. If a community has adopted an inclusionary zoning rule with specific, objective triggers for certain types of outcomes (for example, requiring that 30 percent of the units be affordable in all developments over a certain number of units), some effect may be observable. In most cases, the tools and techniques used are not so objective or obvious; they require some form of community buy-in through a negotiated, legislative process. This creates a different dynamic and, predictably, a different outcome. In Ventura County communities, growth management implementation is a fundamentally political and legislative process. The more politically open the process, the more uncertain the environment and the larger the negative impact on housing production is likely to be.

Conclusion: Trade-Offs and Growth Management

In sum, Carlson and Mathur attempt to assess whether smart growth policies aid or hinder affordable housing, but their study fails to fully address the political economy of growth management polices on the local level or to explore the interactions between public policy and the regional housing market. A fuller, more nuanced discussion of the political context in which smart growth policies are implemented is crucial before we can begin to really understand the practical implications for promoting (or discouraging) affordable housing.

These political trade-offs are even more important in the context of smart growth because it reflects a particular ideology about the urban landscape and the nature of the human footprint. In their conclusion, the authors hint at these trade-offs when they comment: "We speculate that rapid growth in a

59. Fulton and others (2001).

region's housing supply is related to the absence of growth management efforts to concentrate urban and surburban development and to balance development with agriculture and open space." But these "balances" and trade-offs are never really quantified. The "right" balance is never specified, and the presumption is that collective preferences are adequately revealed in the public process. The risk is that smart growth often recommends tools that restrict the supply side of the housing market without recognizing their potential to become obstacles to new housing development, particularly in the low- and moderate-income segments of the housing ladder.

References

Bogdon, Amy. 2001. "Monitoring Housing Affordability." In *Land Market Monitoring for Smart Urban Growth*, edited by Gerrit J. Knaap. Cambridge, Mass.: Lincoln Institute of Land Policy.

Burchell, Robert W., and others. 2002. *Costs of Sprawl: 2000*. Washington: National Academy Press.

Carlson, Daniel, and Shishir Mathur. 2003. "Can We Tell If Growth Management Aids or Thwarts Affordable Housing?" Paper prepared for the Symposium on Growth Management and Affordable Housing, Brookings, May 29, 2003.

Danielsen, Karen, Robert Lang, and William Fulton. 1999. "Retracting Suburbia: Smart Growth and the Future of Housing." *Housing Policy Debate* 10 (3): 513–40.

DiPasquale, Denise, and Matthew E. Kahn. 1999. "Measuring Neighborhood Investments: An Examination of Community Choice." *Real Estate Economics* 27 (3): 389–424.

Fulton, William, and others. 2001. *Smart Growth in Action: Housing Capacity and Development in Ventura County*. Policy Study 288. Los Angeles: Reason Public Policy Institute/Solimar Research Group (www.rppi.org/ps288.pdf [February 11, 2003]).

———. 2003. *Smart Growth in Action, Part II: Case Studies in Housing Capacity and Development from Ventura County*. Policy Study 311. Los Angeles: Reason Public Policy Institute/Solimar Research Group (www.rppi.org/ps311.pdf [February 11, 2003]).

Holtzclaw, John, and others. 2002. "Location Efficiency: Neighborhood and Socioeconomic Characteristics Determine Auto Ownership and Use—Studies in Chicago, Los Angeles and San Francisco." *Transportation Planning and Technology* 25 (1).

Husock, Howard. 1996. *Repairing the Ladder: Toward a New Housing Paradigm*. Policy Study 207. Los Angeles: Reason Public Policy Institute (www.rppi.org/ps207.pdf [February 11, 2003]).

Johnson, Denny, Patricia Salkin, and Jason Jordan. 2002. *Planning for Smart Growth: 2002 State of the States*. American Planning Association. Washington.

Jud, Donald G., and Daniel T. Winkler. 2002. "The Dynamics of Metropolitan Housing Prices." *Journal of Real Estate Research* 23 (1-2): 29–45. Summary available at www.urbanfutures.org/abstract.cfm?ID=57 [February 11, 2003].

Kahn, Matthew. 2001. "Does Sprawl Reduce the Black/White Housing Consumption Gap?" *Housing Policy Debate* 12 (1): 77–86.

King County. 2002. *Affordable Housing: An Annual Bulletin Tracking Housing Costs in King County.* Office of Regional and Policy Planning.

Kleit, Rachel Garshick. 1998. *Housing Mobility and Healthy Communities: Montgomery County, Maryland's Moderately Priced Dwelling Unit Program.* Paper presented at the 1998 Tri-County Conference on Housing and Urban Issues. Fannie Mae Foundation, Washington, D.C.

Kockelman, Kara. 1996. "The Effects of Location Elements on Home Purchase Prices and Rents: Evidence from the San Francisco Bay Area." University of California, Berkeley.

Mathur, Shishir, Paul Waddell, and Hilda Blanco. 2003. "The Effect of Impact Fees on the Price of New Housing." Working paper. University of Washington, Urban Design and Planning.

Mayer, Christopher J., and C. Tsuriel Somerville. 2000. "Land Use Regulation and New Construction." *Regional Science and Urban Economics* 30: 639–62. Summary available at www.urbanfutures.org/abstract.cfm?ID=58 [February 11, 2003].

Montgomery County. 2003. *MPDU Production Table.* Department of Housing and Community Affairs, Moderately Priced Housing Section.

Murakami, Elaine, and Jennifer Young. 1997. "Daily Travel by Persons with Low Income." Paper prepared for NPTS Symposium. Bethesda, Maryland, October.

Nelson, Arthur, and others. 2002. *The Link between Growth Management and Housing Affordability: The Academic Evidence.* Brookings Center on Urban and Metropolitan Policy.

Porter, Douglas. 1997. *Managing Growth in America's Communities.* Washington: Island Press.

Rosen, Kenneth. 1974. "Hedonic Prices and Implicit Markets: Product Differentiation in Pure Competition." *Journal of Political Economy* 82 (1): 34–55.

Staley, Samuel R. 2001. "Ballot-Box Zoning, Transaction Costs, and Urban Growth." *Journal of the American Planning Association* 67 (1): 25–37. Summary available at www.urbanfutures.org/abstract.cfm?ID=35 [February 11, 2003].

Staley, Samuel R., and Leonard C. Gilroy. 2001. *Smart Growth and Housing Affordability: Evidence from Statewide Planning Laws.* Policy Study 287. Los Angeles: Reason Public Policy Institute (www.rppi.org/ps287.pdf [February 11, 2003]).

Tucker, William. 1997. *How Rent Control Drives Out Affordable Housing,* Policy Analysis No. 274 (Washington, D.C.: Cato Institute). Summary available at www.urbanfutures.org/abstract.cfm?ID=27 [February 11, 2003].

3

RICHARD P. VOITH
DAVID L. CRAWFORD

Smart Growth and Affordable Housing

P ROPONENTS OF SMART growth argue that it can limit suburban sprawl, reduce dependence on automobiles, revitalize older communities, and cure other ills associated with current patterns of metropolitan development in the United States. Opponents argue that smart growth policies seldom achieve their goals but often close the door on minority, low-income, and moderate-income families seeking the American dream of affordable suburban housing. Who is right? Before that question can be answered, several more basic questions must be addressed:

—What is smart growth?
—What determines housing prices?
—What does "affordable" mean in this context?
—Can smart growth policies lead to lower housing prices?
—Can smart growth affect employment opportunities, costs of public services, and commuting costs so as to increase the affordability of housing?

The authors gratefully acknowledge the financial support of the Greater Philadelphia Transportation Initiative (GPTI), which is funded by the William Penn Foundation through the Surface Transportation Policy Project and Econsult Corporation. This chapter has been strengthened by comments from Anthony Downs, Michael Schill, Robert Burchell, Sahan Mukherji, Scott Bernstein, Andrew Haughwout, and three anonymous reviewers, who of course share no responsibility for any errors. All opinions expressed are those of the authors and are not necessarily those of the GPTI Board, the William Penn Foundation, or the Surface Transportation Policy Project.

In addressing these questions, we argue in this chapter that there is little reason to expect smart growth policies to systematically make *all* housing less affordable. On the contrary, one would expect properly designed smart growth policies to increase the supply of *less land-intensive* housing of a moderate scale; the increased supply would lead to lower prices for that type of housing, directly enhancing its affordability. It also would be reasonable to expect smart growth to enhance general affordability indirectly, by creating new income opportunities in communities that already have affordable housing, by controlling the cost of public services by reducing the need for new infrastructure, and by reducing the costs of commuting and owning an automobile. At the same time, however, smart growth policies are likely to increase the price of new and existing *land-intensive* housing. The bottom line is that smart growth can close some doors and open others. If the social goal is to provide more affordable land-intensive housing, then smart growth policies will be counterproductive. On the other hand, if affordable housing that is less land-intensive is acceptable, then smart growth policies can help. As Michael Schill points out in his comment on this chapter, the mere fact that smart growth policies *can* help increase affordable housing does not guarantee that they *will*. While this chapter focuses largely on the "can" question, it discusses a few cases in which actual smart growth policies have in fact enhanced the affordability of housing.

What Is Smart Growth?

Despite the lack of consensus on the definition of smart growth, a recent study published by the American Planning Association reports multiple indications of significant legislative activity regarding smart growth policies. For example, the study reports that "in the 2000 election, 533 state or local ballot initiatives in 38 states focused on issues of planning or smart growth, with an approval rate of more than 70 percent."[1] The study also reports that roughly three-quarters of the states are pursuing, augmenting, or implementing statewide smart growth reforms. Smaller jurisdictions such as counties and cities are actively pursuing smart growth policies as well.[2]

1. American Planning Association (2002).
2. See, for example, the Legislative Analyst's Report prepared for the San Francisco Board of Supervisors in August 2000 that describes smart growth initiatives in Seattle, Portland, New York City, and San Francisco (http://sfprospector.com/site/bdsupvrs_page.asp?id=5156 [February 3, 2004]).

Smart growth means different things to different people and in different contexts.[3] Smart growth policies usually are based on some sort of consensus regarding a carefully drawn plan for the use of land in a particular jurisdiction. In principle the area could be of any size, but smart growth advocates usually argue for larger areas, such as an entire county or even an entire state, to prevent developers from "leapfrogging" beyond the controlled area and to minimize the deleterious effects of interjurisdictional competition for taxable development projects.[4] The intention of any such plan and the associated smart growth policies is to channel particular types of economic and real estate development into particular areas in order to revitalize older communities and rationalize newer ones. Plans usually are comprehensive enough to coordinate such development with existing and planned infrastructure for transportation and other services.

Smart growth policies are a mix of carrots and sticks. Carrots include tax incentives or public subsidies for development projects that are consistent with the land use plan; they also include incentives for smaller jurisdictions to make their zoning and other regulations consistent with the plan for the larger region. Another carrot may be streamlining or accelerating the approval process for smart development. Sticks include regulations that prohibit certain types of development outside designated growth boundaries or penalties imposed on jurisdictions that do not follow the plan. Without such sticks it would be difficult or perhaps impossible to confine growth to designated areas. Even given strong incentives to comply with a plan, some developers probably would choose to go outside the designated areas unless they are specifically prohibited from doing so. Of course, public policy can relax regulations as well as impose them. Strategies such as reducing minimum lot sizes in particular areas or allowing the creation of accessory dwelling units could be part of a smart growth plan.

3. Many authors have offered definitions of smart growth. See, for example, Downs (2001) or the Sierra Club, "Stop Sprawl Fact Sheet"(www.sierraclub.org/sprawl/factsheet.asp [December 10, 2003]). Others have avoided the term because of the lack of consensus on its definition. See Nelson and others (2002, p. 2) in which the term "growth management" is used instead of "smart growth." In his comments on this chapter, Michael Schill says, "Since I have never met anyone who has advocated 'dumb growth' and since 'smart growth' seems to mean something different to virtually everyone who uses the term, I feel that the expression is less than optimal." While we find merit in the positions taken by Nelson and others and Schill, we have used the term "smart growth," largely because it was chosen by the organizers of the Symposium on Growth Management and Affordable Housing.

4. In New Jersey, for example, the governor recently put forward a smart growth plan that applies to the entire state.

Smart Growth Policy Goals and Mechanisms

The key elements of smart growth policies, listed in the box on page 86, are actually a mix of policy goals and policy mechanisms.[5] Elements 2, 4, 5, 9, and 13 represent goals. The remaining elements are policy mechanisms intended to help achieve one or more of the goals. For example, while sometimes it is incorrectly described as a goal, limiting outward growth is actually a policy mechanism that some suggest would promote elements 2, 4, 5, and 13. Advocates seek to limit outward growth not as an end in itself but as a means to achieve various objectives.

The distinction between goals and mechanisms is important because the questions that should be of interest to proponents, politicians, and analysts are whether smart growth policy mechanisms can achieve smart growth policy goals and whether it is feasible to implement those mechanisms. This chapter focuses on two more specific questions: whether smart growth policy mechanisms can result in more affordable housing and, if so, whether it is feasible to implement these mechanisms. The diversity of the policy mechanisms makes it difficult to answer both questions.

The Affordable Housing Goal of Smart Growth

While smart growth policies typically are designed to shape the geographic pattern of growth within a metropolitan area, they also can affect housing affordability throughout the region in several ways. They can alter the distribution of housing types and prices across the region, thereby directly affecting affordability. They can alter the geographic distribution of employment opportunities, which affects family income, which in turn affects affordability. Smart growth policies also can enhance the efficiency of public and private infrastructure, thereby lowering the cost of public and private services, which could make housing more affordable. And they can alter the cost of commuting, which, as argued below, is a potentially important component of housing affordability.

Smart growth policy initiatives take many different forms and many of those forms have positive implications for the provision of affordable housing. In a 2001 study, Brown reports that many jurisdictions have implemented

5. The symposium organizers used the term "nearly universal" to mean that when proponents, politicians, or analysts talk about smart growth, they nearly always have at least the first five elements in mind.

Key Elements of Smart Growth Policies

Nearly universal elements
1. Limiting outward growth
2. Reducing dependency on automobiles
3. Promoting compact, higher-density development
4. Preserving open space
5. Redeveloping inner-city areas and infill sites

Occasional elements
6. Placing the cost of infrastructure for new growth on new residents
7. Creating local government incentives for locating growth in limited areas
8. Speeding the approval and entitlement process
9. Increasing the supply of affordable housing
10. Promoting mixed-use development
11. Removing regulatory barriers to new urbanist and other innovative designs
12. Sharing regional resources among local governments
13. Creating a greater sense of community
14. Developing a public-private process for achieving consensus on plans for the region's future.

inclusionary zoning ordinances under which "a developer sells or rents a percentage of units in a new development at prices that low- to moderate-income families can afford, and in return is usually given a 'density bonus,' which gives permission to build more units than local zoning regulations typically allow."[6] The Smart Growth Network Subgroup on Affordable Housing describes several examples of smart growth policies that create affordable housing. These include relaxing zoning restrictions, as in Cary, North Carolina, to encourage the creation of accessory dwelling units (independent housing units created within single-family homes or on their lots); streamlining the review process; reducing or waiving fees; making public investments in infrastructure for projects that are consistent with development guidelines, as in Austin, Texas; and using low-income housing tax credits to help fund the construction of affordable housing units, as in Chicago.[7]

Even though many aspects of smart growth could improve housing affordability, Downs notes that "affordable housing is not high on the priority lists

6. Brown (2002).
7. Arigoni (2001).

of the advocate groups" and that "it is often omitted from their smart growth goals."[8] Recently it has been suggested that smart growth policies are inevitably exclusionary. It is certainly true that zoning restrictions and other local regulations have been used historically to systematically exclude certain racial or economic groups.[9] Commenting on the historical conflict between smart growth and affordable housing, Arigoni says:

> In many communities, initial attempts to deal with growth's negative effects focused simplistically on limiting new development. As a result, tensions rose between efforts to manage growth and perceived threats to affordable housing. The adoption of strict growth management policies which aim to stop growth without making provisions for new development do raise legitimate concerns about increasing housing costs because of a diminishing supply. Unfortunately it is precisely these situations that have created a perception that smart growth and affordable housing are opposing forces. Ensuring an adequate supply, distribution, and quality of affordable housing is a litmus test for smart growth.[10]

It is our view that the creation of affordable housing should be a smart growth goal. Even if it is not considered a goal by smart growth advocates, it clearly is a proper goal of public policy and one that should be considered in evaluating smart growth policy mechanisms.[11]

Although it is difficult to encourage some types of economic or real estate development without excluding other types, smart growth policies do not have to exclude particular groups of people. For example, by reducing minimum lot sizes, a high-income community could facilitate the development of moderate-income housing, which would have the effect of including moderate-income families who were effectively excluded before. Such a change

8. Downs (2001).

9. See Glaeser and Gyourko (2000). They conclude that zoning is a major factor in reducing the affordability of housing.

10. Arigoni (2001).

11. It should be noted, however, that affordability should never be the only guiding principle or goal of a smart growth policy because it is defined with respect to the costs faced by the purchaser alone. Affordability, as usually considered, does not reflect external costs that may be imposed on others. For example, extensive construction of houses on very large lots could lower the price of such houses but create more sprawl, which could impose costs on many other people. Those external costs would not concern most buyers because they would focus only on their private costs. In this case, private decisions could produce bad social outcomes.

might have the effect of excluding some additional high-income families, but such families already would be included in the community. In another example, discussed below, smart growth policies could encourage job creation and housing rehabilitation in older low-income communities with usable housing stock. The important question is whether smart growth policies can be used and are used to make housing more affordable for minority, low-income, and moderate-income families.

What Determines Housing Prices?

Like most prices in the U.S. economy, housing prices are determined by supply and demand, but it is not possible to talk meaningfully about a single housing price because housing is highly differentiated in many dimensions. Contrary to popular wisdom, the value of a housing unit depends on many factors in addition to its "location, location, location." Unit size, other unit characteristics such as style or condition, amount of land, and other land characteristics all are significant determinants of the relative value of different housing units. And location, of course, does matter, because buyers value both locally provided public services such as schools and proximity to employment opportunities and amenities.

To speak meaningfully about demand and supply, one must focus on a particular type of housing, such as existing high-quality, single-family houses on one-acre lots in some area or on new moderate-quality townhouses in another area. Once there is a focus on a particular type of housing, one can think about the demand for and supply of that type. Demand increases or supply decreases can be expected to increase its price, and, of course, demand decreases or supply increases can be expected to decrease its price.

The demand for different types of housing and the preferences of buyers are interconnected. Individual buyers may consider more than one type of housing and choose among types considered to be good substitutes for each other. For example, many buyers would consider an existing single-family house on a one-acre lot—but not a two-bedroom garden apartment—to be a good substitute for a new single-family house on a one-acre lot. A buyer will choose among a set of good substitutes in substantial part on the basis of their relative prices.

Similarly, the supply of different types of new housing and the profit-seeking behavior of developers are interconnected. While no developer is likely to build all types of housing, many developers will consider building more than one type. For example, one developer might consider building detached houses of different sizes and another might consider building one-, two-, or three-bedroom apartments. A developer will choose among a set of feasible alternatives in substantial part on the basis of their relative prices.[12]

So buyers and sellers react to the relative prices, which themselves are determined by the interaction of demand (buyers) and supply (sellers). If real estate markets were unregulated, they would determine the price and quantity of the various types of housing; however, unregulated markets probably do not exist in any U.S. metropolitan areas. When real estate markets are regulated through smart growth policies or any other kind, the markets yield prices and quantities that are different from those that would be observed in the absence of regulation. As argued below, the key to understanding the impact of smart growth on housing prices and quantities is to recognize that *smart growth policies are likely to increase the supply of some types of housing and decrease the supply of others.* In this regard, smart growth policies are not unlike zoning regulations in many American communities.[13]

In one regard, the interaction of supply and demand for housing differs from that for most commodities. Generally, in the long run, competition ensures that the price of a commodity equals its cost of production plus a "normal" profit. For housing, however, this may not be the case because each house's location is unique. The value of a house that enjoys benefits that are unique to its location will exceed its production cost. This is an important issue with regard to the implications of smart growth policies for housing affordability. If smart growth policies make entire neighborhoods or even regions more attractive than others, those policies could in effect raise the prices of all housing in the market—even those housing types favored by smart growth policies.[14] This issue is similar, on a larger scale, to that of gentrification,

12. Supplies of existing housing also respond positively to prices. As the price of a particular type of housing increases, owners of that type of housing are more inclined to offer their units for sale.

13. In a personal communication Andrew Haughwout pointed out to us that low-density zoning used to be considered a smart growth policy and still may be by some observers.

14. One possible example of this phenomenon is Portland, Oregon. After the imposition of comprehensive smart growth policies, densities in Portland have increased and prices have risen. Some argue that the price rise reflects only restrictions on the supply of land available for development. That cannot be the entire story, however, because the Portland metropolitan area has continued to experience strong growth in housing demand, despite increasing prices. Portland, perhaps as a result of policy choices, is viewed as a very desirable location. If housing prices were increasing solely because of supply shortages, the price increases would have choked off the growth of the metropolitan area.

whereby improvements in local neighborhoods increase house values and reduce affordability.

What Does "Affordable" Mean in This Context?

"Affordability" is a highly subjective term because housing that one family can easily purchase may be completely out of reach for another family. Commonly used measures of affordability—like median price or median price as a percentage of median family income—do not tell the whole story.[15] The problem can be illustrated by a simple hypothetical example. Consider a community in which all housing units have the same price, a price that is just within reach of a household with median income. A comparison of the median price and the median income would suggest that the community's housing was affordable, but nearly half of the households would be unable to afford any housing in the community. Generally, one should consider the entire distribution of such costs in relation to the entire distribution of income. For example, one could ask whether households in the 25th percentile of the income distribution can afford housing in the 25th percentile of costs and then ask the same question for the other percentiles.

Acknowledging the need to compare the *distribution* of housing costs with the *distribution* of household income when evaluating housing affordability, Nelson and others call for an effort to frame a definition of affordability, a suggestion with which we concur.[16] They also point out that defining housing affordability is further complicated by the need to address the heterogeneity of housing characteristics, including transportation and other location-specific associated costs.

The heterogeneity problem can be explored though a simple example. Consider two houses that are identical in every detail except that one house has an extra bedroom and therefore commands a higher price. Is the smaller house more affordable? It is in the sense that a larger percentage of households would be able to purchase it, but the comparison is clearly not "apples to apples." Depending on the prices and the value that the households assign to the extra space, the larger, higher-priced house may be a more or less affordable source of *housing services*. Housing services typically are defined as

15. In their comments on this chapter, Robert Burchell and Sahan Mukherji show how alternative measures of housing affordability can yield very different assessments of the scale of the affordability problem.

16. Nelson and others (2002, pp. 3–4).

the flow of services derived from the components of a structure and the land on which it is located—kitchens, bathrooms, bedrooms, garages, yards, and so forth. Transportation, location-specific amenities, and public services such as schools affect the overall cost of living in a particular unit of housing.[17] In assessing affordability, one should consider all the costs associated with housing, not just its price.

Housing services are inevitably bought in bundles, which vary in their composition from one housing unit and one location to another. There are at least two interesting ways to define housing affordability: in terms of *housing units* (bundles of housing services) or of the components of *housing services*. These need not be the same with respect to their affordability. For example, the cost per bedroom may be lower in a large house, but the same large house may be less affordable than a house with fewer bedrooms. We argue below that smart growth policies can expand the supply of lower-cost bundles of housing services or lower the costs of particular housing services. Either outcome would make lower-income families better off.

Like Nelson and others, we can sidestep the problem of not having precise definitions of housing affordability. Why? Because our focus, like theirs, is on the potential and actual impact of smart growth policies on affordability, not on measuring affordability per se. Several changes can make housing more affordable, by any reasonable definition: changes in the composition of the housing stock; directly lowering the price of a given bundle of housing services; increasing income opportunities near the housing; lowering local taxes; lowering the cost of utilities; lowering monetary or time costs of commuting; and substituting public services for private services while holding taxes constant.

Can Smart Growth Policies Lead to Lower Housing Prices?

The typical argument against smart growth is that such policies necessarily raise all housing prices because they restrict the supply of land available for housing. A recent study by Randall Pozdena concludes that

It is difficult to make a case for the site-supply restrictions promoted by advocates of smart growth. It is apparent both from theory and

17. Taxes associated with the provision of public services should be considered in the affordability calculus as well.

the available data that restricting the supply of development sites is bound to raise home prices, everything else being equal.[18]

We return below to Pozdena's conclusion regarding the data, but first we note that the flaw in the theoretical argument is easily demonstrated by a simple example.

Consider a community made up of two areas, one undeveloped and the other filled with single-family homes on one-acre lots. Now consider two alternatives for the development of the undeveloped land: zoning the undeveloped land to require one-acre lots or taking a smart growth approach that requires a more intensive use, such as moderately priced town homes. Which approach will produce higher prices for existing homes on one-acre lots? Which will produce higher value of the undeveloped land? Which will produce higher prices of town homes? And finally, which will produce more affordable housing?

The price of existing one-acre homes will be determined by the demand for and supply of those and comparable homes. Looking first at supply, it is clear that the smart growth policy will reduce the future supply of new comparable homes on one-acre lots because no such homes will be built in the community. Taken by itself, this supply restriction should have the effect of raising the future value of the existing one-acre homes; however, we need to consider how the policy might affect the demand for one-acre homes in the community.

The extent to which the supply restriction dominates the price response for existing homes on one-acre lots depends on two important factors affecting the demand for these homes: homebuyers' elasticity of substitution between homes on one-acre lots and high-density townhouses; and the impact of the smart growth development on the overall attractiveness of the community. The elasticity of substitution between housing types is important because, while the supply of large-lot housing is limited in the smart growth development plan, the overall number of housing units is likely to be larger. If the two types are good substitutes, the smart growth policy may result in a decline in demand for the existing dwellings on large lots. In this case the impact on the price of large-lot housing would be ambiguous because both supply and demand are decreasing. If, on the other hand, town homes are not a very good substitute for one-acre homes, the demand for

18. Pozdena (2002).

one-acre homes is not likely to drop when more town homes become available, and the supply restriction will result in higher prices on large-lot houses.

The second demand-related question is what impact, if any, the mere existence of town homes will have on the attractiveness of one-acre homes in the community. Economists refer to such effects as externalities, and they can be either negative or positive. Negative effects could occur if the town home development led to traffic congestion or overcrowded schools or other facilities or if it somehow diminished the ambience of the community. Positive effects could occur if the town home development led to an expansion of services. So although the supply restriction alone will have a positive impact on the value of existing one-acre homes, the substitution and the externality effects could be positive or negative. Thus the total impact is ambiguous.

The smart growth policy is likely to increase the value of the undeveloped land in this hypothetical community because the land will be used more intensively. Furthermore, the future value of the town home development, including the new buildings, is likely to be higher than the value of a new one-acre lot development. If more land-intensive housing were not more valuable, communities would not need to block it with zoning regulations.[19]

Which policy will produce more affordable housing? The one-acre policy will reduce the price of one-acre homes, but add no new townhouses; the town home development will add to the housing stock and lower the price of town homes. Nelson and others argue that smart growth, which they refer to as growth management, can and sometimes does lead to lower prices for some kinds of housing:

> Land-supply limiting effects of growth management need not lead to higher housing prices if housing density increases (relative to prior conditions), infrastructure is available in a timely manner, and land use decisions are made roughly concurrent with market needs.[20]

Because it restricts the supply of some types of housing, smart growth is unlikely to make all types of housing more affordable, but it could lead to more units of affordable housing. The theoretical impact on median housing price is ambiguous, so evidence regarding changes in median price is unlikely to

19. Note that it is also conceivable that the negative externalities associated with dense development that are imposed on existing large-lot housing may be large enough to lower the aggregate value of land in the community.

20. Nelson and others (2002, p. 35).

resolve the question of affordability. What is needed is an examination of changes in the entire distribution of prices to see whether a particular smart growth plan does increase the supply of affordable housing units.

What is the empirical evidence on smart growth and affordable housing? According to Nelson and others:

> Typical growth management programs have affordable housing and inclusionary elements that are designed to lower the costs of construction and broaden choices to more housing segments. The most important programs include measures to ensure an adequate supply of land for dwellings of many types. Local governments sometimes complement land-supply restrictions with housing subsidy programs and affordable housing requirements. The latter essentially cross-subsidize the construction of low-cost units with profits generated from high-cost units. In general, however, these types of programs do not lower housing unit prices but rather increase the range of housing types available—that is, they assure affordability at the neighborhood or municipal scale, rather than at the scale of the individual dwelling unit. By permitting, or encouraging, the construction of smaller and more dense forms of housing, housing units are made available at lower prices and rents, even though the cost per unit of housing services may be higher.[21]

From her analysis of the impact of inclusionary zoning ordinances (as defined above) in the greater Washington, D.C., area, Brown concludes

> that attaching affordable dwellings to the production of market-rate units not only benefits low- and moderate-income individuals by providing them with housing they can afford, but also helps to create integrated communities where households of different incomes and racial backgrounds live within the same developments. Moreover, inclusionary zoning ordinances create affordable units away from neighborhoods of concentrated poverty, providing moderate-income households with access to areas of jobs and opportunity.

How does one reconcile these positive conclusions with Pozdena's negative conclusion? The explanation lies in the fact that Pozdena focuses narrowly on

---

21. Nelson and others (2002, p. 13).

land-supply restrictions, excluding other smart growth mechanisms. As Nelson and others say, "the housing price effects of growth management policies depend heavily on how they are designed and implemented."[22]

Would any smart growth plan necessarily produce a lower price for some type of housing? No, it is certainly possible that a particular smart growth plan could restrict the supply and increase the price of all types of housing. Our point, which is supported by Nelson and others, is that a carefully designed smart growth initiative could lead to lower prices for some types of housing.

Can Smart Growth Increase the Affordability of Housing?

One way to make a given stock of housing more affordable without lowering prices is to create new nearby job opportunities. Clearly smart growth policies have the potential to do just that because they can focus job-creating development in areas where there already is a relatively inexpensive stock of housing. For example, smart growth policies could encourage new businesses to locate in older communities that are economically depressed and have an excess supply of housing. Restricting the supply of land for commercial and industrial greenfield development would make development in existing communities more attractive. At the same time, brownfield remediation programs could increase the supply of commercial land in older communities. Brownfield programs, which used to focus only on the cleanup of old industrial sites, are now an integral part of many smart growth initiatives. According to a study published in 2000 by the National Governors Association,

> brownfields projects can play a central role in urban and rural revitalization and offer alternatives to new, greenfields developments. Natural areas and green spaces are less likely to succumb to urban sprawl and development when brownfields properties and their existing infrastructure are available and ready to meet development needs. . . . One analysis concluded that brownfields redevelopment appears to be the "politically smartest smart growth policy" because it is a "much less threatening way for federal and state governments to provide alternatives to sprawl."[23]

22. Nelson and others (2002, p. 24).
23. National Governors Association (2000, p. 8), quoting Greenburg and others (2000).

The study reports, among other successes, that roughly 175 brownfield projects in Massachusetts were projected to create or retain more than 30,000 jobs.[24] The former governor of Maryland, Parris Glendening, described a recent project in his state:

> The American Can Company project in the Canton section of East Baltimore has become a poster child for smart growth. It is in a Priority Funding Area where sewer, water and other infrastructure and services already exist. It was one of our first brownfield cleanup sites. And they were able to take advantage of our Heritage and Job Creation Tax Credits. This site was abandoned for years and the area around it suffered. Now it is home to 40 separate businesses, including hi-tech companies, restaurants, cafes, and bookstores and 700 jobs. *As a result of this project and other development nearby, Canton can boast that it is the only neighborhood in Baltimore City where the percentage of home ownership is now rising!* [emphasis added][25]

Clearly, the governor believed that smart growth can create affordable housing, and the nation's mayors shared his enthusiasm:

> According to a recent survey of the U.S. Conference of Mayors, 187 of 231 cities responded that cleaning up existing brownfields sites could generate as many as 540,000 new jobs if the land were returned to production. "Bringing jobs back to the center of town and away from greenfields may also mean that jobs and services in the local economy are more accessible because of availability of other modes of transportation."[26]

When there are more jobs and jobs are more accessible, households will be better able to afford whatever housing is available.

Finally, evidence is growing that a community's fiscal policies affect the location of activities. While uncommon in the United States, one element of smart growth, tax sharing, could be used systematically to address the difference in tax burdens on older and newer communities. Haughwout and others (2000), Haughwout and Inman (2001), and Voith (2002) all present

24. National Governors Association (2000, p. 22).
25. National Governors Association (2000, p. 25).
26. National Governors Association (2000, p. 9), citing the U.S. Conference of Mayors (2000) and quoting Gaspar (1998).

strong evidence that local taxes play a significant role in the location of economic activity.[27] Regional tax sharing is one seldom-used approach to ameliorating fiscal differences.[28] However, there are many examples of regional taxation for particular regional services, especially for transit. Just as important, local fiscal differences can be greatly affected by state policies—which, in most cases, are where smart growth policies originate. States that assume larger financial responsibilities for services such as education implicitly impose tax sharing across communities.[29]

Another way to make a given stock of housing more affordable without lowering prices is to lower the cost of utilities and other public services. By increasing population density (reducing sprawl), smart growth can do just that. It seems fairly clear that providing those services is characterized by economies of density over broad ranges of density.[30] For example, it is clearly less expensive to provide electricity, water, and sewer services to 100 town homes than to 100 houses on single-acre lots. Burchell and others estimated that more compact development would reduce the national cost of water and sewer infrastructure by $12.6 billion, or 7 percent, over the period 2000–25.[31] They also estimated savings on local roads: compact growth would save 180,000 lane miles (9 percent) or $110 billion (12 percent) over the same period.[32]

Still another way to make housing more affordable without lowering prices is to reduce residents' monetary or time costs of commuting. Smart growth can reduce commuting costs in three ways. First, by reducing sprawl, it can reduce the distances that people need to travel, thereby reducing both the monetary and time costs of commuting.[33] Second, by locating new employment sites in the same community with new or existing housing and

27. See Haughwout and others (2000); Haughwout and Inman (2001); and Voith (2002).

28. Explicit regional tax sharing is rare, the Minneapolis/St. Paul metropolitan area being a notable exception. Regional tax sharing also is accomplished in many areas through annexation of suburbs by the central city. This is common in the South and West.

29. In Pennsylvania, for example, Governor Rendell recently proposed a simultaneous increase in state income and decrease in local taxes with the primary goal of shifting a significant portion of education funding from local governments to the state (Senate Education Committee 2003).

30. Such economies may become diseconomies when population density becomes very high, but economies are likely to persist over the ranges of density that would be observed in most communities.

31. Burchell and others (2002, p. 225).

32. Burchell and others (2002, p. 249).

33. Downs (1992, pp.173–85) argues that this effect is likely to be small unless density is increased dramatically.

by locating new housing in the same community with existing employment sites, smart growth can decrease more expensive intercommunity commuting and increase less expensive intracommunity commuting. Third, smart growth can reduce residents' dependence on cars. Living in a community that offers pedestrian, bicycle, or transit access to shopping and employment centers and thereby reduces the need for cars by one car per household could result in a substantial increase in housing affordability. The American Automobile Association estimated the average annual cost of owning and operating a car in 2002 at $7,533; a household needing one car less could afford to spend more on housing.[34] Assuming added public transit expenses of $1,500 annually, the household could afford to pay an additional $500 more per month for housing.[35]

So the answer to the question of whether smart growth policies can work to increase the affordability of housing is "yes": by increasing employment opportunities and reducing the costs of services as well as by reducing commuting costs.

Winners, Losers, and Obstacles to Smart Growth

Smart growth policies will affect families, businesses, developers, and politicians. Smart growth policies will never create "win-win" situations, because they lower some prices and raise others. In addition, because they represent a significant departure from past practices, these policies will frustrate the expectations of investors who did not anticipate them. There will be political implications of winning and losing, and demographic changes also may accompany smart growth.

Families that would like to upgrade the quality of their housing but do not insist on land-intensive housing probably have the most to gain. Families that strongly prefer but do not currently have land-intensive housing are likely to lose out, because the cost of such housing is likely to increase as its

34. American Automobile Association (2002).

35. Consumers may be able to substitute lower-cost housing for longer commutes (Burchell and others, 2002, pp. 455–56). That opportunity could be viewed as a reason why one should be less concerned with the commuting costs associated with sprawl. Nevertheless, if in equilibrium people at the margin are indifferent to a choice between two houses—one with higher prices and lower commuting costs and one with lower prices and higher commuting costs—the introduction of a new, lower-cost commuting option will necessarily increase the attractiveness of the house that can use the new option. This gain will be partially offset as the housing market adjusts and the value of that option is capitalized into the price of the house.

supply is restricted.[36] These are the families that concern the opponents of smart growth. One possible way to help them would be to encourage outward growth—the antithesis of smart growth. It is not at all clear, however, that such a strategy could help these families much. The prices of land-intensive housing would fall, but the costs of services and commuting would increase significantly, perhaps offsetting the price decrease.

The impact of smart growth on low-density high-income communities is ambiguous. They probably would realize capital gains on the increased prices of their houses, benefit from the preservation of nearby open spaces, and enjoy reductions in pollution and congestion. On the other hand, they probably would lose from a fiscal point of view if lower-income families entered the community to live in more land-intensive housing. The more land-intensive housing need not be lower-cost housing and certainly need not be low-income housing, but it could be the former and possibly the latter if smart growth policies are so designed. The total value of real estate and real estate taxes in the community could *increase* due to the more intensive use of land or *decrease* if the land-intensive housing is sufficiently low in value. Either way, property value and tax revenue *per family* are likely to fall, thereby imposing additional net costs of public services on the incumbent families.[37] This conjecture depends, however, on whether the smart growth policies address local fiscal impacts.

Some developers will be winners and others will be losers. Developers tend to specialize in particular types of real estate, so a smart growth policy that encourages one type of development and discourages another will benefit some developers and harm others.[38] Similarly, some landowners will win and others will lose. Smart growth policies will enhance the value of land that will be used more intensively than it would have been without the policies. For example, land value will increase when large-lot zoning restrictions are

36. Gyourko and Voith (2001) argue that the price elasticity of residential demand for land is surprisingly elastic, suggesting that households are generally willing to adjust residential land consumption significantly in response to price. This suggests that many households will be able to adjust to higher-density housing with less utility loss than if demand for residential land were less price-elastic.

37. In a personal communication, Andrew Haughwout pointed out that many communities would not regard a population-increasing policy to be smart growth. Clearly more local perspectives on smart growth may differ significantly from a broader regional perspective. A person may support affordable housing in the region, but not in his or her local community.

38. Nelson and others (2002, p. 28) agree: "Furthermore, single-family housing producers may be unfamiliar with the dynamics of the multifamily housing market and may be unable to enter new markets following changes in the price of land."

relaxed and dense housing, such as townhouses, is allowed. On the other hand, owners of land that is to be preserved as open space will suffer financial losses unless they are compensated for the loss of development rights.

Local politicians are likely to lose power while regional or state politicians gain because a move toward smart growth would likely shift regulatory authority from smaller jurisdictions to larger ones. Politicians also could be affected by intraregional shifts in the demographic and economic characteristics of voters.

Every potential loser is a potential obstacle to the adoption of smart growth policies. One way to remove those obstacles is to compensate—noneconomists would say bribe—the losers. Compensation may be possible because any smart growth plan worth pursuing should create net value. That is, the amount that the winners gain should exceed the amount that the losers lose. If gains do not exceed losses, then most would agree that the particular smart growth plan involved is a bad idea that should be revised.

There are many ways that losers can be compensated. Current owners of what is to be preserved as open space can be and often are paid for the development rights that they surrender.[39] Regional jurisdictions can tax winners and compensate losers through regional taxes and expenditures. To gain political consensus, such fiscal arrangements may have to be made before a smart growth plan is implemented. New fiscal arrangements for financing basic services such as education may be required as well.

The possibility that smart growth results in the cost of public services, especially for education, rising faster than local property tax revenues in some communities suggests that the currently common system of funding public schools through property taxes may be an obstacle to adopting smart growth. If local communities perceive that their education costs will rise faster than property tax revenues because of an increase in lower-priced, denser housing, they are likely to oppose smart growth policies.[40] Some communities also may perceive that smart growth policies limit their ability to attract commercial real estate development, which helps pay for public education. These considerations suggest that smart growth policies may need to look for revenue sources for public education that span entire regions or even states.[41]

---

39. For example, the New Jersey Farmland Preservation Program uses state funds to purchase development easements from farmers who wish to continue farming (www.state.nj.us/agriculture/sadc/overview.htm [February 3, 2004]).

40. As noted above, denser housing is not necessarily lower priced, but it could be if the smart growth policy requires or encourages that outcome.

41. See footnote 28 for an example.

Many may argue that it is highly unlikely that any scheme to address the economic and fiscal consequences of smart growth would be politically feasible. Yet, at the state level at least, there are frequent changes in the extent to which states aid local jurisdictions in many arenas—transportation, education, social services, and economic development. As more state governments look more closely at their patterns of growth, they also have the power to craft incentives to both guide growth and partially compensate those who may lose from a shift in policy.

Will Smart Growth Make Housing More or Less Affordable?

The best answer is "Although smart growth probably will make some housing less affordable, it can make other housing more affordable." The most land-intensive housing, single-family houses on large lots, probably would become less affordable. Less land-intensive housing could become more affordable if smart growth policies are carefully designed.

Do smart growth policies necessarily exclude particular groups from particular communities? Again, not if the plans are well designed. Can they help minority, low-income, and moderate-income families afford better housing? Clearly, yes. Can opposition to smart growth be overcome? Yes, but only with a comprehensive strategy to implement a plan that creates real value.

The next question, then, is whether such strategies will actually be developed and implemented. We have established here that smart growth policies have the potential to create—and on at least a few occasions have created—more affordable housing. However, in his comments on this chapter, Michael Schill says that he believes that "most of the popular support for smart growth is based on a variety of factors that will create strong incentives for municipalities to adopt growth restrictions *without* simultaneously promoting affordable housing."

The question of whether smart growth policies, as actually implemented, are likely to enhance housing affordability requires analysis of the emphasis given to affordable housing, which is largely a political issue. While it clearly is very important, that issue is beyond the scope of this chapter and our expertise.

COMMENT BY
Michael H. Schill

The Achilles' heel of the "smart growth" movement is the impact that many of the proposals put forth by its advocates would have on affordable housing.[42] Fairly intuitive economic models of supply and demand suggest that if one restricts the amount of land that can be used for housing—particularly cheap land at the periphery—one will likely drive up the price of land nearby and whatever is built on it.

Many people who write about smart growth, including Voith and Crawford, seek to rescue the concept from this critique by suggesting that restrictions on land use are only part of the story. They suggest that smart growth encompasses—in addition to urban growth boundaries, up-zoning, and impact fees—tools to promote the construction of affordable housing, such as increased densities in central cities and inner-ring suburbs. They also maintain that inclusionary zoning (with and without density bonuses) can allow us to win the battle against hated sprawl and actually increase housing opportunities for low- and moderate-income families. In the words of Voith and Crawford, "a carefully designed smart growth initiative could lead to lower prices for some types of housing."

I have no doubt that if Dick Voith or his coauthor were governor or county executive of a particular jurisdiction, that jurisdiction would indeed have a fighting chance of restricting development at the periphery and simultaneously promoting more compact, less costly housing in transportation-efficient locations. Unfortunately, we are not so lucky. In this comment, I would like to suggest why I believe that although Voith and Crawford are no doubt correct in stating that smart growth *need not* lead to higher housing prices, it will do so in practice.[43]

I would like to thank David Engel and Randy Lee for their insightful comments on earlier drafts. Of course, all views expressed in this comment are my own and do not necessarily represent those of any other person or institution.

42. Throughout this comment, I will use the term "smart growth" since that term is used by Voith and Crawford. Nevertheless, since I have never met anyone who has advocated "dumb growth" and since "smart growth" seems to mean something different to virtually everyone who uses the term, I feel that the expression is less than optimal.

43. One additional critique of smart growth—which was notably absent from the papers prepared for the Symposium on Growth Management and Affordable Housing and therefore is not be covered in this comment—are its implications in terms of property rights. Smart growth

According to Voith and Crawford, "smart growth can close some doors and open others." In other words, land-intensive housing or housing built on large lots will likely increase in price and therefore become less affordable. At the same time—as a result of up-zoning, parking waivers, streamlining of the approval process, subsidies, and density bonuses—some housing built on less land will become more affordable.

The problem with this formulation, I believe, is that most of the popular support for smart growth is based on a variety of factors that will create strong incentives for municipalities to adopt growth restrictions *without* simultaneously promoting affordable housing. Adherents of smart growth typically are not motivated by the desire to help low-, moderate- or even middle-income families afford their housing. Instead they are typically concerned with traffic and gridlock on the highways, the loss of environmental amenities, and the cost of providing public services—most important, schools. And, of course, there is the omnipresent fear of losing community character, a concern that is even less precise than the concept of smart growth and can encompass everything from the desire to retain an environment with a small-town feel to the desire to retain one that is devoid of racial and ethnic minorities.

Given the strong interest of many suburban families in restricting development, it is highly likely that in the absence of some external pressure—either from the state, the county, the courts, or the local business community—affordable housing will fall off the table. In other words, it might be very easy to enact additional barriers without also adopting the types of policies that Voith suggests would make housing more affordable.

Indeed, in many ways, affordable housing is in direct conflict with most of the motives behind people's desire for smart growth. Although none of us want people to live in substandard housing or to pay more than half their income in rent, we also do not want to have more crowded roads and to pay more in property taxes for local schools.[44] Unfortunately, at present, we have

---

implies that some owners of land (particularly land at the periphery) will suffer losses in value at the same time that other owners of land (unregulated land) will enjoy increases in value. Whether these windfalls and wipeouts are justified as a matter of equity or efficiency is a subject for another day. For an examination of issues of equity and efficiency in the closely related area of development exactions, see Been (1991).

44. According to the 2001 American Housing Survey, 23.3 percent of all renter households in the United States paid more than half their income for housing; among black and Hispanic renters, the proportion with severe rent burdens was even greater (27.1 percent and 25.2 percent respectively).

a collective action problem concerning affordable housing in many of our metropolitan areas. Thanks to Voith's pioneering work on suburban/urban interdependencies, we understand that the good of an entire region—even those rural suburbs at the periphery—may depend on having housing that our retail clerks, our teachers, and our firefighters can afford.[45] Nevertheless, it is difficult for any one municipality to step up to the plate and adopt programs to create more of the housing that Voith envisions because of the perception, accurate or erroneous, that the negative consequences to the community outweigh the benefits.

So, in the end, where will the bulk of the affordable housing likely be built? It seems clear that if smart growth advocates have their way, most new affordable housing will be built in central cities or inner-ring suburbs. Of course, in some respects this may be desirable. Developments in inner areas are more compact, economize on transportation, and may even promote the regeneration of underused land in communities that have lost population.[46]

Nevertheless, there are various reasons to be concerned about a strategy that relies on development in central cities and inner-ring suburbs to make up the shortfall of housing production that would be created by supply restrictions enacted in the name of smart growth. Building affordable housing in urban environments is by no means an easy undertaking. First, even within cities, housing development is not always greeted with enthusiasm. Just like their suburban counterparts, many inner-city residents would be happy not to have new neighbors, new barriers to their views, and new competitors for parking spaces. The desire to maintain the status quo is as strong in city neighborhoods as it is in less dense surroundings. Community opposition to new development manifests itself every day in opposition to rezoning, drawn-out land use and environmental approval procedures, and endless lawsuits, meritorious and frivolous, designed to tie up a project and raise its costs.

Furthermore, even in central neighborhoods where affordable housing would be welcomed rather than opposed and where allowable densities would permit the developer to economize on land, many of the cost savings of compactness could be eaten up by the relatively higher cost of construction in such areas. First, there are the everyday headaches of building in congested environments, including the physical difficulties of transporting mate-

45. Voith (1992).
46. See for example, Schill and others (2002), which shows that subsidized housing increased property values in the immediate area more than other housing in the same neighborhood.

rials through crowded urban roadways. Second, labor costs are likely to be higher in central cities than in more peripheral areas; this typically can be attributed to the greater power of labor unions in cities. Third, site preparation costs also may be higher. Although smart growth advocates argue that infrastructure already exists in central cities, so, in many cases, do buildings. In many instances, existing structures will have to be demolished and carted away. Also, the parcels available often will be brownfields that require expensive environmental remediation.

Perhaps most important, central cities themselves often have erected regulatory impediments to construction ranging from an excessively long land use approval process to burdensome building code regulations and inefficient administrative procedures. In 1999 I coauthored a study on how to reduce the cost of new housing construction in New York City.[47] We found that regulatory barriers and labor practices together did indeed add more than 25 percent to the cost of housing development.

Therefore, even if a locality has the political will and the cooperative spirit needed to tie growth management restrictions at the periphery to higher-density development in the city or inner-ring suburbs, we must not take it as an article of faith that affordable housing could be built there without deep subsidies.

While I am on the subject of subsidies, the fragmented nature of our metropolitan areas leads me to wonder whether central cities and inner-core suburbs might be getting the short end of the stick in the version of smart growth that promotes housing construction in the city core. To the extent that affordable housing is built and that the households who move into the housing consume public services whose costs exceed the tax revenues they generate, growth management at the periphery could well be a losing proposition for cities and inner-ring suburbs, widening existing fiscal disparities.[48]

A final reason to be concerned about efforts to steer development into denser environments is what such an effort might mean in terms of equity for racial and ethnic minorities. According to the 2000 census, minorities have made significant strides in terms of moving to the suburbs.[49] Although much of this increase has taken place in inner-ring suburbs, some significant growth

---

47. Salama and others (1999).

48. Of course, some thoughtful smart growth advocates suggest a series of fundamental reforms that would allay many of these problems, including tax-base sharing and metropolitan government. See, for example, Katz (2002). Although many of these proposals are extremely sensible, many would be extremely difficult to achieve for political reasons.

49. See Frey (2003).

has taken place in developments at the periphery where land is relatively cheap. There is something ironic, and potentially unfair, about closing the door on minority families to the type of suburban residence long enjoyed by their white counterparts just at the time they seem to be walking through it.[50]

I believe (in keeping with the Greek mythology metaphor of my opening paragraph) that smart growth has the potential to be a Trojan horse for advocates of affordable housing, most of whom tend to be politically progressive and open to the idea of government intervention to preserve the environment. History has shown that government regulation in the urban environment has repeatedly been misused, frequently to the detriment of low- and moderate-income families and racial and ethnic minorities.

The answer to our housing problem lies not with more government regulation, but with less. As government budgets become ever more tight, we must seek to stretch every subsidy dollar as far as it can go. This requires us to tear down regulatory barriers to new housing construction rather than build new ones.

COMMENT BY
Robert W. Burchell and Sahan Mukherji

Overall, the Voith-Crawford chapter was nicely done by competent people who know housing well. It covers the topic comprehensively and is an excellent resource on the relationship between smart growth and affordable housing. However, we believe two key points need clarification: the definition of affordable housing and how to calculate an optimal percentage of affordable housing in any project in an inclusionary zoning program.

An Appropriate Definition of Affordable Housing

In most analyses, the operative definition of housing affordability stipulates that occupancy costs should not exceed 30 percent of household income. In other words, the costs of principal, interest, taxes, and insurance (PITI) or

---

50. In addition, if demand for housing in central locations increases as a result of suburban growth management practices and if regulatory barriers keep the market from responding with additional supply, existing residents of cities could be hurt by rising prices.

Table 3-1. *Affordable Home Price for a Buyer at 60 Percent
and 80 Percent of Median Income*
Dollars, except as indicated

Item	60 Percent of median (1)	80 Percent of median (2)
Square footage	1,800	1,800
Number of bedrooms	3	3
Type of housing	Townhouse	Townhouse
Mortgage rate (percent)	6.50	6.50
Mortgage cost per $1,000	6.321	6.321
Common charges	50	50
Insurance	25	25
Real estate taxes	145	210
Electricity	50	50
Oil	100	100
Sewer	15	15
Water	28	28
Total	413	478
1. Region median income	70,000	70,000
2. 60 percent or 80 percent of item 1	42,000	56,000
3. 30 percent of item 2	12,600	16,800
4. Divide item 3 by 12	1,050	1,400
5. Housing cost assumptions	413	478
6. Mortgage payment (4 – 5)	637	922
7. Maximum mortgage	100,775	145,863
8. Maximum sales price (10 percent down)	111,888	162,070

rent, plus expenses (heat, electricity, water/sewer, routine maintenance, and community association dues) should not be more than 30 percent of all the combined income sources of the household. Sometimes single-person households and unrelated individuals are eliminated from this standard and the term "family" is attached to the definition of qualifying income. The latter usually raises any area average because single-person household income generally is low and lowers the overall median.

Table 3-1 shows how much a family of four with an income of 60 or 80 percent of median income can afford to pay for housing, under this definition.

With a 10 percent down payment and an interest rate of 6.5 percent, a household making $42,000 (60 percent of a $70,000 median) can afford a home costing about $112,000 and a household making $56,000 (80 percent of the same median) can afford a home costing about $162,000. While these numbers obviously are affected by housing expenses, interest rates, and down payments, when they do not vary, the ratio of price to income moves upward with income, from 2.67 to 2.90.

The above standard may be useful in deciding whether a household is paying more than it can afford for housing. But according to surveys of American housing conditions, 50 to 75 percent of households whose incomes are below 80 percent of median pay more than 30 percent of their income for housing. By this definition, they "cannot afford" the housing they actually occupy, so they "need" affordable housing. In a community of 4,000 housing units, about 1,600 units are occupied by households whose incomes fall below 80 percent of median (table 3-2). If one assumes that an average of 60 percent of those households pay more than 30 percent of their incomes for housing, then 960 of these units are deemed "unaffordable" by this definition. Assume that on average, housing of all types added to the existing stock annually through new construction equals 1.5 percent of that stock (sixty units). Assume further that one in ten of the new units is dedicated affordable housing under inclusionary zoning rules, for a total of six such units per year. It would take 160 years to meet the current affordable housing need defined in this way (960 units/6 units a year). Obviously, this definition poses an insurmountable obstacle to meeting the "housing affordability needs" of the community within a reasonable period, if housing to answer those needs comes primarily from inclusionary programs imposed on market-rate housing developers.

An alternative approach is to define the need for affordable housing differently—specifically, as affecting all households in two groups. The first group contains all households in the community that currently meet two conditions: they have incomes below 80 percent of the area median income, and they live in deteriorated housing. The second group contains all households likely to enter the community in the future who meet two conditions: they have incomes below 80 percent of median, and the market will not provide housing for them through such secondary sources as filtering, conversion, spontaneous rehabilitation, and subsidies to housing developers. (About 70 percent of low- and moderate-income households receive housing from those sources.) This approach produces much more realistic targets for programs aimed at creating affordable housing. Calculating the housing needs of

Table 3-2. *Providing a Smart Growth Housing Solution*

Community A population	10,000
Number of housing units	4,000
Median household income of community	$70,000
Median household income of region	$70,000
Households below 80 percent of median	1,600
Households that cannot afford housing at 30 percent standard	960
Deteriorated units in community (2 percent)	80
Deteriorated units occupied by poor (0.6 × 2 percent)	48
Growth of community	60 units/year
10 percent inclusion (twelve years)	72 units
Households in ten years for which market will not provide	72 units
	(600 × 0.40 × 0.30)
10 percent inclusion (twelve years)	72 units
	(60 × 0.10 × 12)

these groups projected into the future produces the results that follow below. For current Section 8 eligible households,

—Approximately 2 percent of the overall housing stock (0.02) is deteriorated using the three prime indicators of housing occupancy and structure condition (nonoverlapping crowding, plumbing, kitchen) occupied by all income groups.[51]

—Approximately 40 percent of the population's households have incomes below 80 percent of median income. About 0.8 percent of them live in deteriorated housing (0.40 × 0.020 = 0.008).

—The poor are found in deteriorated housing at about 1.5 times the rate of the population at large (0.008 × 1.5 = 0.012).

—For an average community of 4,000, poor households living in deteriorated housing occupy forty-eight units (4,000 × 0.012).

—If an increment of 1.5 percent of the existing housing stock is delivered as new units each year (sixty units) and one in ten new units is dedicated to meeting rehabilitation needs (six units), the currently deteriorated stock occupied by the poor could be corrected in eight years (60 × 0.1 × 8 = 48).

51. Crowding = >1.00 persons per room in units built in 1939 or earlier; this indicates a crowded, old unit likely to be lost from the stock. Shared or incomplete kitchen and plumbing indicate a unit with basic deficiencies. Kitchen is multiplied by 0.45 to avoid double counting. Plumbing is presented by the census in non–double-counted form.

This is certainly a workable schedule; in fact, it is close to the ten-year period that New Jersey specifies for compliance with its rehabilitation regulations. In addition, if the population of this community grows, the following affordable housing provision would take care of the needs of future Section 8 eligible households:

—Housing needs for those below 80 percent of median[52] (focusing on units not provided by secondary sources of supply—30 percent of total[53]) equal seventy-two units, the number of units delivered each year multiplied by 40 percent times 0.30 (60 × .40 × 0.30 × 10 = 72 units).

—A 10 percent inclusionary requirement on sixty units per year equals six units a year, or seventy-two units in twelve years (60 × 0.10 × 12 = 72). This averaged with the rehab requirement would involve a combined set-aside of 20 percent for ten years.

Thus the definition of affordable housing used in calculating "need for affordable units" is the key to estimating how large the burden of creating such units will be. A definition that classifies all those who pay more than a certain percentage of their income for housing as "needing affordable units" is not workable within the confines of a zoning solution. Certainly that is the case if the standard used is 30 percent of income. If the standard were increased to 50 percent of household income, the number of households that cannot afford housing would be one-third of the number at the 30 percent level. This still results in too much required housing (that is, delivery would take fifty-three instead of 160 years), which would have to be developed coterminously with normal additions to the existing stock.

On the other hand, if the definition is changed to include only the poor living in deteriorated housing plus the future poor for whom the market will not provide housing, then a smart growth or land use plan can realistically deliver the required housing as part of an inclusionary zoning solution. This could take the form of one unit in five (that is, 20 percent) over a reasonable period of time (approximately ten years—between, for instance, releases of the decennial U.S. census). A recent census could be used both to gauge the number of deteriorated units occupied by the poor (current affordable housing need) and to project future population in order to estimate future affordable housing needs.

52. 80 percent of median is about equivalent to 40 percent of the total distribution.

53. Approximately two-thirds of low- and moderate-income housing need is met through filtering, conversion, spontaneous rehabilitation, and subsidies to housing developers (low-income housing tax credits).

Optimal Density Bonus

A related issue is how large the density increase or "bonus" given to a developer must be to make an additional 20 percent inclusionary requirement economically feasible. The assumption is that to be affordable, housing must sell at a fraction of the selling price of the other housing in a development. To have an affordable unit for a household at 60 percent of median income, the house-value-to-income multiplier is 2.67, as shown above. If median income is $70,000, 60 percent of median is $42,000; using the multiplier, the house must sell for not over $112,000. If a developer was building 100 townhouses at $400,000 each and was required to provide twenty affordable units, the density increment should be very close to the inclusionary requirement. In other words, the developer should be allowed to build an additional twenty units to offset the twenty units of affordable housing. This is true because the bonus will be enough to build the extra units without additional land costs. Moreover, the developer can finish the development and move on to another without taking an excessive amount of time or creating an excessive impact on the price of existing units due to the increase in density.

Assume that initially a developer plans to build 100 townhouses at $400,000 each. Desired profit is approximately 20 percent of total costs. Column 1 of table 3-3 shows the developer's costs and revenues: costs are about $33.6 million and revenues about $40 million, yielding a profit of $6.35 million, or approximately 19 percent. In this scenario (scenario 1), the developer is not asked to provide affordable housing. It is assumed that the developer fully understands the market and density reflects the maximum permitted by local laws.

In scenario 2A, the developer is allowed an extra twenty units to deliver twenty units of affordable housing. In this scenario, it is assumed that the density bonus and the presence of affordable units will have no impact on the selling price of market units. The cost of the construction loan increases because the construction schedule increases from twelve to fourteen months. The developer's profit as a share of equity (his land) remains essentially the same; he secures a similar 19 percent profit ($6.60 million) and actually makes an additional $250,000, based on the profit from the affordable units. In scenario 2B, the developer's market units decrease in price by 0.25 percent, or $1,000 for each of the twenty units of affordable housing. Thus market units sell for $380,000 instead of $400,000. This is not an unrealistic assumption, given that there will be two affordable units for every ten market units on site;

Table 3-3. *Development Profit with Inclusionary Development at Various Densities*
Dollars, except as indicated

Components of development	Scenario 1[a]	Scenario 2A[b]	Scenario 2B[c]	Scenario 3[d]	Remarks
Total units	100	120	120	150	
Market units	100	100	100	120	
Below-market units	0	20	20	20	
1. Land	7,500,000	7,500,000	7,500,000	7,500,000	$7.5 million for project, constant
2. Housing units	18,750,000	19,950,000	19,950,000	24,300,000	$75 per square foot
3. Hard costs	1,000,000	1,100,000	1,100,000	1,350,000	$10,000/$5,000 per unit (market/nonmarket)
4. Financing fee	525,000	549,000	549,000	636,000	2 percent of land and housing unit cost
5. Construction interest	2,062,500	2,560,982	2,560,982	4,009,500	11 percent of housing unit cost per year
6. Design and engineering	1,312,500	1,372,500	1,372,500	1,590,000	5 percent of land and housing unit cost
7. Sales	1,600,000	1,689,600	1,609,600	1,814,400	4 percent of total price
8. Legal and inspections	100,000	120,000	120,000	150,000	$1,000 per unit
9. Soft costs	800,000	800,000	800,000	800,000	$800,000 for project, constant
10. Total costs	33,650,000	35,642,082	35,562,082	42,149,900	Total of above
11. Revenues/sales	40,000,000	42,240,000	40,240,000	45,360,000	Sales price times number of units
12. Profit	6,350,000	6,597,919	4,677,919	3,210,100	Revenue minus costs

	a	b	c	d	
Return on equity (12 ÷ 1)	0.85	0.88	0.62	0.43	Profit divided by land
Return on investment	0.19	0.19	0.13	0.08	Profit divided by total costs
Development specifics					
Market units	100	100	100	120	
Sales price	400,000	400,000	380,000	350,000	
Square feet	2,500	2,500	2,500	2,500	
Below-market units	0	20	20	30	
Sales price	—	112,000	112,000	112,000	
Square feet	—	800	800	800	
Time	12 months	14 months	14 months	18 months	

a. No affordable housing set-aside.
b. Twenty units affordable, twenty additional units.
c. Twenty units affordable, twenty additional units.
d. Twenty units affordable, fifty additional units.

the site therefore is more crowded and contains some lower-income house-holds, and both conditions may reduce the desirability of the market-price units in the eyes of potential buyers. In this case, the developer's profit is reduced to $4.68 million (13 percent) due to the effect of increased density on the price of market units. The density bonus has driven down the value of market units and driven down profit accordingly. There is not a huge differ-ence in selling price of the market units but the decrease in price has a large impact on profit. This is also a much more realistic view of a density bonus impact.

In scenario 3, the developer is allowed fifty additional units for providing twenty affordable units—a 50 percent density bonus. Again the price of the market units is reduced by 0.25 percent, or $1,000 for each affordable unit. Market units now sell for $350,000 instead of $400,000. In addition, the developer is now obligated for eighteen months of a construction loan. The developer's profit ($3.21 million—8 percent) is only 50 percent of what it was originally. The construction loan is somewhat more costly, yet the decrease in the price of market units has had a significant impact on profit. Again, it is not unrealistic to expect prices of market units to decrease by 12.5 percent if den-sity increases by 50 percent. The inclusionary component does not lead to a significant increase in profits even when the density bonus is significant.

Conclusion

The mathematics of affordable housing—relating to both the definition of affordable housing and the amount of the density bonus—is not straightfor-ward. Defining "lack of affordability" as including all households that pay more than 30 percent of income for housing is an unworkable approach for a smart growth or land use solution to the housing affordability problem. Given typical new construction rates and a 10 percent inclusionary require-ment, it would take 160 years to provide housing under this approach. More-over, people pay more than 30 percent of their housing for a variety of rea-sons: housing tenure alternatives, housing type alternatives, public service advantages (better schools, lower taxes), neighborhood advantages (people with similar life-styles), and other reasons. Further, when new units are pro-vided in response to cost concerns, there is too much housing in the market. If it is a one-for-one response, there is twice as much affordable housing as actually needed in the market. This definition of affordable housing lends itself to an income subsidy solution to affordability problems, rather than a solution based on influencing the behavior of developers through inclusionary zoning and density bonuses.

On the other hand, if the definition of need for affordable housing includes only the poor who currently live in deteriorated housing plus the future poor for whom the market will not provide housing, net of secondary sources of supply (in both cases "poor" being defined as those who qualify for Section 8 income subsidies), the definition is much more in accord with a solution that can be provided through land use policies. A 20 percent inclusion requirement answers both current and future need in a ten-year period, on average.

This is also true concerning the inclusionary percentage. Assuming that the land is infinitely capable of taking additional units with no impact on the selling price of existing units is incorrect. When the selling price of market units is affected by the additional affordable units and the resulting higher density and the construction schedule is extended because of the additional units, monies are lost from revenues and added to costs. This has a dramatic effect on profits. A 12.5 percent decrease in market unit price resulting from having 50 percent more units on site and an additional half-year added to the term of a construction loan can reduce original profits by 50 percent. A 50 percent density bonus could actually cost a developer a 58 percent reduction in profit. Care must be taken to pay attention to the mathematics of development. Often the math is hard to understand—and it is even more difficult to craft public policy solutions that take it into account.

References

American Automobile Association. 2002. *Your Driving Cost: 2002.*

American Planning Association. 2002. "Planning for Smart Growth: 2002 State of the States." February.

Arigoni, Danielle. 2001. "Affordable Housing and Smart Growth: Making the Connection." Smart Growth Network Subgroup on Affordable Housing (www.smartgrowth.org/pdf/epa_ah-sg.pdf [January 16, 2004]).

Been, Vicki. 1991. "Exit as a Constraint on Land Use Exactions: Re-thinking the Unconstitutional Conditions Doctrine." *Columbia Law Review* 91 (3): 473–45.

Brown, Karen Destorel. 2002. "Expanding Affordable Housing through Inclusionary Zoning: Lessons from the Washington Metropolitan Area." Brookings Center on Urban and Metropolitan Policy. October.

Burchell, Robert W., and others. 2002. "The Costs of Sprawl: 2000." TCRP Report 74. Transportation Research Board.

Downs, Anthony. 1992. *Stuck in Traffic: Coping with Peak-Hour Traffic Congestion.* Brookings.

Downs, Anthony. 2001. "What Does 'Smart Growth' Really Mean?" *Foresight* 8 (2).

Frey, William F. 2003. "Melting Pot Suburbs: A Study of Suburban Diversity." In *Redefining Urban and Suburban America: Evidence from Census 2000*, edited by Bruce Katz and Robert E. Lang. Brookings.

Gaspar, Christine. 1998. "Brownfield Development as Smart Growth." *Getting Smart!* July.

Glaeser, Edward, and Joseph Gyourko. 2000. "The Impact of Zoning on Housing Affordability." Working Paper 395, Wharton School, University of Pennsylvania.

Greenburg, M., and others. 2000. *Brownfield Redevelopment as a Smart Growth Option*. National Center for Neighborhood and Brownfields Redevelopment, Rutgers University. January.

Gyourko, Joseph, and Richard Voith. 2001. "The Price Elasticity of Demand for Residential Land." University of Pennsylvania.

Haughwout, Andrew, and Robert Inman. 2001. "Fiscal Policies in Open Cities with Firms and Households." *Regional Science and Urban Economics* 31 (April 2001).

Haughwout, Andrew, and others. 2000. "Local Revenue Hills: A General Equilibrium Specification with Evidence from Four U.S. Cities." Working Paper 7603. Cambridge, Mass.: National Bureau of Economic Research.

Katz, Bruce. 2002. "Smart Growth: The Future of the American Metropolis" (www.brookings.edu/dybdocroot/es/urban/publications/20021104katzlse2.htm [January 21, 2004]).

National Governors Association. 2000. "Where Do We Grow from Here?" *New Mission for Brownfields: Attacking Sprawl by Revitalizing Older Communities*.

Nelson, Arthur C., and others. 2002. "The Link between Growth Management and Housing Affordability: The Academic Evidence." Brookings Center on Urban and Metropolitan Policy. February.

Pozdena, Randall J. 2002. "Smart Growth and Its Effects on Housing Markets: The New Segregation." QuantEcon, Inc. November.

Salama, Jerry J., and others. 1999. *Reducing the Cost of New Housing Construction in New York City*. New York: Furman Center for Real Estate and Urban Policy.

Schill, Michael H., and others. 2002. "Revitalizing Inner-City Neighborhoods: New York City's Ten-Year Plan." *Housing Policy Debate* 13 (3): 529–66.

Senate Education Committee. 2003. "Governor Unveils Education and Tax Proposals." *Education Update*, April 7.

U.S. Conference of Mayors. 2000. "Recycling America's Land." *A National Report on Brownfields Redevelopment*, vol. 3.

Voith, Richard. 1992. "City and Suburban Growth: Substitutes or Complements?" *Business Review* (Federal Reserve Bank of Philadelphia) 126 (September–October).

———. 2002. "Philadelphia City Tax Structure and the Metropolitan Economy." Philadelphia: Econsult Corporation.

4

ARTHUR C. NELSON
ROLF PENDALL
CASEY J. DAWKINS
GERRIT J. KNAAP

The Link between
Growth Management and
Housing Affordability:
The Academic Evidence

INTEREST IN URBAN growth management may have reached an all-time high. What was once the practice in a few obscure places such as Ramapo, New York; Lexington, Kentucky; Boulder, Colorado; and Petaluma, California, has moved on to the national agendas of organizations such as the American Planning Association, the National Association of Home Builders, the Sierra Club, and the Urban Land Institute. Despite rapidly growing support for managing urban growth, there remain lingering concerns about the impact of growth management on the affordability of housing; some organizations allege that many policy instruments used to manage growth can adversely affect land and housing markets and contribute to the affordability problem. Fortunately, the effects of growth management on housing affordability have been the subject of considerable research by scholars in economics, planning, and real estate for the past generation. Though no consensus has yet to form, this body of research offers considerable insight into the influence of growth management on land and housing markets.

To understand fully the effect of growth management policies on housing prices, the researcher must answer several related questions. Have housing prices been affected by such policies? If so, are price increases due to supply-side restrictions or demand-side amenities attributed to growth management?

If supply restrictions are the culprit, how competitive is the market for developable land? What barriers do housing producers face in producing higher-density housing? Finally, how elastic are the supply of and demand for housing in growth-managed communities? The empirical studies examined in this review address many of these questions, but several still remain—particularly with respect to growth management, not just growth control or traditional land use regulation.

In this chapter we review the literature in order to address these questions. Our intent is not to condemn or promote the practice of urban growth management. To do either would be naïve; growth management comes in many forms, and each has different effects on housing prices. Whether and how to manage urban growth, we believe, is a decision that must be made by state and local governments after careful consideration of all the potential costs and benefits of doing so, including the potential impact of growth management on housing affordability. The purpose of this review is to assess the available evidence in order to identify what the impacts might be.

Our analysis is based on the information and evidence presented mostly in the scholarly literature, which includes articles published in refereed journals and a few other publications written by researchers whose work routinely appears in such outlets. We do not give much weight to constituency publications issued by those affected by this subject, such as development and environmental interests. Nor do we develop new theory or engage in new or refined empirical analysis. We do offer concluding observations, in the hope that they reflect a balance between what is known based on reasonably defensible evidence and what is not yet known. For example, considerable consensus exists in the literature that traditional land use regulations and some forms of growth control raise housing prices, but little consensus exists on whether growth management as we define it does the same.

Definitions

Notably absent from our report is use of the term "smart growth." We do not enter the smart growth arena because as yet no clear consensus exists on how to define it, although efforts by Downs, Kalinowski, and Nelson help.[1] Instead, we use the terms "growth management" and "affordable housing" throughout. It therefore is important to discuss what we mean by both terms.

1. Downs (2001a), Kalinowski (2001), and Nelson (2001).

Growth Management

We define "urban growth management" as the deliberate and integrated use of the planning, regulatory, and fiscal authority of state and local governments to influence patterns of growth and development in order to meet projected needs. Included in this definition are such tools as comprehensive planning, zoning, subdivision regulations, property taxes and development fees, infrastructure investments, and other policy instruments that significantly influence the development of land and the construction of housing. Excluded from the definition are general policies designed to stimulate economic development (such as enterprise zones, industrial recruitment policies, and other tax abatement programs) and general policies designed to improve social welfare, such as community service programs, public health services, and other social services.

Growth management often is distinguished from growth control.[2] Whereas growth management accommodates projected development in a manner that achieves broad public goals, growth control limits or rations development. Typical growth control tools are building moratoriums, permitting caps, development quotas, and the like. It is not always possible, however, to tell the difference between a growth control and a growth management tool simply on the basis of a label or the presence of an ordinance; a particular growth management tool can have vastly different impacts in different municipalities.[3] While our primary focus is on the relationship between growth management and affordable housing, we necessarily consider the relationship between growth control and affordable housing, particularly in the context of the literature. We find generally that growth management as we have characterized it appears to have fewer impacts on the provision and distribution of affordable housing than traditional land use regulations and perhaps somewhat fewer impacts than growth control. Yet even in some growth control communities we find significant efforts to expand the supply of affordable housing through inclusionary zoning requirements (such as in Petaluma and Boulder).

Housing Affordability

Housing affordability is more difficult to define. Generally, it involves the capacity of households to consume housing services; specifically it involves

2. See also Nelson and Duncan (1995).
3. Landis (1992).

the relationship between household incomes and housing prices and rents. An often quoted rule of thumb is that households should spend no more than 30 percent of their income on housing unless they choose to do so. Measuring housing affordability therefore is complicated by the inability to determine whether households spend more than 30 percent of their income on housing by necessity or by choice. Other measurement problems involve the definition of income (whether permanent or transitory, liquid or illiquid, personal or household) and the definition of housing expenditure (whether voluntary or involuntary, total or per unit of housing services, nominal or real rents, mortgage payments or down payments).

Another definition of housing affordability, the shelter poverty measure, uses a sliding scale to reflect that upper-income and smaller households can afford to spend much more than 30 percent of their income on housing and still have enough left over to satisfy other basic needs, whereas extremely low-income households that pay even 10 percent of their income on housing costs may be forced to forgo essential medical care and healthful food.[4]

The Housing Opportunity Index, published by the National Association of Home Builders (NAHB), shows for each metropolitan statistical area the share of homes that a median-income household can afford.[5] The NAHB index also reveals some disadvantages of some of these homes, however. For example, housing affordability scores generally are more favorable in metropolitan areas that also are rated as the least desirable places to live according to *Places Rated Almanac*.[6] Neither the NAHB nor the federal government has a lock on how to view affordable housing; this is due in part to limitations in their formulations. For example, neither considers transportation costs. We know from the Consumer Expenditure Survey that the typical American household earned $42,770 in 1999 and spent $11,843 on housing, or about 27 percent of income.[7] For the typical household, therefore, housing is affordable. But the typical household also spent $6,815 for transportation. Housing plus transportation costs consumed 44 percent of household income in 1999. If a household's transportation costs were zero but its housing costs were 44 percent of income, we would say that its housing was unaffordable, when in fact the household would be no worse off than the typical American household.

Moreover, no definition of housing affordability considers that a household's satisfaction with housing depends not so much on housing prices and

4. Stone (1993).
5. National Association of Home Builders (2001).
6. Savageau and Loftus (1997).
7. U.S. Bureau of Labor Statistics (2001).

rents as on consumption of housing services (the role of housing in providing shelter, storage, assembly, access to work, and so forth), which must be broadly defined. In London, for example, the share of income spent on housing greatly exceeds the share spent in Beijing, where rents are almost zero. That does not imply that housing consumers are better off in Beijing than in London. Residents of Los Angeles who live near the beach, whether rich or poor, pay more for housing than those who live inland, but that does not mean that those who live inland are better off than those who live near the beach. Most existing assessments of growth management's effects on housing prices provide only limited information. A more comprehensive assessment of the virtues of growth management would take into account its direct effects on housing services and the indirect effects of such services on a household's satisfaction with its housing.

We recommend that a coalition of interests be formed to define just what "affordable housing" means. Such a definition would need to consider all forms of housing, reflect accurately all costs of housing, and establish a transparent relationship between income from all sources and those costs. The U.S. Department of Housing and Urban Development and the NAHB have jointly sponsored several housing production programs; perhaps they could sponsor the effort we recommend.

For our purposes, fortunately, these measurement issues are not consequential. We are concerned here with the influence of growth management on housing affordability and therefore need not measure the extent of the problem precisely; we need only examine the degree to which the problem is exacerbated by growth management. Further, although growth management can affect household income, such an effect is likely to be small compared with its effect on housing prices (given our definition of growth management); therefore we focus on the effects of growth management on housing prices and rents. Finally, adverse effects on housing prices and rents are likely to impose the greatest affordability problem on those with the lowest income. Therefore we consider explicitly the effects of growth management on housing prices and rents for those at the lower end of the income scale.

The following sections discuss what growth management is and how it is undertaken in a variety of regimes, the historic connection between traditional land use regulations and exclusionary housing, and the theoretical relationship between growth management and housing prices. The scholarly literature is reviewed, and the question of whether growth management mechanisms intentionally exclude certain groups is addressed.

Why Growth Management?

Rapid suburbanization following World War II created many of the problems we face today. Roads intended to relieve congestion have become congested. Cookie-cutter subdivisions have replaced scenic landscapes. Once-vital downtown stores have been shuttered as shoppers have transferred their allegiance to more convenient suburban malls. The spread of low-density residential development has made public transit impractical, and the car has become virtually the only viable transportation choice. The use of automotive vehicles has degraded the air quality in some places to alarming levels. Once-tranquil communities with their own special character have become engulfed by people, automobiles, and look-alike shopping centers. But the problem is not growth itself. Growth is inevitable. The problem is how to manage growth in ways that both minimize its costs and maximize its benefits to individuals and to the larger public.

Growth management has emerged in response to the unintended and often perverse consequences of restrictive growth controls. Instead of inhibiting market-driven development altogether, growth management tries to tame development to yield environmentally sound, fiscally efficient, and socially just outcomes. Although growth management certainly leads to plans, what distinguishes it from traditional planning is its emphasis on implementation. Growth management combines regulations and incentives to guide new development in changing land markets. Douglas R. Porter characterizes growth management as a dynamic process of evaluating current trends, managing results, and updating objectives and methods; a means of anticipating and accommodating development needs; a forum and process for determining an appropriate balance between competing goals; and the recognition of local needs in relation to regional concerns.[8] Ultimately, effective growth management allocates available land to uses that meet economic demands, human needs, and environmental quality requirements.[9]

Often missing from the popular characterizations of growth management are its goals. Ervin and others argue that growth management has three essential goals:[10]

—*Preserve public goods.* Certain resources are available to everyone (such as air, water, and significant landscapes); no one can be excluded and adding

8. Porter (1997).
9. Clawson (1962).
10. Ervin and others (1977).

one more person does not deprive another of their enjoyment. Yet polluting the air does deprive people of its enjoyment. Growth management should preserve if not enhance the provision of public goods.

—*Minimize negative externalities.* Certain land uses have adverse effects on others, such as siting landfills near areas planned for new community development. Growth management should minimize if not prevent adverse land use impacts. Related to this but not advanced by Ervin and others is that growth management should also maximize the positive impacts of land uses.

—*Minimize public fiscal costs.* Growth management should minimize cost per unit of development to provide public facilities and services.

In recent years two other goals have been added:[11]

—*Maximize social equity.* Growth management should maximize the jobs-housing balance within small areas; provide equal access to work, shopping, services, and recreational areas; ensure life-cycle housing opportunities within neighborhoods; and offer socioeconomic balance within neighborhoods.

—*Enhance quality of life.* Ultimately, growth management should ehance quality of life more than alternative planning regimes do. Elements of quality of life may be satisfaction with housing and neighborhood, security from crime and natural or man-made catastrophic events, and flexibility in housing and location choices.

Growth management is thus an attempt to assess the reasonable development needs of the community, region, or state and to accommodate those needs in a manner that preserves public goods, minimizes fiscal burdens, minimizes adverse but maximizes positive interactions between land uses, promotes the equitable distribution of the benefits of growth, and enhances quality of life. At its heart, growth management aims to achieve these goals by choreographing public infrastructure investments, land use and development regulations, and the use of incentives and disincentives to influence the rate, timing, intensity, mix, and location of growth.

Growth management policies are not adopted in isolation, though often these land use regulations are studied in isolation. Rather, they are adopted as components of local *regulatory regimes,* defined as the sum of formal and informal institutions that regulate the delivery of housing and community services in a particular place. For low-income households especially, it may be the local regulatory regime as a whole and not particular land use controls that affects their ability to find an affordable place to live. Hence our earlier admittedly simplistic distinction between growth *management* and growth

11. Nelson (1999).

control is refined here by comparing regulatory regimes on the provision of affordable housing, usually in the form of higher-density housing.

Growth management regulatory regimes vary across the United States. Analyzing the results of a 1994 survey on local land use controls in the country's twenty-five largest metropolitan areas, Pendall found three broad sets of these regimes, summarized below:[12]

—The Northeast and Midwest are characterized by fragmented metropolitan areas in which municipalities tend to use large-lot zoning to control growth. These municipalities seldom adopt affordable housing programs to mitigate the price effects of their land-use regulations. The development approval process in most Northeastern and Midwestern states tends to be idiosyncratic and unpredictable from one municipality to the next, and over time. County government plays very little or no coordinating role to assure that regional housing markets are responsive to the long-term requirements of the economy and to the needs of the entire population.

—The South (except Florida) and the Great Plains regions tend to be more laissez-faire. They seldom impose growth controls of any kind, nor do they adopt affordable housing programs. County governments are important, especially in the South, but their regulatory role is often very slight and usually designed to facilitate development rather than to control it (Lowry and Ferguson 1992).

—The West, Florida, and Maryland are all characterized by stronger growth management programs, often coordinated at the county level, with combinations of such techniques as urban growth boundaries (UGBs), building permit caps, and adequate public facilities ordinances. Exclusionary zoning is very rare in suburban and newly developing parts of these regions; municipalities and especially counties tend to use large-lot zoning primarily to protect resource lands and open space rather than to create low-density residential environments. Environmental regulation is also strong in many of these locations, and as a consequence of project- and plan-level impact assessment requirements of various sorts, the development approval process can be very long for complicated projects. For routine subdivisions, and even fairly large ones, however, state laws in many of these states have established a process that makes development more predictable than the average in the Northeast. Many municipalities in the West also adopt a large number of creative local affordable housing programs.

12. Pendall (1995).

Traditional Land Use Regulation and Exclusionary Housing: The Historic Connection

One of the main criticisms of growth management is that it is a form of exclusionary land use regulation.[13] Growth management may have exclusionary tendencies, but there must be no mistaking the fundamental and explicit purpose of traditional land use controls, which was to exclude undesirable land uses and often people from entering a community.[14] There are various ways in which land use regulations can—and have been shown to—limit the ability of low-income households and people of color to find suitable housing in decent neighborhoods.

Local land regulations arose from the desire of landowners and municipalities to stop nuisances before they started, to stabilize property values, and to separate people of different income levels and ethnicities. Early zoning ordinances throughout the South explicitly designated districts for black and for white residents and although such zoning was ruled unconstitutional in 1917,[15] municipalities continued to adopt racial zoning ordinances for at least ten years afterward.[16] Efforts after 1917 to exclude people from neighborhoods on the basis of their ethnicity shifted toward private deed restrictions and covenants between land developers, homeowner associations, and property buyers. These racially restrictive covenants were rendered unenforceable by a 1948 U.S. Supreme Court decision, but like racial zoning, they persisted afterward.[17] New developments in Kansas City, for instance, carried racially restrictive covenants well into the 1960s.[18]

The idea that minorities, especially African Americans but also Hispanics and Asians, threaten property values was not just conventional wisdom; it was incorporated in federal and state policy until the 1960s. From the armed forces to public housing to transportation to urban renewal, most major federal institutions and programs were explicitly designed to separate Anglos (non-Hispanic whites) from minorities until at least mid-century. The Federal Housing Administration (FHA), created in 1934 to provide low-cost mortgage insurance, favored the most "stable" neighborhoods and downgraded

13. Pendall (2000).
14. Juergensmeyer and Roberts (1998).
15. *Buchanan* v. *Warley*, 245 U.S. 60.
16. Silver (1997).
17. *Shelley* v. *Kraemer*, 334 U.S. 1.
18. Gotham (2000).

mixed-race and minority neighborhoods.[19] The FHA also promoted "modern" subdivision controls and zoning ordinances, both of which were thought to maintain neighborhood stability and thereby guarantee predictable property values.[20]

Land use regulations thus were initially designed in part to separate people by ethnicity, and they arose during a period of unprecedented government action to construct a U.S. version of apartheid.[21] It is therefore only natural to suspect that land use regulations might still be complicit in creating and maintaining racial and ethnic segregation. But land use controls do not explicitly demarcate Anglo and minority neighborhoods. Instead, they work indirectly by shaping local housing markets—encouraging or prohibiting the construction of certain types of housing and thereby influencing the tenure of housing (renter- versus owner-occupied) and its price.

Local regulations that reduce the availability of rental housing are strongly exclusionary. For a host of reasons (such as discrimination in mortgage lending and insurance underwriting, low incomes, limited assets, and limited or unconventional credit histories), African Americans and Hispanics in the United States have much lower rates of homeownership than do Anglos: between 45 percent and 50 percent, compared with more than 70 percent for Anglos. To the extent that municipalities enact regulations that encourage the construction of mainly owner-occupied housing, they also limit access of the majority of African American and Hispanic households that rent.

Local regulations that directly or indirectly raise housing prices also have important exclusionary impacts. When jurisdictions deliberately or unintentionally raise their housing prices, they indirectly exclude a larger proportion of minority than Anglo households. In the three-year period between 1997 and 1999, the median Hispanic and African American household earned approximately $29,100 and $26,600 respectively, compared with about $43,300 for the median Anglo household.[22] Their lower incomes also have made wealth accumulation more difficult for them, reducing their ability to afford the substantial move-in costs for owner-occupied housing and even average-price rentals in many markets.

Unmistakably, the fundamental purpose of traditional land use controls is to exclude undesirable land uses from entering communities. Such regulations also can limit the ability of low-income households and people of color

19. Jackson (1985).
20. Weiss (1987).
21. Massey and Denton (1993).
22. U.S. Census Bureau (2000).

to find suitable housing in decent neighborhoods. Growth management is an attempt to regulate land uses in ways that do not result in social exclusion.

The Role of Growth Management in Determining Housing Prices

Since this chapter discusses the relationship between growth management and housing prices, it must discuss the determinants of housing prices. Understanding how housing prices are set in a market economy is simple, yet complicated. In effect, we call "rent" our housing price. Housing rents, whether explicit (money paid) or implicit (nonmonetary costs such as pollution or benefits such as access to jobs) are determined by the demand for and supply of housing services. Housing prices are determined by the capitalized value of housing rents. "Capitalization" is the process of converting annual income into a lump sum. For example, if one earns income from renting a home for $18,000 annually ($1,500 monthly), the expenses (utilities, taxes, insurance) bring the "net" income to $12,000. If the current market capitalization rate is 10 percent, the price of the home is $120,000 ($12,000 / 0.10).[23] Even if a household owns its home, there is a market rental value for it based on the capitalization rate. We consider *direct* and *indirect* effects of land use regulation regimes.

Direct Effects

Any land use regulation regime can raise housing prices by increasing the demand for housing, decreasing the supply, or increasing the rate of rent capitalization. The degree to which growth management policies affect housing prices depends on the *elasticity* of supply and of demand—that is, the degree to which housing consumers or suppliers can escape from (or capture) the effects of growth management by migrating to (or from) other markets. For this reason, land use policies are likely to have greater price

23. Conceptually, capitalization is the rate of return necessary to reward risk given opportunity costs such as investing in federally backed thirty-year Treasury notes (currently bearing about 6 percent interest). The higher the "cap" rate, the riskier the investment and the higher the needed rate of return but the lower the price. In this example, if the cap rate rose to 12 percent, the price of the house would fall to $100,000 ($12,000 / 0.12). Alternatively, the lower the cap rate, the less risky the investment and the lower the needed rate of return but the higher the price. Here, if the cap rate fell to 8 percent, the price of the house would rise to $150,000 ($12,000 / 0.08).

impacts when imposed at the regional level than at the local level, holding other factors constant.

DiPasquale and Wheaton created a simple way of considering housing prices. In effect, the price of a house can be expressed as the present value of five factors:[24]

—*Price* equals agricultural value + structural value + infrastructure value + present location value + future location value.

—*Agricultural value* equals the opportunity cost of using the land for agriculture. The higher the agricultural productivity of the land, the higher the value of this component.

—*Structural value* equals the opportunity cost of the resources used to construct the house. The higher the construction cost, the higher the value of this component.

—*Infrastructure value* equals the opportunity cost of resources used to provide urban infrastructure such as schools, police and fire services, water and sewer systems, and transportation services. The higher the cost of services, the higher the value of this component.

—*Present location value* equals the value of the house's location. The closer the house is to centers of employment, shopping, recreation, or other attractive features relative to other houses, the higher the value of this component.

—*Future location value* equals the expected future value of the house's location. The faster the city grows or the more attractive the attributes of the site become, the higher the value of this component.

From this we can conceptualize the relationship between land use regulations, growth management, and housing affordability.

AGRICULTURAL VALUE. In an indirect way, growth management policies can affect this first component of housing price. Nelson shows that when agricultural land is preserved because of growth management, the value of land for agricultural uses rises.[25] One would expect, however, that this effect would be small in the urban areas of a region.

STRUCTURAL VALUE. Many traditional land use regulations influence the actual structure of housing and thereby its price. For example, building codes and design reviews that require expensive materials or designs can add to construction costs and increase housing prices. Zoning ordinances with exclusionary purposes can specify minimum sizes for houses or apartments, thereby raising the price of each unit. Likewise, growth controls using build-

24. DiPasquale and Wheaton (1994b).
25. Nelson (1986).

ing permit caps are sometimes implemented through "beauty contest" regulations that favor one housing type over another (for example, custom
homes), they often entirely exempt the construction of single houses on preexisting lots from building caps, and they encourage builders to load their
houses and subdivisions with expensive amenities. Although these controls
may not directly affect the cost or price of each dwelling, they do raise the
aggregate price of all housing affected by them.

Traditional land use regulations also affect housing prices through controls
on the type of housing that may be built in a neighborhood, a town, and
even (cumulatively) a region. Zoning ordinances usually designate specific
zones in which only single-family detached residences are allowed; sometimes
entire municipalities or even blocs of municipalities are zoned exclusively for
single-family detached homes. Zoning ordinances also can ban the construction of secondary dwellings in single-family zones and often place severe limits on manufactured housing and mobile homes or even prohibit these housing types entirely. (Zoning ordinances also can promote higher density, of
course.) Finally, zoning can limit the supply of duplexes, "granny flats," and
other housing styles by ruling out conversion of existing structures to smaller
units.

Since housing markets often are segmented by location, type, style, and
density, it is difficult to predict how supply restrictions imposed on certain
housing types will affect the entire regional housing market. Because cus-
tomers and housing producers can substitute among various housing submarkets in response to submarket supply restrictions, the ultimate price
impact of this type of traditional land use regulation will depend on the type
of regulation imposed (such as density restriction, allowable use restriction,
lot-size restriction) and the elasticity of demand for housing in each submarket.[26] If the submarkets operate independently of one another and the
demand for the restricted land use is more elastic than the demand for the
unrestricted land use, then the regulation may actually serve to reduce the
aggregate price of new housing. This results from the fact that the supply of
land available for the unrestricted land use increases, causing prices in that
market to fall to an amount that is greater than the higher price in the
restricted market.[27]

Under certain circumstances, restrictions on housing supply can influence
the type of housing built. For instance, the housing stock in Seoul and in

26. Grieson and White (1981).
27. Ohls, Weisberg, and White (1974).

London, both of which are encircled by tight greenbelts, has shifted decisively toward multifamily structures.[28] Building permit caps or quotas, by contrast, sometimes indirectly encourage builders to build large houses rather than attached housing units; since they are not guaranteed permission to build the volume of attached housing necessary to attain their desired profit, they may shift upmarket to obtain a higher total profit per unit. Several studies have shown that fast-growing metropolitan areas make more progress toward integration.[29] Since young households tend to move more often than older ones, and since young households tend to be more ethnically diverse than older ones, movers tend to be more diverse and places with growing housing stock tend to have more diverse households. The effect of supply restrictions is to deny low-income households (regardless of ethnicity or age) the opportunity to move into such areas. This outcome may be the desired effect of some forms of traditional land use regulation and of certain growth controls, but it is not a purpose of growth management as we have characterized it.

Growth management is instead oriented toward meeting development needs, not displacing them. Typical growth management programs have affordable housing and inclusionary elements that are designed to lower the cost of construction and broaden the choice of housing types. The most important programs include measures to ensure an adequate supply of land for dwellings of many kinds. Local governments sometimes complement land-supply strategies with housing subsidy programs and affordable housing requirements. The latter essentially cross-subsidize the construction of low-cost units with the profits generated from high-cost units. In general, however, these types of programs do not lower housing unit prices but rather increase the range of housing types available—that is, they ensure affordability at the neighborhood or municipal level, rather than at the level of the individual dwelling unit. By permitting or encouraging the construction of smaller and more dense forms of housing, they make housing units available at lower prices and rents, even though the cost per unit of housing services may be higher.

INFRASTRUCTURE VALUE. Traditional land use regulations can have a substantial impact on the infrastructure value of housing prices in three respects. First, modern subdivision regulations require housing developers to provide costly infrastructure improvements and other neighborhood ameni-

---

28. Bae (1998); (Evans 1991).
29. Frey and Farley (1996); South and Crowder (1998).

ties before lots are divided and sold. Seidel observes that these regulations
have grown increasingly more burdensome since their introduction in the
late 1800s.[30] Initially designed to regulate the division of property, subdivision requirements now are commonly used to exact "gold-plated" community infrastructure improvements, the cost of which falls on those buying the
homes. Second, lacking a growth management perspective, many communities using traditional land use regulations "overzone" land; that is, more land
is zoned for certain land uses than is justified by near- or long-term market
conditions. Yet because owners of such land can develop it on the basis of its
zoning, the outcome is a haphazard extension of publicly provided infrastructure that raises the cost of infrastructure per unit of development
served.[31] Third, in some cases such communities use adequate public facilities ordinances (APFOs) and concurrency requirements to limit growth: if
adequate facilities do not exist at the time of development then development
cannot go forward. The effect is to reduce the supply of development relative
to need—and thus increase prices.

Alternatively, growth management programs can lower the cost of infrastructure per unit by increasing housing densities, using existing capacities
before constructing new facilities, leveraging impact fees to decide the location of public infrastructure investment, and capturing economies of scale
through regionalization.[32] This can occur by removing prior density constraints. Infrastructure costs can affect more than just housing price, however;
they also can change developers' calculations about which type of unit to
provide. For example, APFOs and impact fee programs within growth management regimes can favor the construction of attached or higher-density
housing to make more efficient use of infrastructure, whose cost is borne by
landowners and new residents instead of the general public. It is important,
then, to consider the effect of infrastructure-related regulation on a jurisdiction's and a region's entire housing portfolio, including both the types of
units provided and their cost.

PRESENT LOCATION VALUE. Growth management programs can alter
location values by shaping the supply and demand for residences at particular locations. Although again this can lead to either higher or lower prices,
growth management programs tend to increase locational values; they do so
by increasing accessibility or in some other way making a location more
attractive. Traditional land use regulation also can raise value but only by

30. Seidel (1978).
31. Nelson (1999).
32. Knaap and Nelson (1992).

limiting the supply of properties with favorable locational features. Both regimes increase housing prices, but growth management raises aggregate welfare by making all residents and landowners better off, while traditional land use regulation lowers aggregate welfare by limiting potential interaction between present and future residents.

The relative impact of a local supply constraint created by traditional land use regulation or certain growth controls depends on the relative "openness" of the housing market being constrained. In an open regional housing market, households are perfectly mobile and move within and between jurisdictions to obtain their desired housing. In such a market, a land supply constraint imposed by any particular jurisdiction would simply cause housing developers to look for land in another jurisdiction. Assuming that land for housing is perfectly substitutable across jurisdictions, home builders would be unable to raise prices following this type of land supply constraint, because homebuyers unwilling to pay the higher price would simply move to another jurisdiction. Any local housing price increase could result only from an increase in the level of housing amenities produced within the community. Such is not the case in a closed housing market. Here, housing is either heterogeneous across communities or the population is immobile. Therefore housing supply constraints imposed by individual communities are binding and serve to increase local housing prices in areas wherein which the constraints are imposed.[33] To offset housing affordability impacts, adequate access and mobility are needed across the region. This is one objective of regional growth management efforts.[34]

FUTURE LOCATION VALUE. The value of location can rise in the future under traditional land use regulation and under growth management, but for different reasons. For example, if traditional land use regulations create a community that is economically exclusive, then that community will become more attractive as a place to live in the future; values will rise with the expectation that supply relative to future demand will fall. On the other hand, growth management can elevate the value of an entire region by making more efficient use of infrastructure, creating or enhancing agglomeration economies, and improving the quality of life; values will rise because demand will rise. This expectation can increase housing prices even though changes in demand or supply may never actually occur.[35]

33. Courant (1976); Katz and Rosen (1987).
34. Nelson and Duncan (1995).
35. Titman (1985).

Indirect Effects: Housing Tenure and Occupancy

Land use regulations have an indirect but very important connection with housing tenure that derives in part from their effects on agricultural, structural, infrastructure, and supply values. Single-family houses tend to be owned by their occupants; multifamily dwellings tend to be rented. Any regulation that promotes the construction of single-family houses and discourages the development of attached dwellings will tend to attract more owner-occupants and fewer renters. Zoning ordinances can also exert a very direct influence on the occupancy of housing units by reserving certain zones for narrowly defined families, further limiting options for unrelated low-income individuals who wish to share a house.

Summary Observations

This model of housing price determination illustrates a number of important points. First, it suggests that traditional land use policies can affect housing prices in a number of ways: by altering the costs of construction and of infrastructure, by making the community more attractive, by limiting the supply of attractive residential locations, and by altering consumer expectations. In addition, these effects can interact in what Pendall calls a "chain of exclusion" that links housing supply, type, and tenure to affordability.[36] The chain of exclusion, discussed in more detail later, is an innovative way in which to assess how communities become exclusionary or inclusionary in social composition. Growth management policies can have the same tendencies, but they do not always affect housing affordability.

Second, the model illustrates that the net community welfare effects of both traditional land use policies and growth management depend on more than their effects on housing prices or housing affordability, however defined. Both increases in demand and decreases in supply can increase the price of housing relative to income; but only increases in demand will make all residents and landowners better off (because wealth increases). This can happen under both traditional land use policies (by restricting supply relative to demand) and growth management (by increasing demand relative to supply). Moreover, the model implies that housing prices can be significantly affected by expectations about future urban growth. This has two important implications. On one hand, only fast-growing communities are likely to adopt growth

36. Pendall (2000).

management or growth control policies; such policies therefore are likely to arise only in cities with high and rising housing values. On the other hand, growth management policies can affect housing prices even if they alter nothing more than expectations; that is, growth management policies can raise housing values if they raise expectations that future locational values will rise.

Finally, it is important to note that this simple model is limited. Most important, as an aggregate model, it is limited by the inability to address variations in submarkets and complications in implementing growth management policies. A state growth management policy, for example, may be undermined by local policies; at the local level, a generous permitting process may be undermined by restrictions on sewer access. Submarkets can be affected asymmetrically. Traditional land use regulations might encourage the construction of single-family homes, while discouraging the construction of multifamily housing. Alternatively, local governments might favor high-density condominiums yet exclude mobile homes. These caveats suggest that the relationship between the affordability of housing and the regulation of development—whether through traditional means or growth management—can be considered in a simple economic framework, but that general relationships at the aggregate level often mask subtle yet important distinctions at the submarket level.

Growth Management and Housing Prices

Most research on the effect of land use controls on housing prices and affordability has focused on single-family owner-occupied housing. Many studies have considered the effects of regulations in some of the most expensive housing markets in the United States, especially in California, Florida, Oregon, and metropolitan Washington, D.C. These studies tend to focus narrowly on one question: How does a particular regulation, or in limited cases a battery of regulations, affect the sale price of a house? Since local governments adopt housing regulations as a component of regulatory regimes, it would seem logical to investigate the way in which local regulatory regimes influence the type, pattern, and affordability of housing that is delivered. Such investigation has not, however, occurred in a very systematic way, although Lowry and Ferguson offer an interesting and helpful point of departure through case studies of the development approval process in Orlando, Sacramento, and Nashville.[37]

---

37. Lowry and Ferguson (1992).

A useful way to organize the empirical literature is according to the intergovernmental framework within which land use policies are implemented. As Pollakowski and Wachter suggest, the impact of a land use policy on the housing market should vary according to the fraction of metropolitan land controlled by an individual jurisdiction.[38] If this is true, a local growth management policy should affect the land market to a degree that is quite different from that of state, regional, or national management policies. One can imagine therefore a continuum of growth management. At one extreme are the national growth management policies that exist in England and South Korea. Toward the middle are state policies that require local governments to adopt growth management and involve state oversight of local activities. Florida, Hawaii, and Oregon come to mind.[39] Moving farther away are state enabling acts that encourage or sometimes mandate local growth management programs, but without state oversight. California comes to mind.[40] At the other extreme are purely local efforts that receive no guidance from the state or national government (Ramapo, New York; Lexington, Kentucky; Brooklyn Park, Minnesota; and Boulder, Colorado).[41]

For the most part, we find that the literature surrounding the housing market effects of growth management policies is characterized by many facts in search of a unified theory. Although studies consistently find that growth management policies contribute to housing price inflation in areas where they are imposed, there is general disagreement among scholars over the size of these effects and the appropriate way to measure them.

Comparative Analyses and Local Case Studies

Basically, growth management regulates development. The central theoretical issue is therefore obvious: How do regulatory policies per se affect housing prices? This basic question has been addressed in several studies. For example, Black and Hoben classified all metropolitan statistical areas (MSAs) as "restrictive," "normal," or "permissive" in terms of accepting growth, usually through expanding the supply of developable land (either by increasing the actual acreage available or by allowing higher densities, or both).[42] They

38. Pollakowski and Wachter (1990).
39. DeGrove (1983).
40. Burby, French, and Nelson (1999).
41. Porter (1992) and Bollens (1992) provide an alternate scheme for categorizing intergovernmental growth management policy implementation regimes.
42. Black and Hoben (1985).

developed a ten-point scale in which −5 reflected MSAs with the most restrictive orientation and +5 reflected MSAs with the most permissive orientation. They found a simple correlation of +0.7 between their index and prices for finished lots, the interpretation being that more restrictive orientations led to higher land costs and presumably higher housing prices. Using a similar continuum, Guidry, Shilling, and Sirmans found that the average finished lot price in the "most restrictive" cities was $50,659 (in 1990 dollars) but $23,842 in the "least-restrictive" cities.[43]

In another survey, Segal and Srinivasan used information collected from planning officials to estimate the share of undeveloped land in several MSAs taken out of production under land use regulations. Using an ordinary least squares (OLS) regression model of single-family house prices, they found that reducing the supply of developable land was associated with higher prices.[44] Later, Rose measured the extent to which land removed from development by natural constraints (usually water) and by regulatory constraints affected housing prices in forty-five cities for which the Urban Land Institute provided land price data.[45] He found that constraints of all kinds explained about 40 percent of the variation in house prices, with about three-quarters of that attributable to natural and one-quarter attributable to regulatory constraints.

These early comparative works faced three critical shortcomings. First, although most of them controlled or adjusted for local growth factors, usually population growth, none controlled for changes in income. Growth per se contributes to housing demand, but so does household income. Second, none addressed the extent to which differences among communities reflected the benefits of regulation. Those benefits could include improved access to employment, services, and shopping centers (because higher density may create more routes and support more modes of transportation), improved public services, more desirable neighborhoods, and greater sense of community. These are not easy things to measure, but if growth management is successful, then it should generate such benefits, which should be reflected in the value of finished lots and homes. Third, in his review of those studies Malpezzi surmised that no models of the housing market "pay much atten-

---

43. Guidry, Shilling, and Sirmans (1991).

44. Segal and Srinivasan (1985). Ordinary least squares (OLS) regression is a commonly employed statistical technique that involves fitting a linear relationship between a dependent variable and independent variables so as to minimize the sum of the squared differences between the observed and predicted dependent variable.

45. Rose (1989a, 1989b).

tion to direct measures of regulation."[46] None of those studies measured growth management outcomes directly.

Several later studies employing more direct measures of regulation generally find that while restrictive land use constraints increase housing prices, the housing price impact depends on the type of regulation adopted, the overall regulatory regime within which the regulation is implemented, and the demand for new housing. Seidel's extensive nationwide survey of homebuilders found that at least seven different types of land use regulations affect land development costs in unique ways.[47] Chambers and Diamond conducted an updated version of the Black and Hoben study using more direct measures of restrictiveness and found that regulatory delay and the lack of zoned land increased land prices.[48]

Luger and Temkin examined the impacts of land use regulation in several North Carolina and New Jersey communities.[49] On the basis of nine different case studies constructed from numerous interviews with local developers, planners, and engineers, the authors contend that many regulatory requirements impose "excessive" costs, beyond those necessary to preserve health, safety, and environmental quality. The authors were interested not in examining the impacts of regulation per se but in determining the relative burden of regulations that they deemed to be excessive, such as the unnecessary project approval delays that cause developers to forgo immediate market and financing opportunities. They estimated the direct costs of these excessive regulations to be from $10,000 to $20,000 per new housing unit. Although the ultimate impact on housing prices and affordability depends on the level and elasticity of demand for housing—that is, the extent to which households are sensitive to changes in the price of housing compared with changes in their income—the authors contend that in a housing market with strong but inelastic demand (in which households have to pay a higher share of their income for housing because they have no substitute locations), "excessive" regulation could put an additional $40,000 to $80,000 on the price of a new house.

Other recent studies point to the importance of examining the entire metropolitan regulatory regime rather than single regulations in isolated communities. Pollakowski and Wachter examined the impact of land use controls

46. Malpezzi (1996, p. 217).
47. Seidel (1978).
48. Chambers and Diamond (1988); Fischel (1989, footnote 45).
49. Luger and Temkin (2000).

within and across individual planning areas within Montgomery County, Maryland.[50] The authors derived measures of constraints imposed by the county's adequate public facilities requirement and zoning regulations and found that the constraints, particularly zoning, have cumulative effects within and across individual planning areas. This suggests that the collective regional impact of land use restrictions may be much larger than the aggregate impact of each individual restriction, especially if a single entity controls land use policy for the entire region and there are few substitutes for housing in restricted communities.

Lowry and Ferguson examined the aggregate impacts of land use regulation in three different housing markets: Sacramento, California; Orlando, Florida; and Nashville, Tennessee.[51] They found that housing affordability was affected more by the type of land use regulations and processes in place than by their sheer number. Land supply constraints together with rapid increases in housing demand contributed to rampant price inflation and a decline in housing affordability in Sacramento. Orlando, on the other hand, was able to keep pace with the demand for new development by increasing the supply of developable land. Housing price inflation in Orlando during the same period was modest, despite the complex web of state, regional, and local regulations. Interestingly, housing prices rose more rapidly in Nashville's unregulated market than in Orlando's regulated market. Despite abundant land supplies, Nashville developers engaged in rampant speculation during the 1980s and constructed far more homes than residents demanded; short-term prices were high because developers needed to recover their speculative investments. Of course, in the long term, many could not recover their costs. Lowry and Ferguson speculate that perhaps a more stringent and complex regulatory process in Nashville would have benefited both developers and residents by dampening rampant land speculation. On the other hand, the authors did not consider long-run and cyclical trends in their case studies; failing to do so can make such "event" studies problematic.

More recently Green examined the impact of various zoning constraints on the price of housing, on other aspects of housing affordability (such as rental prices) and tenure, and on the share of new housing constructed within an "affordable" range.[52] Green found that, in effect, zoning sets a minimum price floor for housing construction that makes small, inexpensive

---

50. Pollakowski and Wachter (1990).
51. Lowry and Ferguson (1992).
52. Green (1999).

houses unprofitable relative to large, expensive homes; the former therefore are not produced.

The results of earlier case studies of urban growth boundaries and other "urban containment" programs are mixed. A study conducted by Gleeson in Brooklyn Park, Minnesota, examined the assessed value of unimproved land parcels following the adoption of a local limitation on infrastructure extensions, a policy similar in function to an urban growth boundary.[53] Gleeson defined land parcels as "developable" or "undevelopable" on the basis of the location of the parcel relative to the urban development boundary. Significant findings from this study include the observed differences between values of undevelopable and developable farmland parcels and the lack of an observed difference between the values of developable and undevelopable "urban" parcels. Gleeson suggests that the differentials were most likely due to the relative "openness" of the metropolitan land market. Since Brooklyn Park was only one jurisdiction within a larger metropolitan area, landowners were unable to exact higher rents due to competition for land in neighboring jurisdictions.

One of the earliest studies to examine the effect of urban growth boundaries as part of a growth management strategy is Correll, Lillydahl, and Singell's study of the Boulder, Colorado, greenbelt program. By estimating a hedonic model (a statistical model that allows one to estimate the price buyers are willing to pay for each attribute of a house, such as square footage, land area, age, number of bathrooms, and so forth), Correll and others found that landowners placed a price premium on relative proximity to the edge of the greenbelt.[54] Also, the preservation of open space was capitalized into land prices. They concluded that benefits of open space preservation are reflected in local housing prices.

A crucial component of the Boulder growth management policy is a restriction on the total number of new housing units constructed each year. Boulder also adopted a citywide height limit of thirty-five feet in the mid-1970s. Although one would expect these constraints to eliminate affordable housing, Miller contends that due to the mix of policies designed to encourage higher-density housing and the demand for small units, adequate affordable housing was provided despite the constraints.[55] By the late 1990s, however, Boulder's housing prices had risen dramatically, raising questions about

53. Gleeson (1979).

54. Correll, Lillydahl, and Singell (1978). Hedonic analysis is a type of analysis that uses multiple variate regression to estimate the contribution of structure, location, neighborhood, and other attributes on the observed price of housing. Hedonic analysis applies only to observable and measurable relationships.

55. Miller (1986).

the long-term viability of a strict urban containment system that does not also accommodate more substantial increases in density than Boulder's residents have been ready to accept. Although Miller provides only descriptive statistics to support his claim, he reiterates an important point: since housing producers are likely to vary the type and style of housing to economize on regulatory costs, conclusions about the effect of growth management policies should not be drawn without examining the dynamics of the entire housing market.

To summarize, several comparative analyses and case studies have examined the housing price effects of various types of development regulations. From these studies, we can conclude that when traditional land use regulations and certain growth controls act as supply constraints, especially in closed regional land markets with strong demand for new housing, housing price inflation can be substantial. On the other hand, communities engaging in growth management, including some that also use growth controls, may actually expand the supply of higher-density housing. Fewer studies have directly examined the potential amenity benefits of these regulations; however, those effects may also be driving housing price increases. Several studies also suggest that when one considers the impact of a growth management program, one should examine the entire regulatory regime for a given region rather than one or more specific regulations in individual jurisdictions. We can infer that at the regional level, efforts to expand the supply of land for housing should have a *modifying* impact, reducing housing price inflation and increasing housing affordability. To address this, we now zero in on California and Portland, Oregon, to gain further insight into the effects of particular types of growth controls and growth management regimes.

CALIFORNIA. In California, growth management policies often are adopted explicitly to restrict the local supply of housing. To control the volume of new development in rapidly growing suburban communities, many local governments have adopted various types of growth controls that are designed either to directly limit the number of housing units produced or to indirectly limit housing production through constraints on the supply of land. Anthony Downs suggests that these local antigrowth regulations have contributed, in part, to a 46 percent decline in California housing production from 1986 to 1990.[56]

Two studies by Schwartz, Hansen, and Green examined a growth control measure in Petaluma, California, designed to directly control the supply of

56. Downs (1992).

new housing.[57] In their 1981 study, they found that the price of new housing was significantly higher in Petaluma than in two nearby communities that did not impose growth controls. In the 1984 study, they found that the production of low- and moderate-income housing had been curtailed in Petaluma as a result of growth control. It is important to note that this result was observed despite Petaluma's policy of awarding points to developers to produce affordable housing units.[58] Additional studies of San Francisco Bay area communities found similar housing price effects attributable to the imposition of growth control ordinances.[59]

A study conducted by Landis provides evidence that different growth management regimes affected housing markets differently.[60] Landis compared the growth management programs of three California cities using a variety of local and national data sources. His analysis is interesting because each community pursued different forms of growth management. At one extreme was Sacramento, a community that allowed flexible urban growth boundary expansions and frequent plan amendments. Fresno's growth management approach was unique in that it was implemented through a charge or tax placed on new development that varied with distance to existing urban development; the idea was that one could build closer to the city center to avoid the tax. Unlike Sacramento and Fresno, San Jose relied primarily on growth controls designed to slow the rate of rural land conversion.

According to Landis, these differences in growth management policy created distinctly different types of housing and land markets in each community. In Sacramento, a competitive market was maintained and new homebuilders face no barriers to entering or exiting the market. As a result, housing was provided in a wide range of prices and styles. In the Fresno market, the highly concentrated structure of the homebuilding industry created a uncontestable housing market where incumbent homebuilders consistently held a competitive advantage over new entrants. The aggregate effect of the uncontestable nature of the Fresno market was to limit house choices for a given price range, which at the time of the study was moderate by California

57. Schwartz, Hansen, and Green (1981; 1984).

58. This evidence of the ineffectiveness of the Petaluma point system does not suggest that all such measures to reduce the price impacts from growth controls will be ineffective. In fact, a study by Zorn, Hansen, and Schwartz (1986) finds that a requirement to construct a percentage of new housing at affordable prices results in a 13 percent decline in the number of low-income persons excluded from housing in Davis, California.

59. Dowall and Landis (1982); Rosen and Katz (1981); Katz and Rosen (1987); Elliott (1981).

60. Landis (1986).

standards. In San Jose, the primary effect of the growth control policy was to raise land costs, thus creating market entry costs for all developers. Higher land prices forced small homebuilders from the market, and the price and size of new homes has increased. Gruen, Gruen, and Associates quantified the extent of these entry costs in San Jose and found that the growth management system in San Jose accounted for 32 percent of the increase in housing price for one homebuilder and 43.4 percent of the housing price increase for another.[61] The growth management regimes used in Sacramento and Fresno did not necessarily raise housing prices, but the growth controls used in San Jose did.

Dowall made a similar comparison between Santa Rosa and Napa. His comparison suggests that the housing price effects of growth management can be understood only by looking at the complex interaction between housing supply and demand over time.[62] Napa, a community with a relatively restrictively drawn urban growth boundary, has seen only moderate increases in housing prices due to the relatively low demand for housing there. Santa Rosa, on the other hand, allocates sufficient land for housing but still experiences housing price inflation because of speculative hoarding of land by large developers.

Research conducted in the 1990s began to cast doubt on the uniform assumptions about the general effects of growth controls on housing supply, price, and affordability in California. Landis compared seven growth-controlled cities with six similar non-growth-controlled cities in California to determine the effect of growth controls.[63] He found slower population increases in only three of the seven controlled cities than in their matched, uncontrolled partners. Similarly, housing shortfalls were not always higher in the growth-controlled communities than in their uncontrolled partners. Landis also found that median single-family home prices did not increase more rapidly in the growth-controlled than in the non-growth-controlled cities.

Warner and Molotch conducted detailed case studies and a briefer statistical analysis of growth patterns in three Southern California areas containing eleven political jurisdictions (cities and counties) with and without growth controls, including downzoning (reductions in permitted residential

---

61. Gruen, Gruen, and Associates (1977). We should point out here that the entry costs in San Jose are also attributable to growth management policy–induced costs that have nothing to do with the urban containment boundary per se. These costs include land development charges and other planning-related costs.

62. Dowall (1984, p. 153).

63. Landis (1992).

and commercial development capacity), moratoriums, permit caps, and incorporation policies. In all, they found that "growth continues under growth control . . . only two growth control measures had any statistically detectable negative impact on building activity."[64]

Glickfeld and Levine did a comprehensive study of all 907 local growth control measures adopted in 443 California jurisdictions, including fourteen specific measures affecting the pace, intensity, infrastructure quality, and geographical extent of new residential, commercial, and industrial development.[65] Testing only the permit value of construction (for both residential and nonresidential development), they found that the annual number of growth control measures enacted did not affect the value of construction three years later; population and the prime lending rate accounted for most of the difference among communities.

In a more recent study, Levine found that reductions in permitted zoning density were associated with strong displacement of housing from coastal locations to cities and counties as much as fifty miles away from the controlled communities.[66] In contrast, "weak measures," including (among other measures) urban growth boundaries, building permit caps, and adequate public facility ordinances, did not consistently affect the location or supply of housing.

Why are these studies on growth control so ambiguous? In most of Landis's cases, the controls were enacted in response to unusually high growth rates in previous years—rates that would not have been attained in later years even without the controls. Furthermore, growth controls often have numerous loopholes that preclude stringent implementation, including exemptions for affordable housing and small projects.[67] Perhaps it could be that growth controls do not slow growth in these cities or that housing consumers are finding substitute housing nearby. On the other hand, perhaps the "uncontrolled cities," special districts, or state and federal agencies were actually using ad hoc or informal growth controls.[68] Developers use opportunities creatively, elected officials approve projects they value, and environmentalists make compromises when they must. Glickfeld and Levine concluded that growth controls do not stop growth because there is still substantial demand for construction because of population growth; there is leakage from one

64. Warner and Molotch (1992, p. 2).
65. Glickfeld and Levine (1992).
66. Levine (1999).
67. Landis (1992, pp. 496–97).
68. Landis (1992).

community to another in the system; many measures are political compromises; and many "controls" may be symbolic rather than real.[69]

One can draw a general conclusion from these California studies that is similar to a conclusion drawn from other studies: the housing price effects of growth management policies depend heavily on how the policies are designed and implemented. If they serve to restrict land supplies, then housing price increases would be expected. However, the extent of these effects depends on the relative effect on development costs for new developers and incumbent developers as well as the strength of the local and regional market.

METROPOLITAN PORTLAND, OREGON. One of the strongest U.S. statewide growth management efforts comes from Oregon; it is known locally as Senate Bill 100, adopted in 1973. In Oregon, local governments are required to adopt urban growth boundaries to curb sprawl and preserve farmland. Because of the political consequences of enacting a statewide policy of restricting outward growth, policymakers were particularly keen to incorporate additional policy levers to ensure that urban containment does not constrain the supply of land for housing and economic growth. This has meant substantial increases in densities allowed, emphasis on mixed-use development, and efforts to streamline the permitting process.[70] The relevant question in the Oregon case is whether the policy instruments adopted to facilitate the provision of adequate housing supplies have been effective in increasing housing output and in controlling housing price inflation.

Most earlier studies of the price effects of Oregon's growth management policies focused on land prices; all found a positive association between land prices and UGBs and other growth management features, such as infrastructure provision, timing of infrastructure expansion, and zoning density.[71] That was to be expected. What those studies did not address were housing price effects.

---

69. Glickfeld and Levine (1992, pp. 80–81).

70. Knaap and Nelson (1992); Nelson and Duncan (1995).

71. Nelson (1985; 1986) found a lag between initial adoption of urban growth boundaries and market response, but the lag was only two years or so. Otherwise, he found that land value within UGBs rose and land value outside UGBs fell when the market perceived that the boundary was not flexible and that land outside the boundary could not be urbanized. Knaap (1985) found that within the UGB, urban land was valued higher than nonurban land within the UGB and that nonurban land inside the UGB was valued higher than nonurban land outside the UGB. He also found that an IGB (intermediate growth boundary) had a similar differential effect on nonurban land but had no effect on urban land. Urban land was defined as any land that can be developed at urban densities given existing zoning designations. Knaap's theoretical explanation for the different effects of UGBs on land zoned for urban uses and land zoned for nonurban uses is that UGBs, by specifying the expected date of future zoning changes, affect only

Knaap and Nelson argued that the Oregon land use program, of which UGBs are an important part, was effective in reducing the potential negative supply-side effects associated with growth management.[72] That was in part because densities were increased and each community had housing supply targets. To support their claim, they constructed supply and demand curves for Portland's share of the U.S. housing market, pointing out the cyclical pattern of price and quantity movements from the late 1970s until the late 1980s and arguing that the pattern closely approximates the timing of demand shocks in Oregon during that period. Although both the price and quantity of housing increased during the 1970s, they argued that it was due primarily to the fact that many local plans during that time had not been reviewed for compliance with state objectives. During the early 1980s housing prices declined, along with housing production, due to the recession in Oregon and the reduced demand for housing. When the demand for housing recovered in the late 1980s, relative prices did not rise to their previous levels. Knaap and Nelson concluded from this that housing supplies in the late 1980s were sufficient to meet rising demand at a relatively lower price than in the 1970s.

Two recent studies corroborate Knaap's and Nelson's findings. A study by Phillips and Goodstein measured differences in metropolitan Portland housing prices compared with all other western U.S. metropolitan areas over the period 1991 through 1996.[73] After controlling for differences in income, unemployment rate, climate, and other factors, they found no statistically significant association between metropolitan Portland's UGB and housing prices. The rapid rise in housing prices in Portland during the study period was apparently attributable to rapid growth in employment and in income more than to regulatory factors associated with the UGB. They also found that metropolitan Portland's housing prices were approximately $20,000 less than predicted by their ordinary least squares model of western metropolitan area housing prices. They surmise that although the UGB can reduce the supply of developable land, higher-density housing can offset the reduction. Not wanting to leave the reader with the impression that growth management of the sort practiced in metropolitan Portland is good for housing prices, they draw a worst-case scenario, concluding that "the results . . . [provide] weak

the value of unzoned land. Land already zoned for development should not be affected by the boundary and should command normal urban rents.

72. Knaap and Nelson (1992).

73. Phillips and Goodstein (2000).

evidence that the UGB has probably increased median housing prices . . . [by] less than $10,000." During the study period, metropolitan Portland's housing prices averaged $144,000. The worst-case interpretation of coefficients therefore implies a price effect of about 7 percent. Phillips and Goodstein did not measure the extent to which this price effect was related to improved benefits.

Another recent study, conducted by Downs, comes essentially to the same conclusion by using different approaches.[74] First, using data from the National Association of Realtors and from Freddie Mac, Downs found that the only period since 1980 that Portland's housing prices rose substantially faster than the national average was from 1990 to 1994. This corresponds to Portland's emergence from the recession of the 1980s, which hit Oregon's timber-based economy particularly hard. Second, using regression analysis he found no statistically significant association between Portland's housing price changes relative to those in other metropolitan areas since 1994. Although he found a statistically significant relationship for the period 1990 to 1994, he attributed it mostly to rapid job and wage growth. Downs found that the existence of a UGB—even a stringent one—does not necessarily cause regional housing prices to rise more than those in comparable regions without a UGB. However, a tightly drawn and enforced UGB can—at least for a short period—exert upward pressure on the rate of increase of housing prices, if it is combined with factors that strongly stimulate the regional demand for housing. He concluded that there clearly was "no simple relationship between containment programs and housing prices. Therefore condemnations of UGBs and other containment programs as always undesirable because they inevitably cause higher housing prices are as unwise and unreliable as unqualified claims that UGBs never accelerate rates of housing price increase. The truth lies somewhere between those extremes."[75]

Housing Supply Studies

Housing price studies have little relevance to housing supply. A more useful model would directly examine the differences in housing investment decisions resulting from the imposition of a growth management policy. Although a version of this supply-side approach has been adopted by several researchers, the literature on housing supply suggests that many more methodological hurdles must be overcome. First, housing producers do not

74. Downs (2002).
75. Downs (2002, p. 21).

immediately adjust housing stocks in response to demand or supply shocks.[76] Due to the durability of the existing housing stock and the time required to construct new housing units, only a small fraction of the gap between actual and desired housing quantities is eliminated in one year.[77] This suggests that the effect of a growth management policy on housing construction may take several years to materialize and may be difficult to distinguish from regional and national economic effects.

A second dilemma is the relative paucity of adequate information on housing stocks and services. Although the U.S. Census of Construction publishes monthly data on new construction and improvements, data on the value of existing housing stocks are incomplete. Median housing values published by the U.S. Census are published only every ten years and may not accurately reflect the true value of housing due to errors associated with the census's use of stated valuation data. Many also argue that housing stock data are an imperfect measure of housing services, the more appropriate unit of analysis. "Housing services" is a term used to refer to the quantity of service yielded by one unit of housing stock per unit of time.[78] The more common unit of analysis, the individual dwelling unit, does not take into account the variations in housing quality among different housing units.

Two studies help advance knowledge of the relationship between growth management and affordable housing production. In the first, Pendall found that "low-density-only" zoning (limiting density to eight dwellings, essentially single-family detached "cluster" homes, or fewer) consistently reduced jurisdictions' housing supply, shifted their housing stock away from multifamily and rental housing, and reduced the affordability of their rental housing.[79] Zoning did not exert an independent effect on jurisdictions' racial and ethnic composition, but supply restrictions (especially reductions in the share of rental housing) strongly reduced the growth of the black and Hispanic population. The chain of exclusion was, he concludes, a powerful reality for low-density zoning. To a lesser extent, building permit caps and moratoriums also had consistent exclusionary results. He goes on to show that, in contrast to low-density-only zoning, both urban growth boundaries and adequate public facilities ordinances were associated with shifts toward multifamily housing. Since multifamily housing often is rented and since black and Hispanic residents depend heavily on rental housing to gain entry into a jurisdiction, urban

76. Voith (1996).
77. Muth (1960); DiPasquale and Wheaton (1994a).
78. Muth (1960).
79. Pendall (2000).

growth boundaries and adequate public facilities ordinances may have inclusionary benefits that help balance any tendency they may have to raise housing prices.

In the second study Downs notes that the key to separating supply-side from demand-side effects is to examine the interaction between the price of housing and the quantity of housing produced, since demand-side price increases suggest concomitant increases in the volume of housing units produced, whereas supply-side increases suggest the opposite.[80] Although this approach appears on the surface to disentangle the dynamics of a growth management–induced price effect, few studies have employed housing quantity variables in their investigations. Downs applied this approach to metropolitan Portland, Oregon, for the period extending from the late 1970s to the late 1990s and found that during the entire period, Portland's housing prices rose at the same rate as those of its peers (about thirty metropolitan areas). Downs notes that the much-advertised spike in housing prices seen in the early 1990s was attributable more to substantial increases in employment and income than to supply-restricting effects of the regional urban growth boundary and other growth management efforts. Since then, Portland's housing prices have flattened to a level lower than those of other large metropolitan areas.

Summary Observations

Many studies find some evidence of housing price inflation attributable to the imposition of traditional land use regulations and certain growth controls. Microeconomic theory, however, suggests two possible explanations for this outcome. On one hand, in the face of rising demand for housing, reductions in the supply of developable land may reduce the quantity of new housing units produced and increase the price of new housing relative to existing housing. If housing consumers can costlessly transfer their housing expenditures to neighboring communities or elsewhere within the existing housing market, the aggregate effect of a supply constraint may be merely to reduce the total quantity of new housing units produced in the affected community. If the demand for housing and developable land is perfectly elastic (meaning that households are free to come and go depending on housing price), no aggregate price increase should result from a supply constraint. Available empirical evidence suggests, however, that the demand for housing is rela-

80. Downs (2002).

tively inelastic (meaning that households are not very free to come and go and must essentially pay a higher share of their income for housing than if demand were elastic) but that the long-run supply of housing is perfectly elastic (meaning that supply will always meet demand in some form).[81] We therefore should expect housing supply constraints to increase the price of housing.

We also expect to see aggregate housing price increases following the imposition of a supply constraint due to the highly segmented nature of housing markets. If the total supply of urban fringe land available for housing construction is reduced, provision of the most affordable housing becomes unprofitable and average housing prices rise due to the overabundance of higher-priced new units. Affordable housing production becomes even more unlikely if the supply of developable land is concentrated in the hands of a small oligopoly of landowners. Since any regulatory regime can reduce the number of landowners along with the number of land parcels, the additional land rents exacted by newly created landowner oligopolies may create a minimum price floor for new housing.

Granted, if housing producers are flexible and able to economize on costly land inputs, they may continue to provide affordable housing by increasing new housing densities. Unfortunately, exclusionary zoning regulations often prohibit the kind of densities required to produce the most affordable housing. Furthermore, single-family housing producers may be unfamiliar with the dynamics of the multifamily housing market and may be unable to enter new markets following changes in the price of land. Finally, if sufficient demand exists for higher-priced multifamily units, housing producers may produce sufficient quantities of new high-density housing but still fail to produce a sufficient quantity of new affordable units.[82]

A final possible explanation for housing price increases is that growth management policies can increase housing prices when they create *localized* amenities and *regional* amenities. Localized amenities include the open space benefits that are largely enjoyed by homeowners who live adjacent to an urban boundary. Regional amenities include increased efficiency in the provision of public services and infrastructure; a sense of place associated with compact, contiguous urban forms; and increased access due to the closer proximity of housing and neighboring commercial and recreational land uses.[83]

81. Mayo (1981); Hanushek and Quigley (1980); Follain (1979).
82. Danielsen, Lang, and Fulton (1999).
83. Nelson and Duncan (1995).

Do Growth Management Policies Mean to Exclude?

Why do local governments adopt land use regulations? They may be motivated by the desire to exclude low-income and minority residents, but they also do so to maximize or at least balance the local budget (so-called "fiscal zoning"); to create and maintain amenities for local and even regional constituencies; to ensure that adequate infrastructure is available; to safeguard against natural hazards; to smooth the rate of change; to support productivity of agricultural and forest land; and to create positive externalities (for instance, by encouraging complementary land uses to locate close to one another). Many of these motivations overlap, hindering efforts to distinguish unethical or even illegal exclusionary land use regulations from regulations to promote the public welfare. Yet a growing body of evidence permits some generalizations about the extent to which land use regulations of various sorts are motivated primarily by the intent to exclude. Broadly speaking, the literature suggests that exclusive large-lot zoning, when adopted as the primary land use control in a municipality, often tends to be adopted to exclude low-income households. With other residential controls and growth management measures, it is difficult to distinguish such narrow motivations.

There is strong support from both case law, popular accounts, and the academic literature that local governments often adopt exclusive large-lot zoning and minimum house size requirements and bans on secondary units precisely to make their housing more expensive and thereby indirectly exclude lower-income racial and ethnic minorities.[84] Kirp, Dwyer, and Rosenthal and Haar, for example, delve into the history of the conflicts in Mount Laurel, New Jersey, that led to the best-known legal decisions overruling exclusionary zoning ever handed down by a court in the United States.[85] Federal courts, by contrast, have been more deferential to local zoning and have tended to uphold the right of communities to exclude low-income residents, at least on constitutional grounds, as long as there is no direct evidence that they intended to exclude racial or ethnic minorities.[86] The adjudication of these cases and their

---

84. Babcock (1966); Danielson (1976).

85. Kirp, Dwyer, and Rosenthal (1995) and Haar (1996). These cases, known as Mount Laurel I (*Southern Burlington County NAACP* v. *Mount Laurel*, 336 A.2d 713 [N.J. 1975]) and Mount Laurel II (*Southern Burlington County NAACP* v. *Township of Mount Laurel*, 456 A.2d 390 [N.J. 1983]), set forth a statewide fair share housing system, which was modified and incorporated into state law in 1985 as the New Jersey Fair Housing Act (N.J. Stat. Ann. 52:27D-301 to 329).

86. In *Village of Arlington Heights* v. *Metropolitan Housing Development Corp.*, 429 U.S. 252 (1977), the U.S. Supreme Court established a nearly impossible standard for exclusionary zon-

tendency to be decided in favor of exclusionary jurisdictions show that local governments not only know that their large-lot zoning ordinances will exclude but embrace them for precisely that reason. Rolleston, studying the intensity of local residential zoning ordinances in metropolitan Chicago, found that communities with smaller minority populations than surrounding communities tend to practice more restrictive zoning, supporting the idea that exclusionary motives contribute to local zoning decisions.[87] But other motives, especially the desire to maximize or at least balance the local budget, are simultaneously at work in many cases; Rolleston also found that communities with growing tax bases practiced less restrictive residential zoning.

Some unsympathetic observers of land use regulation infer from the well-documented connections between large-lot zoning and exclusionary intent that all land use controls, especially controls on new housing, are adopted primarily to exclude low-income residents and to increase property values.[88] This "exclusionary hypothesis" has been tested widely on measures that limit local residential growth. These tests can be separated into two main types: adoption studies and attitude surveys.

Adoption Studies

Adoption studies look for features shared by jurisdictions that adopt growth measures of certain kinds. They tend to find that jurisdictions that adopt growth controls tend to be growing faster and to have more professional and white-collar residents, wealthier households, and fewer minorities, but these results are neither universal nor direct evidence of exclusionary intent.[89] Some places adopt growth measures after a spurt of rapid growth in response to the desire of newcomers to maintain the quality of environment and public services that were present when they arrived.[90] Comparing voters for and against a growth control ballot measure in Riverside, California, Gottdiener and Neiman found no relationship between support for the measure and socioeconomic status; rather, support tended to correlate with "liberal" sentiments "generally favoring more government activity in providing public

---

ing cases brought under the equal protection clause of the Constitution. Proof of disproportionate impact on minorities is not enough to invalidate a zoning ordinance for constitutional violations; plaintiffs are required to demonstrate intent to exclude.

87. Rolleston (1987).

88. Frieden (1979); Ellickson (1973).

89. Dowall (1980); Donovan and Neiman (1992); Protash and Baldassare (1983).

90. Rosenbaum (1978); Dubbink (1984).

services."[91] Dubin, Kiewiet, and Noussair, analyzing precinct-level returns from competing 1989 growth measures in the city and county of San Diego, support the Gottdiener and Neiman results.[92] They also found that minority voters, mostly renters, tended to oppose growth control measures much more often and that homeowners tended to support them; this tends to support the exclusionary model. Brueckner found that the adoption of growth control does not occur in a vacuum; instead, the choice to adopt local growth control ordinances is affected, to some extent, by the adoption of similar measures in nearby communities.[93] Brueckner speculates that this may be due either to the interdependence of jurisdictions' share of regional land supplies or to copycat behavior among nearby policymakers.

Attitude Surveys

Attitude surveys ask people about their position on growth control, usually correlating them with actual growth conditions and sometimes with their socioeconomic status. Surveys of citizen attitudes offer support for the idea that slow-growth sentiments arise in response to perceptions that growth has been fast and that infrastructure is deteriorating;[94] such perceptions sometimes matter more than the real rate of growth.[95] Liberalism also tends to be associated with support for controls in many attitude surveys; the surveys lend less support, however, to the idea that people who favor controls are wealthier than those who oppose them. A retrospective on these surveys suggests that the sources of support for growth control and management may change through time, producing contradictory results even within jurisdictions, not to mention among different jurisdictions.[96]

Studies that analyze only the effects of regulation on the sale price of single-family housing are of limited usefulness because they provide little direct evidence that regulations affect the affordability or supply of housing for people with very limited incomes. They also are related only indirectly, if at all, to the issue of whether and how regulations result in the exclusion of people of color from neighborhoods or from entire jurisdictions. Pendall's work, which shows that the chain of exclusion is a powerful reality for low-

91. Gottdiener and Neiman (1981, p. 62).
92. Dubin, Kiewiet, and Noussair (1992).
93. Brueckner (1998).
94. Baldassare and Wilson (1996); Anglin (1990).
95. Baldassare (1985).
96. Baldassare and Wilson (1996).

density zoning, therefore is very instructive. To a lesser extent, building permit caps and moratoriums also have consistent exclusionary results. Pendall also found that, in contrast to low-density-only zoning, both urban growth boundaries and adequate public facilities ordinances were associated with shifts toward multifamily housing. Since multifamily housing often is rented and since black and Hispanic residents depend heavily on rental housing to gain entry into a jurisdiction, urban growth boundaries and adequate public facilities ordinances may have "inclusionary" benefits that help balance any tendency they may have to raise housing prices. Indeed, in some states, such as Florida, Oregon, and Washington, varying degrees of inclusionary housing are required as part of local and regional growth management efforts.

Conclusions

Rising concerns over traffic congestion, loss of farmland, urban disinvestment, and the cost of public infrastructure have led an increasing number of state and local governments to adopt new policies to better manage metropolitan growth. Such policies often involve the use of zoning, comprehensive plans, subdivision regulations, building permits and fees, and infrastructure investment, and they sometimes are described as growth control, growth management, sustainable development, or smart growth. Despite the increasing popularity of such efforts, some observers are still concerned that growth management programs adversely affect land and housing markets and lead to housing affordability problems. In reviewing the academic and professional literature, we find that

Market demand, not land constraints, is the primary determinant of housing prices. We cannot emphasize strongly enough that housing prices depend more on the relative elasticity of demand, especially within metropolitan regions, than on any other factor, including growth management. If location is relatively substitutable, growth management in one community may shift demand to other communities that do not pursue growth management; the overall effect is that housing prices throughout the region remain about the same. Even if locations are not substitutable (and therefore local supply is relatively inelastic), prices are linked more to the lack of substitution than to the presence of growth management.

Dowall points out that relative differences in the demand for housing contributed to housing market outcomes that were the opposite of what one would expect upon simple examination of the restrictiveness of local regulations.[97] Knaap and Nelson also demonstrate that regional economic shocks affected the Oregon housing market and that the statewide planning program might have been successful in mitigating housing price inflation.[98]

Related to the issue of aggregate housing demand is the relative demand for housing in various submarkets. If the demand for multifamily homes is weak or difficult to assess, housing producers may not economize on high land costs by constructing higher-density housing even if they are allowed or encouraged to do so by local land use regulations. Similarly, if central city characteristics such as crime, poor schools, and poor infrastructure exert a "push factor" that increases the demand for nonurban housing, new housing prices will continue to rise in areas in which land is likely to be the cheapest: the suburbs and exurbs.[99]

Both traditional land use regulations and growth management policies can raise the price of housing. One thing is certain about the studies reviewed: traditional land use regulations and many forms of growth control can and do raise housing prices, either by raising input prices or by restricting supply relative to demand, or both. What is not clear is whether these outcomes apply to growth management regimes as we have characterized them. Yet, as Nelson argues, if no price effects can be attributed to growth management policies then we should question their effectiveness.[100] After all, if one of the primary purposes of growth management is to increase the desirability of the subject community, prices there should rise, but not because of supply-side constraints. The question for the affordability of housing is not whether prices rise because of growth management but whether the distribution of housing types has exclusionary outcomes among communities.

We can classify growth measures into two sets: a clearly exclusionary set and an ambiguous set. Exclusive low-density zoning often is motivated by the intent to limit the supply and accessibility of affordable housing, thereby raising home prices by excluding lower-income households. It also is the land-use control that has most consistently been found to displace growth and exclude low-income and racial and ethnic minority residents, as designed.[101]

On the other hand, growth management often is designed to overcome the exclusionary effects of low-density-only zoning. Oregon's growth policies,

97. Dowall (1984).
98. Knaap and Nelson (1992).
99. Nelson and Sánchez (1999); Nelson and Dueker (1990).
100. Nelson (1986).
101. Pendall (2000).

for example, include both urban growth boundaries to protect rural resource land and a host of strong measures to reduce regulatory barriers in developing areas.[102] The Portland Metropolitan Housing Rule establishes targets for multifamily housing in every jurisdiction; Oregon bans moratoriums and building permit caps. Many growth management policies improve the supply and location of affordable housing and accommodate other development needs, thereby increasing the desirability of the community and thus the price of housing.

A larger group of local land use regulations has more ambiguous effects that depend largely on how the regulations are implemented. UGBs, for example, can be drawn so tightly around a city that housing prices rise dramatically, supply falls, and poor residents are priced out or forced to overcrowd. This arguably has happened in Boulder and in parts of California.[103] But they can also, as in the Portland case, be mechanisms for shaping urban form, raising density, and promoting more affordable housing types. Adequate public facilities ordinances, too, can raise density and thereby encourage more affordable types of housing, while limiting the need for local governments to raise property taxes that are passed along to all households, whether owners or renters. They also can encourage up-market shifts and reduce the supply of new affordable housing. In most cases, regulations with more ambiguous effects are adopted to meet a host of public purposes; if state governments and local planners design them properly and in tandem with affirmative measures to promote housing affordability, the evidence suggests that not only can they be neutral, they also even may help promote a more inclusive housing market.

The land supply limiting effects of growth management need not lead to higher housing prices if housing density is increased, infrastructure is available in a timely manner, and land use decisions are made to be roughly concurrent with market needs. Growth management need not reduce the supply of housing units even if land supply is restricted. But growth management also promises to improve benefits, and housing prices may rise in response to improvements. Some benefits may be measurable, but others are not. Malpezzi found ambiguous relationships between regulatory regimes and benefits that he could measure, but he notes there were many more benefits than he could measure.[104] In addition, he could not distinguish between growth management, growth control, and traditional land use regulation regimes. In

102. Knaap (2000).
103. Fulton, Glickfeld, and Levine (1996); Lorentz and Shaw (2000).
104. Malpezzi (1996).

reviewing Malpezzi, Knaap observes that "there are no measures of land and housing prices that are well suited for research on the determinants of inter-metropolitan property values," thus rendering it difficult at best to estimate differences in regulatory regimes among metropolitan areas, let alone differences in benefit outcomes.[105]

The effect of growth management on housing prices depends mostly on policy implementation, the structure of local housing markets, the existing pattern of land ownership, and the stringency of other local regulations. It appears that whether policies are state or local is less important than whether those charged with implementation actively monitor land supplies and adjust regulations to facilitate the development of higher-density housing. It appears that growth controls of the kind used throughout California significantly contribute to housing price inflation by limiting the supply of housing units. In contrast, it appears that the kinds of growth management policies used in metropolitan Portland do not themselves influence housing prices.

Increasingly, the choice is between exclusionary zoning and growth management—not between regulation and no regulation. More and more people are becoming dissatisfied with increasing traffic, disappearing open space, crowded schools, and other manifestations of poorly managed growth. Inevitably, they will pressure local decisionmakers to respond. Often, leaders see only two politically acceptable choices, exclusionary zoning or growth management; clearly, growth management is better for promoting housing opportunity. Suburbs with exclusionary zoning encircle Boston, New York, Philadelphia, Pittsburgh, Cleveland, Atlanta, and many other regions throughout the United States, reducing the affordability of housing and promoting sprawl.[106] Growth management, at best, incorporates deliberate policies to ensure not only an adequate supply of land but also a range of housing types and densities. This pro-diversity strategy is, in fact, at work in metropolitan Portland and less effectively so in California, and it was imposed as a remedy for exclusionary zoning by the New Jersey supreme court in the famous Mount Laurel II case. By ensuring that land is available explicitly for the construction of higher-density housing and by removing barriers to the construction of such housing, growth management can help overcome exclusionary zoning.

One of the most important policy implications to be gleaned from this review is that the work of local planners plays a significant role in determin-

105. Knaap (1998, p. 276).
106. Pendall (2000).

ing the extent of housing price inflation attributable to growth management policies. As Miller and Zorn and others suggest and as evidence from Portland makes apparent, stemming housing price inflation requires planners to enact proactive measures to guarantee affordability as well as to ensure an adequate supply of land and housing.[107] Miller, Zorn, and other researchers have shown that programs requiring developers to include affordable housing in their new projects deliver more affordable housing than incentive-based programs, but incentives and mandates together—along with supportive land use policies—are likely to make the most positive contribution to increasing housing opportunity.

If left to their own devices, however, local governments often avoid affirmative measures. The literature suggests that state or substate regional growth management programs, coupled with strong state-level housing programs, promise to help overcome parochialism. Knaap suggests that the overall effect of statewide and metropolitan growth management policies is to lower the restrictiveness of local land use regulations, a result that can have the effect of lowering housing rents and prices.[108] Indeed, Fischel observes that it was a regional growth management hearing board in Washington state that overturned a local government's downzoning of land for being inconsistent with the state's Growth Management Act, restoring to the landowner all prior density rights.[109]

Finally, any further discussion of housing affordability must consider a broad range of externalities. Simply examining the cost of housing is not adequate when considering what is or is not "affordable." Services and amenities—such as increased efficiency in the provision of public services and infrastructure, lower overall transportation costs, and increased access due to the increased proximity of land uses—must be factored into such calculations. In short, researchers and policymakers need to consider housing costs the same way families do: as a portion of their overall wealth. We recommend that a coalition of interests be formed to agree on just what is meant by "affordable housing"; the definition would need to consider all forms of housing and to accurately reflect all costs and amenity benefits.

We conclude that a substantial body of research suggests that instruments used to manage urban growth can affect housing prices and thus affordability. In the context of strong housing demand, growth management can

107. Miller (1986) and Zorn, Hansen, and Schwartz (1986).
108. Knaap (1998).
109. Fischel (1999).

adversely affect housing affordability by making the community even more desirable—which is, after all, its intent. Growth management programs can mitigate adverse effects, however, by lowering the costs of providing public infrastructure, minimizing regulatory delays, and prohibiting exclusionary zoning practices. The implications of our interpretation of the literature are clear: successful growth management programs are those that include policy instruments designed to mitigate the adverse effects of urban growth *and* to expand housing opportunities for lower-income households.

COMMENT BY
William A. Fischel

The authors of this chapter have done several important studies of land use and metropolitan structure.[110] Their present work, however, is disappointing. Its conclusions, if one looks past the numerous qualifications, do not follow from the evidence offered.

The two main conclusions are that the market, not growth management, is mainly to blame for high housing costs and that all regulations can raise housing prices, but growth management does so less than traditional zoning. True, the latter is a much balder statement than the authors actually make. The conclusions, especially the second, are hedged by phrases such as "may cause," "can cause," and "when crafted properly." The numerous qualifications of the statements in the chapter suggest that the authors' views are less than unified. The reader gets the impression that one faction wants to make a strong statement to show that growth management does not create affordability problems but that another faction—or maybe the other side of each author's brain—is not convinced that the evidence supports such a claim. The tone of the paper therefore might be best characterized as "cautiously tendentious." There is a feeling that growth management ought to be let off the hook on the affordability issue, but there is a countervailing sentiment that the evidence is kind of mushy or maybe not supportive at all.

The authors need not have worried, if worried they were, that their cautions would undermine the influence of the chapter. Earlier versions (the original draft was done in 2001) have been hailed by growth management

110. Among those I admire are Knaap (1985), Nelson and others (1992), and Pendall (1999).

advocates as the absolute, no-doubt-about-it, final proof that growth management can proceed without any worry that it might create affordability problems. For example, the website of Smart Growth America summarizes the paper thus:

> Critics of growth management accuse it of driving up housing prices. However, this study found that lower-middle and lower-income families often are priced out of housing in areas that lack any growth-management measures. Indeed, they frequently are deliberately screened out through exclusionary zoning practices. Smart-growth policies that attempt to ensure each jurisdiction provides its fair share of affordable, workforce housing can mitigate . . . these problems, the authors conclude.[111]

A news release by 1000 Friends of Oregon, a pioneer in promoting urban growth boundaries, began enthusiastically:

> February 21, 2002: A landmark report from the Brookings Institution confirms what Oregon growth management advocates have said for years: even though urban growth boundaries limit the supply of land for development, those limits do not play a significant role in housing price increases.[112]

The American Planning Association press release was headlined "Growth Management Act: Good Intentions Coming True." The Regional Plan Association's newsletter of January 24, 2003, cites the report in claiming "that there is no inherent connection between limiting development of open land, which should be a goal of Smart Growth plans, and limiting the production of housing."[113]

Growth Management Has a Metropolitan Focus

These optimistic views are unwarranted. The largest number of studies reviewed in this chapter actually show that tighter land-use controls of any type cause higher housing prices. Unambiguous examples (the sources are

111. See www.smartgrowthamerica.com [January 20, 2004].
112. See www.friends.org [January 20, 2004].
113. Regional Plan Association (2003).

given in the chapter references) are Black and Hoben (1985), Brueckner (1998), Dowall (1984), Evans (1991), Frieden (1979), Green (1999), Grieson and White (1981), Gruen and Gruen (1977), Katz and Rosen (1987), Lowry and Ferguson (1992), Malpezzi (1996), Pollakowski and Wachter (1990), Rose (1989), Segal and Srinivasan (1985), Seidel (1978), and Schwartz, Hansen, and Green (1981, 1984). The chapter's authors subject several of these studies to rather demanding econometric standards and in most cases dismiss their relevance to growth management. The few studies that suggest the opposite—and most do no more than suggest it—are embraced as evidence confirming the innocence of growth management.

Their ability to maintain growth management's innocence depends on distinguishing it from some other regulatory regimes. The authors are to be commended for not adopting the rhetoric of many antisprawl tracts, which go on about "unplanned, unregulated suburban development," when in fact nearly all suburban development since the 1920s has been exquisitely planned and regulated. The authors know that zoning was not invented yesterday, and they more or less acknowledge that it is part of the reason housing prices are high.

Their distinction between growth management and other regulations is based on an analysis of the intentions of their advocates. It appears that if growth management advocates say they will not be exclusionary and will respond to the affordability issue, they should be judged to have actually accomplished those goals. But such statements often are rhetorical smokescreens. The original constitution of the former Soviet Union guaranteed all sorts of freedoms, but no social scientist would accept that as evidence that freedom of expression actually existed under Lenin and Stalin. And even if they were sincere statements, a social scientist would want to know whether the stated guarantees had the desired effects.

A more effective distinction that the authors use to differentiate the good guys from the bad guys is the scope of the body doing the regulation. Purely local controls, which is what I take their reference to "traditional zoning regulations" to mean, are problematic. They use devices such as "ten-acre minimum lot size" and discourage high-density housing to keep out the poor. Growth management, on the other hand, takes a metropolitan-wide view. There is something to this distinction. At the level of a small local government, land use regulation looks like "them against us," and "us" usually wins out for the simple reason that the existing residents ("us") are the only voters. At the metropolitan level, regulation is more often a matter of "us against us," because the people affected by land use regulations are those who vote for the officials who adopt them. Now, I must admonish the reader that the authors do not explicitly adopt this distinction between metropolitan and local growth management. I apply it mainly because their best example, Portland, Oregon, takes the metropolitan approach and their cautionary examples are the sins of smaller local governments. I take it then that the real distinction between growth management and traditional zoning has to do with the level of government.

It is important, I would add, to distinguish real metropolitan-wide regulations from regimes that are simply "double-veto" systems. In double-veto systems, both local and metropolitan regulators get to shoot down a development, but neither can force the other to accept development that it does not want. This makes zoning more restrictive, not less so. The contrast between localism and metropolitanism is sharpest when growth management calls for urban growth boundaries. Outside the boundaries, away from the traditional city core, land is zoned to preserve farms and forests and other rural open spaces. The typical means of preserving these uses is to require minimum lot sizes of various dimensions that would embarrass most advocates of traditional zoning: minimum lot sizes of ten, twenty-five, fifty, and 640 acres have been adopted to discourage suburban development from seeping through the urban growth boundary.

Inside the growth boundary, however, things really are different under the modern growth management plans that the authors contemplate. Such plans envision smaller lots, higher density, and a wider range of housing types than found with traditional local zoning. This sets up the possibility that removing developable land outside the growth boundary from the market, which by itself would restrict total supply and thereby raise housing prices, might be offset by allowing a larger number of housing units inside the growth boundary. (I neglect here the academic point that the law of diminishing returns makes higher-density housing more costly per unit of usable floor space. Given the multiacre minimum lot size that characterizes most existing suburban zoning, an increase in density is unlikely to raise building costs.) The legitimate form of growth management, I infer, calls for growth boundaries with required infill.

Portland—The Best Available Paradigm

The real problem in evaluating programs that call for growth boundaries along with high-density infill development is that they are quite rare. All metropolitan growth management programs are imposed on a preexisting layer of zoning regulations that are jealously guarded by municipalities and neighborhoods. For a program that combines a growth boundary with infill development to work, it must overcome local resistance to high-density rezoning. That is exceedingly difficult to do. The jurisdiction that has worked hardest at doing it is Oregon, and most of the credible evidence about the influence of metropolitan growth management comes from studies of its largest metropolitan area, Portland.

Portland's empirical preeminence arises from four factors. One is that it started in the 1970s, years before most others, so there has been time for its effects to become observable. The second is that Portland's growth boundaries have bite. They are not completely inelastic over time, but, as two of the authors have clearly established in other work, land values are affected by the presence of the boundary. Buyers of land think about what can be done now and in the future, and buyers outside the growth boundary pay less for land there. This distinguishes Portland's regulations from those of many other areas, whose boundaries are set so liberally or expanded with such alacrity that they could be described better as "sprawl promoters" rather than "sprawl containers." Portland's third distinction is that Oregon formulated independent, metropolitan-wide boards to administer its growth management system. A critical fact is that board members are not selected by local government officials. They are elected without regard to municipal boundaries, and so the influence of neighborhood groups, which would usually stop infill development at the local level, is kept at a manageable level.

The fourth distinction is that Oregon's growth management boards have the authority to require local officials to rewrite municipal plans and rezone for higher densities. This authority, combined with the political independence of its metropolitan land use board, makes Portland highly unusual. Most other areas that have growth boundaries contain hortatory language about the need for infill development and affordable housing, but few of their requirements have any teeth. As anyone familiar with the formulation of local master plans knows, it is easy to insert infill and affordable housing as one of many plan goals. When it comes to implementing the plan, however, it is equally easy to explain that infill and affordable housing are not appropriate in a given place because they conflict with other goals in the plan.

Therefore the real test of the "white hat" aspect of growth management falls more or less by default to Portland, Oregon. Its growth management plan ought to make it different from other fast-growing metropolitan areas of the West. If it is successful in offsetting the restrictive effects of downzoning rural land outside the growth boundary by "upzoning" land within the growth boundary, then its housing prices ought to be *lower* than those in otherwise comparable areas outside of Oregon.

To find that Portland's housing prices have gone up at the same rate as those of less enlightened urban areas is to say that the Oregon plan has not succeeded in mitigating the housing price impacts of urban boundaries. Bad old California, where local government never loses when it wants to stop development, has exclusionary zoning and no true metropolitan growth boundaries.[114] (There are plenty of local growth boundaries, but these are more likely to exacerbate the metropolitan-wide problem, since they induce developers to leapfrog to other jurisdictions in the area.) It is no wonder that California housing prices, which in the 1960s were about the national average, are now consistently the highest. But all the evidence indicates that Portland has kept pace with California in the decades since Portland adopted its growth boundaries.[115]

Of course, Portland's growth management plan could have caused its housing prices to exceed those in California. If one wants to be optimistic on this front, one could say that the evidence suggests that Portland's program does not produce housing that is less affordable than traditional zoning. But that was not the position of Portland's growth management advocates. They clearly claimed that overriding parochialism in land use would make housing cheaper inside the boundary. If statistical evidence is to be believed, that has not happened.

Other Recent Studies Are More Pessimistic

The chapter does not address two rather important studies of the impact of land use regulation, perhaps because they are fairly recent. Two well-known urban economists, Edward Glaeser and Joseph Gyourko, used a previously unexploited (for this purpose) data set, the American Housing Survey, to examine why housing has become so expensive in many areas of the United States.[116] While they found that a great deal of housing in inner cities and in the Midwest is priced at close to reproduction cost, they also found that housing prices on the West Coast and in the Northeast, especially in the suburbs, usually are well above the cost of construction.

114. Fischel (1995).
115. Downs (2002).
116. Glaeser and Gyourko (2002).

In computing the cost of constructing new homes, Glaeser and Gyourko took account of the fact that land for housing is more expensive in cities and more expensive still in big cities than in small cities. Even after those factors were controlled for, an often-enormous premium was paid in the areas of the country with the heaviest land use regulations. Since 1975, land use regulations have become more restrictive—for reasons that are not well understood—in the West and in the Northeast, and that is where single-family housing prices have become much more expensive. Glaeser and Gyourko have put on firmer statistical grounds what developers and land use experts have said for years. First California and now the Northeast have come to have housing prices that are way out of line with those in the rest of the country. I would not vouch for every claim in the Glaeser and Gyourko study, but it does offer a comprehensive evaluation that requires a serious response.

The other set of studies comes from England, home to the growth management systems envied by American proponents. Growth boundaries have long been a component of British planning, and two scholars, Paul Cheshire and Stephen Sheppard, have constructed elaborate economic models to evaluate their effects.[117] An important aspect of their approach is that it allows both the benefits and the costs of growth boundaries to play out in the results.

Cheshire and Sheppard find that the chief benefit of growth boundaries is one that their American advocates have pointed to: there is less commuting because homes inside the boundary are closer together. But this comes at a cost that is many times the economic value (time saved and lower pollution) of less commuting. It is not a close calculation, and no plausible variation in the parameters of their model could dispel the conclusion that British urban growth boundaries make British housing much more expensive than it needs to be. American planners seem unaware of this evidence. The experience with comprehensive urban growth boundaries in South Korea is similarly cautionary.[118]

The Issue Is Regulation, Not Demand

A joke in the 1950s told of an American who was shown the Moscow subway by a Russian acquaintance. After half an hour of the Muscovite's lecture on the design, artwork, and cleanliness of the subway, the American said,

117. Cheshire and Sheppard (2002).
118. Hannah, Kim, and Mills (1993); Mayo and Sheppard (1996).

"This is all very nice, but we've been here half an hour and not a single train has come through." To which the Russian angrily retorted, "What about the Negroes in the South?"

This chapter's contention that demand for housing is really responsible for price increases is along the same vein of "Let's change the subject." Of course house prices will not rise if no one wants to buy houses. But that's not the question.

The question is why supply has not responded to increases in demand. Demand for computers has risen quite steadily in the last thirty years, and suppliers have responded so vigorously that their prices have declined. Closer to the present subject is that the region of the country with the highest population growth and highest growth in personal income in the last thirty years has been the South. Yet housing prices in the South have risen quite a bit less than in the West and the Northeast. Maybe it is a coincidence that regulatory regimes have been less restrictive in the South, but it does form a powerful counterexample to the proposition that the highly regulated places have housing price inflation just because demand has shifted. Moreover, the population of the West actually grew faster in the 1950s and 1960s than in later decades, yet housing prices did not start taking off until the new regulatory regimes of the 1970s were put in place.

Monopoly Zoning or Rational Regulation?

A question that the chapter only briefly addresses is whether higher housing prices are a bad thing. (The authors note in passing that the *Places Rated Almanac* gives lower ratings to places that have low housing prices.) Economists often use high housing prices as examples of successful local policies: if the local schools get better, housing prices should rise. But before jumping to that conclusion for land use regulations, economists would usually want to know something about the nature of the policy. If the policy simply made one of the inputs for housing—land—more scarce without providing offsetting benefits, then we would be inclined to say that the policy reduced the well-being of those who had to purchase after the policy was put in place. (Those who purchased before, of course, enjoy an extra capital gain on their homes, but we generally do not think that the well-being of the beneficiaries of monopolies outweighs the losses of the victims of monopolies.)

In this respect, the establishment of Portland's growth boundaries looks like the formation of a monopolistic cartel whose purpose is to raise the value of insiders' homes at the expense of outsiders, who naturally do not vote. The mildly xenophobic comments of Oregon governor Tom McCall, who was a promoter of the growth boundary movement in the 1970s, seem consistent with this. He was famous for having urged out-of-staters (Californians in particular) to "visit but don't stay."

There is a more benign economic analogy that could be used to justify Portland's growth boundaries and the higher housing prices associated with them. Petroleum, where it exists near the surface, usually lies beneath the property of many landowners. Under traditional property rights, each owner is entitled to take out all he or she wants without regard to what the neighbors do or think. If all owners avail themselves of that right, they will take the oil out too quickly. Rapid extraction would for a short time keep oil prices low, but later prices would be too high, because oil would be consumed too quickly, oil is costly to store once removed, and rapid extraction of oil depletes the natural-gas pressure that would otherwise reduce pumping costs. Moreover, as a result of the higher extraction costs, some oil would be left in the ground. The solution to this problem is called "unitization." All landowners retain the right to withdraw oil under unitization, but only at a collectively determined rate. This keeps oil prices higher than they would otherwise be, but it makes supplies go further and in the longer run actually keeps prices down. Unitization is a win-win system in that both owners of oil-bearing property and consumers are better off.

Rural space around an urban area might be seen as a similar resource. Individual governing bodies might zone to develop it too quickly. Then, after an initial spate of development, the newcomers vote to downzone the rest for exclusionary reasons or just to maintain their own property values. This process of independent local zoning is the major cause of sprawl—excessive use of land in the process of suburbanization.[119] One way to retard this process would be to "unitize" the local governments and have them zone land collectively. Initially this would cause housing prices to be higher than they would be otherwise. In the long run, however, the policy would keep housing prices lower by preventing individual suburbs from zoning for multiacre lots. Thus Portland's Metro board could be seen as a rationalizer of property rights, like the landowners who unitize their oil fields, rather than a devious monopoly.

It often is hard to tell the difference between a monopolist and a rationalizer of property rights. I once heard someone defend OPEC, which raised oil

---

119. Downs (1994); Fischel (1999).

prices in the 1970s by tightening the spigot, as just a means of establishing long-run property rights. The western oil companies in the Middle East anticipated that they would be expropriated, so they pumped too much out in the 1950s and 1960s, keeping the price of oil low. After the Middle East nations in fact nationalized their resources in the 1970s, prices went up. But this was not, according to this apologist, due to monopoly. It was due only to the fact that the new owners—mostly Arab potentates—took a longer-range look and adopted a conservation-minded ethic.

If you believe that, I know of a bridge in Brooklyn you can buy, but it does illustrate a real problem. It is nearly impossible to distinguish benign intentions from self-serving ones. The rhetoric of conservation is something that monopolists have little trouble adopting. Residents faced with a low-income housing project moving in next door usually are not so foolish as to say that they just do not want poor people nearby. They talk about the possibility of threatening endangered species, the effects of traffic on school children, and the historic character of the neighborhood. There is no truth serum that can reveal what is really bothering them, so outsiders have to evaluate the results with a skeptical frame of mind. This chapter is not helpful in this endeavor.

COMMENT BY
Robert Lang

My read of the academic literature on the link between growth management and housing affordability is that there is *no* theoretical reason why growth management should lead to less affordable housing. The authors clearly show that growth management schemes exist that can be neutral in this regard and that can even increase the supply of affordable housing. The other chapters find the same. This is good work, and the researchers should be applauded.

On a purely technical or mechanical level, growth management strategies can be devised that should have little impact on house prices. But in practice, growth management generally affects house prices. The problem is not with the mechanics of growth management, but with politics and perceptions— in particular, its use by homeowners to maintain the status quo. The authors go to great pains to distinguish enlightened "growth management" from old-fashioned, exclusionary "growth control," but in the public debate over growth such a distinction grows fuzzy. Growth control is one tool that home-owners *think* will help maintain their home's value.

Consider William Fischel's concept of the "home voter."[120] Fischel notes that the most liberal people seem to turn deeply conservative when it comes to defending the turf around their homes. He argues that homeowners are an especially conservative bunch because what is typically their single largest asset is at risk. Homes cannot be readily moved, which means that they are linked to the fate of their neighborhood. Further, there is no insurance that one can take out as a hedge against depreciation in the value of one's home. The solution is to always vote in local elections in the interest of your home. And how do you vote? To stop all land uses that you think may reduce the value of your property—which is to say, basically all change.

I add one more twist to the home voter phenomenon. Let's call it the "vicarious home voter." Virginia Tech recently completed a report for HUD that looks at developing accessory housing, specifically granny flats. One of the report's authors asked me what I would think if such an ordinance were proposed for our neighborhood. I told her that while I supported accessory units in theory, I might just resist accessory units in the neighborhood.

I live in a neighborhood that contains only single-family homes, two units to an acre. It is my impression that the value of my home is based in part on the absence of any form of multifamily housing nearby. If my neighbor suddenly picks up an extra unit, I think that my property value might drop 5 or even 10 percent, so we are talking about thousands of dollars. Some others may be willing to take a chance, but I am not—and clearly I am not alone.

Do I have a personal problem with an accessory unit? No. I have lived in cities for the past twenty-five years. I am not shocked by density. But someday I will sell this house, and a potential buyer may object. Perhaps some progressive person will buy it, but why limit my market to people with this political view? The important point here is that the most conservative purchaser lives in the heads of liberals, because they may have to sell their house to a conservative. So in expressing vicariously the preferences of the next buyer, I may vote to not increase the intensity of development in my neighborhood.

It turns out that my fears may be well founded. In the new journal *Opolis*, I report that a recent study by Sirmans and Macpherson using hedonic modeling shows that granny flats can actually lower house values.[121] I find that neighborhood context may determine in part the relative value of some housing characteristics. In general, features that add to a property's "urban intensity" can lower the sales price of single-family detached suburban homes.

Sirmans and Macpherson analyzed 28,828 home sales during two periods: 1996–99 and 2000–03. Their study covered twenty-one counties in a

120. Fischel (2001).
121. Lang (2004); Sirmans and Macpherson (2003).

region stretching from central New Jersey to northern Maryland. The sample included only single-family detached homes. The typical home analyzed was a mid-range suburban dwelling: "the average selling price was $213,335 . . . the average house had 3.5 bedrooms, 1.80 full baths, and 0.68 partial baths. About three-fourths of the homes had a regular garage. . . . Two-thirds of the homes had central air conditioning."[122]

Buried in the data is a striking pattern that shows a distinct bias against housing elements that make a single-family home more utilitarian. Sirmans and Macpherson report that an "in-law suite" (or a granny flat) drops a house price by 5.2 percent. Likewise a "professional office" can shave 5 percent off the price. Believe it or not a sidewalk can cost a homeowner 4.5 percent of value at sales time, while fencing shaves off 2.8 percent. On face value, all of these elements would seem to be "improvements," in that they allow for more complete use of a house. But in the market for suburban single-family detached dwellings all these features count against the price.

Yet not every buyer has an anti-urban bias. In fact, cities regained some popularity in the 1990s, especially their downtowns.[123] Even many new suburban developments are getting denser and more urban in look and feel.[124] There is some evidence that people will pay a price premium of about 15 percent to live in a New Urbanist (or neotraditional) community over a comparable conventional suburban subdivision.[125] How do these facts reconcile with the house price data presented above?

The most likely answer is that dual housing markets exist: one for conventional low-density suburbs and one for cities and denser suburbs. Hughes, Danielsen, and I (using target market data) developed the concept of "suburban urbanites" to argue that some suburbanites show a preference for city living, including higher density housing.[126] Myers and Gearin find that a large share of older households also seek more densely built and compact housing units than are found in low-density suburbs.[127]

Growth management advocates who seek to introduce urban elements into suburban settings should better understand what impact these changes have on house values. In July 2003 California passed a bill that requires local agencies to routinely approve applications for granny flats without public hearings if the new structures meet local guidelines. The bill triggered a nasty

---

122. Sirmans and Macpherson (2003, p. 3).
123. Sohmer and Lang (2003).
124. Danielsen, Lang, and Fulton (1999).
125. Eppli and Tu (1999).
126. Lang, Hughes, and Danielsen (1997).
127. Myers and Gearin (2001).

fight between California municipalities and the state, as many places rushed to enact local ordinances that make it almost impossible to build such units. The state is now considering a new law to prevent the practice. But what California really needs is an accurate assessment of impact showing in which cases granny flats lower house values. Perhaps then the state could target the law to localities where house values are the least affected by accessory dwellings. For now, many home voters are right to resist what may be a real loss to their prime asset.

References

Anglin, Roland. 1990. "Diminishing Utility: The Effect on Citizen Preferences for Local Growth." *Urban Affairs Review* 25 (4): 684–96.

Babcock, Richard F. 1966. *The Zoning Game: Municipal Practices and Policies.* University of Wisconsin Press.

Bae, Chang-Hee Christine. 1998. "Korea's Greenbelts: Impacts and Options for Change." *Pacific Rim Law & Policy Journal* 7 (3): 479–502.

Baldassare, Mark. 1985. "The Suburban Movement to Limit Growth." *Policy Studies Journal* 4 (4): 613–27.

Baldassare, Mark, and Georjeanna Wilson. 1996. "Changing Sources of Suburban Support for Local Growth Controls." *Urban Studies* 33 (3): 459–71.

Black, J. Thomas, and James Hoben. 1985. "Land Price Inflation." *Urban Geography* 6 (1): 27–49.

Bollens, Scott A. 1992. "State Growth Management: Intergovernmental Frameworks and Policy Objectives." *Journal of the American Planning Association* 7 (3): 211–26.

Brueckner, Jan. 1998. "Testing for Strategic Interaction among Local Governments: The Case of Growth Controls." *Journal of Urban Economics* 44 : 438–67.

Burby, Raymond J., Stephen P. French, and Arthur C. Nelson. 1999. "Plans, Code Enforcement, and Damage Reduction: Evidence from the Northridge Earthquake." *Earthquake Spectra* 14 (1): 59-74.

Chambers, Daniel N., and Douglas B. Diamond Jr. 1988. "Regulation and Land Prices." Washington, D.C.: National Association of Realtors and National Association of Home Builders.

Cheshire, Paul, and Stephen Sheppard. 2002. "The Welfare Economics of Land Use Planning." *Journal of Urban Economics* 52 (2): 242–69.

Clawson, Marion. 1962. "Urban Sprawl and Land Speculation." *Land Economics* 38 (1): 99–111.

Correll, Mark R., Jane H. Lillydahl, and Larry D. Singell. 1978. "The Effects of Greenbelts on Residential Property Values: Some Findings on the Political Economy of Open Space." *Land Economics* 54 (2): 207–17.

Courant, Paul N. 1976. "On the Effects of Fiscal Zoning on Land and Housing Values." *Journal of Urban Economics* 3 (1): 88–94.

Danielsen, Karen A., Robert E. Lang, and William Fulton. 1999. "Retracting Suburbia: Smart Growth and the Future of Housing." *Housing Policy Debate* 10 (3): 513–40.

Danielson, Michael N. 1976. *The Politics of Exclusion*. Columbia University Press.

DeGrove, John M. 1983. *Land, Growth, and Politics*. Chicago: APA Planners Press.

DiPasquale, Denise, and William C. Wheaton. 1994a. "Housing Market Dynamics and the Future of Housing Prices." *Journal of Urban Economics* 35 (1): 1-27.

———. 1994b. *Urban Economics and Real Estate Markets*. Prentice-Hall.

Donovan, Todd, and Max Neiman. 1992. "Citizen Mobilization and the Adoption of Local Growth Control." *Western Political Quarterly* 45 (3): 651–75.

Dowall, David E. 1980. "An Examination of Population-Growth-Managing Communities." *Policy Studies Journal* 9 (3): 414–27.

———. 1984. *The Suburban Squeeze: Land Conversion and Regulation in the San Francisco Bay Area*. Los Angeles: University of California Press.

Dowall, David E., and John D. Landis. 1982. "Land-Use Controls and Housing Costs: An Examination of San Francisco Bay Area Communities." *Journal of the American Real Estate and Urban Economics Association* 10: 67–93.

Downs, Anthony. 1992. "Regulatory Barriers to Affordable Housing." *Journal of the American Planning Association* 58 (4): 419–22.

———. 1994. *New Visions for Metropolitan America*. Brookings.

———. 2001a. "What Does 'Smart Growth' Really Mean?" *Planning* (April): 67, 20–25.

———. 2001b. *"Have Housing Prices Risen Faster in Portland than Elsewhere?"* Working paper. Brookings Institution.

———. 2002. "Have Housing Prices Risen Faster in Portland than Elsewhere?" *Housing Policy Debate* 13 (1): 7–31.

Dubbink, David. 1984. "I'll Have My Town Medium-Rural, Please." *Journal of the American Planning Association* 50 (4): 406–18.

Dubin, Jeffrey A., D. Roderick Kiewiet, and Charles Noussair. 1992. "Voting on Growth Control Measures: Preferences and Strategies." *Economics and Politics* 4 (2): 191–213.

Ellickson, Robert C. 1973. "Alternatives to Zoning: Covenants, Nuisance Rules, and Fines as Land Use Controls." *University of Chicago Law Review* 40 (3): 681–782.

Elliott, Michael. 1981. "The Impact of Growth Control Regulations on Housing Prices in California." *Journal of the American Real Estate and Urban Economics Association* 9: 115–33.

Eppli, Mark J., and Charles C. Tu. 1999. *Valuing the New Urbanism: The Impact of the New Urbanism on Prices of Single-Family Homes*. Washington: Urban Land Institute.

Ervin, David E., and others. 1977. *Land Use Control: The Economic and Political Effects*. New York: Ballinger.

Evans, A. W. 1991. "Rabbit Hutches on Postage Stamps: Planning, Development, and Political Economy." *Urban Studies* 28 (6): 853–70.

Fischel, William. 1989. *Do Growth Controls Matter? A Review of Empirical Evidence on the Effectiveness and Efficiency of Local Government Land Use Regulation*. Cambridge, Mass.: Lincoln Institute of Land Policy.

———. 1995. *Regulatory Takings: Law, Economics, and Politics*. Harvard University Press.

———. 1999. "Does the American Way of Zoning Cause the Suburbs of Metropolitan Areas to Be Too Spread Out?" In *Governance and Opportunity in Metropolitan America*, edited by Alan Altshuler and others. Washington: National Academy Press.

———. 2001. *The Homevoter Hypothesis: How Home Values Influence Local Government Taxation, School Finance, and Land-Use Policy*. Harvard University Press.

Follain, James R., Jr. 1979. "The Price Elasticity of the Long-Run Supply of New Housing Construction." *Land Economics* 55 (2): 190–99.

Frey, William H., and Reynolds Farley. 1996. "Latino, Asian, and Black Segregation in U.S. Metropolitan Areas: Are Multiethnic Metros Different?" *Demography* 33 (1): 35–50.

Frieden, Bernard. 1979. *The Environmental Protection Hustle.* MIT Press.

Fulton, William B., Madelyn Glickfeld, and Ned Levine. 1996. "Home Rule: Local Growth . . . Regional Consequences." Ventura, Calif.: Solimar Research Group.

Glaeser, Edward, and Joseph Gyourko. 2002. "The Impact of Zoning on Housing Affordability." Discussion Paper 1948. Harvard Institute of Economic Research (March).

Gleeson, Michael E. 1979. "Effects of an Urban Growth Management System on Land Values." *Land Economics* 55 (3): 350–65.

Glickfeld, Madelyn, and Ned Levine. 1992. *Regional Growth . . . Local Reaction: The Enactment and Effects of Local Growth Control Measures in California.* Cambridge, Mass.: Lincoln Institute of Land Policy.

Gotham, Kevin Fox. 2000. "Urban Space, Restrictive Covenants and the Origins of Racial Residential Segregation in a U.S. City, 1900–50." *International Journal of Urban and Regional Research* 24 (3): 616–33.

Gottdiener, Mark, and Max Neiman. 1981. "Characteristics of Support for Local Growth Control." *Urban Affairs Quarterly* 17 (1): 55–73.

Green, Richard K. 1999. "Land Use Regulation and the Price of Housing in a Suburban Wisconsin County." *Journal of Housing Economics* 8 (2): 144–59.

Grieson, Ronald E., and James R. White. 1981. "The Effects of Zoning on Structure and Land Markets." *Journal of Urban Economics* 10 (November): 271–85.

Gruen, Gruen, and Associates. 1977. *Effects of Regulation on Housing Costs: Two Case Studies.* Washington: Urban Land Institute.

Guidry, Krisandra A., James D. Shilling, and C. F. Sirmans. 1991. "An Econometric Analysis of Variation in Urban Residential Land Prices and the Adoption of Land-Use Controls." Working Paper. Madison: University of Wisconsin Center for Urban Land Economics.

Haar, Charles M. 1996. *Suburbs under Siege: Race, Space, and Audacious Judges.* Princeton University Press.

Hannah, Lawrence, Kyung-Hwan Kim, and Edwin S. Mills. 1993. "Land Use Controls and Housing Prices in Korea." *Urban Studies* 30 (February): 147–56.

Hanushek, Eric A., and John M. Quigley. 1980. "What Is the Price Elasticity of Housing Demand?" *Review of Economics and Statistics* 62 (3): 449–54.

Jackson, Kenneth. 1985. *Crabgrass Frontier: The Suburbanization of the United States.* Oxford University Press.

Juergensmeyer, Julian Conrad, and Thomas E. Roberts. 1998. *Land Use Planning and Control Law.* St. Paul, Minn.: West Publishing.

Kalinoski, Leah. 2001. *Smart Growth for Neighborhoods: Affordable Housing and Regional Vision.* Washington: National Neighborhood Coalition.

Katz, Lawrence, and Kenneth T. Rosen. 1987. "The Interjurisdictional Effects of Growth Controls on Housing Prices." *Journal of Law and Economics* 30 (1): 146–60.

Kirp, David L., John P. Dwyer, and Larry A. Rosenthal. 1995. *Our Town: Race, Housing, and the Soul of Suburbia.* Rutgers University Press.

Knaap, Gerrit J. 1985. "The Price Effects of Urban Growth Boundaries in Metropolitan Portland, Oregon." *Land Economics* 61 (1): 26–35.

————. 1998. "The Determinants of Residential Property Values: Implications for Metropolitan Planning." *Journal of Planning Literature* 12 (3): 267–82.

————. 2000. "The Urban Growth Boundary in Metropolitan Portland, Oregon: Research, Rhetoric, and Reality." American Planning Association (www.metroregion.org/growth/ugbursa/apa_article.html [July 2001]).

Knaap, Gerrit J., and Arthur C. Nelson. 1992. *The Regulated Landscape: Lessons on State Land Use Planning from Oregon.* Lincoln Institute of Land Policy.

Landis, John D. 1986. "Land Regulation and the Price of New Housing." *Journal of the American Planning Association* (Winter): 9–21.

————. 1992. "Do Growth Controls Matter? A New Assessment." *Journal of the American Planning Association* 58 (4) : 489–508.

Lang, Robert E. 2004. "Valuing the Suburbs: Why Some 'Improvements' Lower Home Values." *Opolis: An International Journal of Suburban Studies* 1 (1) (forthcoming).

Lang, Robert E., James W. Hughes, and Karen A. Danielsen. 1997. "Targeting the Suburban Urbanites: Marketing Central City Housing." *Housing Policy Debate* 8 (2): 437–70.

Levine, Ned. 1999. "The Effect of Local Growth Controls on Regional Housing Production and Population Redistribution in California." *Urban Studies* 36 (12): 2047–68.

Lorentz, Amalia, and Kirsten Shaw. 2000. "Are You Ready to Bet on Smart Growth?" *Planning* 66 (1): 4–9.

Lowry, Ira S., and Bruce W. Ferguson. 1992. *Development Regulation and Housing Affordability.* Washington: Urban Land Institute.

Luger, Michael I., and Kenneth Temkin. 2000. *Red Tape and Housing Costs: How Regulation Affects New Residential Development.* New Brunswick, N.J.: Center for Urban Policy Research.

Malpezzi, Stephen. 1996. "Housing Prices, Externalities, and Regulation in U.S. Metropolitan Areas." *Journal of Housing Research* 7 (2): 209–41.

Massey, Douglas S., and Nancy A. Denton. 1993. *American Apartheid: Segregation and the Making of the Underclass.* Harvard University Press.

Mayo, Stephen K. 1981. "Theory and Estimation in the Economics of Housing Demand." *Journal of Urban Economics* 10 (1): 95–116.

Mayo, Stephen, and Stephen Sheppard. 1996. "Housing Supply under Rapid Economic Growth and Varying Regulatory Stringency: An International Comparison." *Journal of Housing Economics* 5 (3): 274–89.

Miller, Thomas I. 1986. "Must Growth Restrictions Eliminate Moderate-Priced Housing?" *Journal of the American Planning Association* (Summer): 319–25.

Muth, Richard F. 1960. "The Demand for Non-Farm Housing." In *The Demand for Durable Goods,* edited by Arnold C. Harberger. University of Chicago Press.

Myers, Dowell, and Elizabeth Gearin. 2001. "Current Preferences and Future Demand for Denser Residential Development." *Housing Policy Debate* 12 (4): 633–64.

National Association of Home Builders. 2001. *Housing Opportunity Index.*

Nelson, Arthur C. 1985. "Demand, Segmentation, and Timing Effects of an Urban Containment Program on Urban Fringe Land Values." *Urban Studies* 52 (2): 439–43.

————. 1986. "Using Land Markets to Evaluate Urban Containment Programs." *Journal of the American Planning Association* (Spring): 156–71.

————. 1999. "Comparing States with and without Growth Management: Analysis Based on Indicators with Policy Implications." *Land Use Policy* 16: 121–27.

————. 2001. "How Do You Know Smart Growth When You See It?" In *Smart Growth: Form and Consequences*, edited by Terry Szold and Armando Carbonelle. MIT Press and Lincoln Institute of Land Policy.

Nelson, Arthur C., and Kenneth J. Dueker. 1990. "The Exurbanization of America." *Journal of Planning Education and Research* 9 (2): 91–100.

Nelson, Arthur C., and J. B. Duncan. 1995. *Growth Management Principles and Practices*. Chicago: American Planning Association.

Nelson, Arthur C., John Genereux, and Michelle Genereux. 1992. "Price Effects of Landfills on House Values." *Land Economics* 88 (November): 359–65.

Nelson, Arthur C., and Thomas W. Sánchez. 1999. "Debunking the Exurban Myth: A Comparison of Suburban Households." *Housing Policy Debate* 10 (3): 689–709.

Ohls, James C., Richard C. Weisburg, and Michelle White. 1974. "The Effect of Zoning on Land Values." *Journal of Urban Economics* 1 (October): 428–44.

Pendall, Rolf. 1995. "Residential Growth Controls and Racial and Ethnic Diversity: Making and Breaking the Chain of Exclusion." Ph.D. dissertation, University of California at Berkeley.

————. 1999. "Do Land-Use Controls Cause Sprawl?" *Environment and Planning B: Planning and Design* 26 (4): 555–71.

————. 2000. "Local Land Use Regulation and the Chain of Exclusion." *Journal of the American Planning Association* 66 (2): 125–42.

Phillips, Justin, and Eben Goodstein. 2000. "Growth Management and Housing Prices: The Case of Portland, Oregon." *Contemporary Economic Policy* 18 (3): 334–44.

Pollakowski, Henry O., and Susan Wachter. 1990. "The Effects of Land-Use Constraints on Housing Prices." *Land Economics* 66 (3): 315–24.

Porter, Douglas R. 1992. "Issues in State and Regional Growth Management." In *State and Regional Initiatives for Managing Development*, edited by Douglas R. Porter. Washington: Urban Land Institute.

————. 1997. *Managing Growth in America's Communities*. Washington: Island Press.

Protash, William, and Mark Baldassare. 1983. "Growth Policies and Community Status: A Test and Modification of Logan's Theory." *Urban Affairs Review* 18 (3): 397–412.

Regional Plan Association. 2003. "Spotlight on the Region" 2 (2) (www.rpa.org/pdf/Spotlight20.pdf [February 12, 2004]).

Rolleston, Barbara Sherman. 1987. "Determinants of Restrictive Suburban Zoning: An Empirical Analysis." *Journal of Urban Economics* 21 (1): 1–21.

Rose, Louis A. 1989a. "Topographical Constraints and Urban Land Supply Indexes." *Journal of Urban Economics* 26 (3): 335–47.

————. 1989b. "Urban Land Supply: Natural and Contrived Restrictions." *Journal of Urban Economics* 25 (3): 325–45.

Rosen, Kenneth T., and Lawrence F. Katz. 1981. "Growth Management and Land Use Controls: The San Francisco Bay Area Experience." *Journal of the American Real Estate and Urban Economics Association* 9 (3): 321–43.

Rosenbaum, Nelson. 1978. "Growth and Its Discontents: Origins of Local Population Controls." In *The Policy Cycle*, edited by Judith V. May and Aaron B. Wildavsky. Sage.

Savageau, David, and Geoffrey Loftus. 1997. *Places Rated Almanac*. Macmillan.

Schwartz, Seymour I., David E. Hansen, and Richard Green. 1981. "Suburban Growth Controls and the Price of New Housing." *Journal of Environmental Economics and Management* 8: 303–20.

————. 1984. "The Effect of Growth Control on the Production of Moderate-Priced Housing." *Land Economics* 60 (1): 110–14.

Segal, David, and Philip Srinivasan. 1985. "The Impact of Suburban Growth Restrictions on U.S. Residential Land Value." *Urban Geography* 6 (1): 14–26.

Seidel, Stephen R. 1978. *Housing Costs and Government Regulations: Confronting the Regulatory Maze.* New Brunswick, N.J.: Center for Urban Policy Research.

Silver, Christopher. 1997. "The Racial Origins of Zoning in American Cities." In *Urban Planning and the African American Community: In the Shadows*, edited by June Manning Thomas and Marsha Ritzdorf. Sage.

Sirmans, G. Stacy, and David A. Macpherson. 2003. "The Value of Housing Characteristics." Washington: National Association of Realtors (December).

Sohmer, Rebecca R., and Robert E. Lang. 2003. "Downtown Rebound." In *Redefining Cities and Suburbs: Evidence from Census 2000*, edited by Bruce Katz and Robert E. Lang, 63–74. Brookings.

South, Scott J., and Kyle D. Crowder. 1998. "Leaving the 'Hood: Residential Mobility between Black, White, and Integrated Neighborhoods." *American Sociological Review* 63 (1): 17–26.

Stone, Michael E. 1993. *Shelter Poverty: New Ideas on Housing Affordability.* Philadelphia: Temple University Press.

Titman, Sheridan. 1985. "Urban Land Prices under Uncertainty." *American Economic Review* 75 (3): 505–14.

U.S. Census Bureau. 2000. Money Income in the United States, 1999.

U.S. Bureau of Labor Statistics. 2001. *Consumer Expenditure Survey.*

Voith, Richard. 1996. "The Suburban Housing Market: The Effects of City and Suburban Job Growth." *Federal Reserve Bank of Philadelphia Business Review* (November): 13–25.

Warner, Kee, and Harvey Molotch. 1992. "Growth Control: Inner Workings and External Effects." CPS Report. Berkeley: California Policy Seminar.

Weiss, Marc A. 1987. *The Rise of the Community Builders.* Columbia University Press.

Zorn, Peter M., David E. Hansen, and Seymour I. Schwartz. 1986. "Mitigating the Price Effects of Growth Control: A Case Study of Davis, California." *Land Economics* 62 (1): 46–57.

5

GEORGE C. GALSTER

The Effects of Affordable
and Multifamily Housing
on Market Values
of Nearby Homes

Tнеre are two distinct dimensions involving the relationship
between so-called growth management policies for developing metropolitan areas and housing prices in these areas. At the regional scale, the issue
is whether changes in the elasticity of housing supply or the level or nature
of housing demands associated with growth management policies ratchets up
the overall level of housing prices. At the neighborhood scale, the issue is
whether the types of housing developments typically associated with growth
management policies—higher density, multifamily dwellings, and "affordable" residences set aside for lower-income and special needs households—
adversely affect the prices of single-family homes nearby.

This chapter focuses on the second issue. It reviews the voluminous statistical literature on the home price impacts of affordable and multifamily
housing and attempts to extract common themes and findings. A typology is
employed that categorizes impacts according to building type (single family
or multifamily), tenure (owner or renter occupied), clientele (market rate,
low income, or special needs) and development technique (new construction
or rehabilitation). Unlike many reviews that do not challenge the validity or
accuracy of studies' conclusions, however, this chapter proceeds from a

The author gratefully acknowledges the helpful comments of Ingrid Ellen, William Fischel,
Jill Khadduri, and anonymous reviewers on an earlier draft, and the research assistance of Jackie
Cutsinger.

methodological foundation on which a critique of extant studies is made. I argue that findings from the vast majority of studies in this field must be heavily discounted because they suffer from serious methodological weaknesses. The handful of recent studies that overcome these weaknesses reveal an emerging consensus: the direction and magnitude of home price impacts are contingent on concentration, context, and type of the development.

Neighborhood externalities are of central importance to the broader discussion of growth management in several ways. First and most obviously, growth management proposals often involve increasing density of suburbs by including multifamily buildings in new developments and infill sites in existing neighborhoods. These proposals frequently specify that a minimum share of these new dwellings be subsidized to make them more affordable. Even in the absence of such specifications, middle-quality apartments may offer opportunities for low-income tenants holding housing vouchers. Fears about whether such multifamily and subsidized dwellings harm residential property values nearby is a root of local opposition, conventionally termed the "not in my backyard" (NIMBY) effect.[1] Second, proposals for managing growth typically encourage the revitalization of underutilized sites in core urban areas, often with large-scale rehabilitation and construction efforts. The externalities associated with such efforts are also crucial to ascertain if one is to obtain a full accounting of their social benefits.[2]

Some comments on the terminology in this chapter are in order. "Affordable housing" means housing that is subsidized in its development or operation to make it sell or rent for less than its market value. When appropriate, variants of affordable housing will be identified, such as site-based (newly constructed or rehabilitated structures) or tenant-based assistance (vouchers); generic lower-income or special needs programs (group living quarters for the mentally ill, disabled, recovering substance abusers, nonviolent offenders, frail elderly, and others); and ownership or rental programs.[3] "Multifamily housing" means any structure types that are not single-family occupied; distinctions among numbers of units in multifamily structures or the ownership status or occupant incomes of such units will be made when

---

1. Galster and others (2003).

2. Quercia and Galster (1997).

3. Note that I do not consider in this chapter housing that may command low prices or rents because it offers minimal quantity or quality of housing services. Such dwellings typically are supplied in U.S. housing markets by downgrading associated with filtering and neighborhood decline (Rothenberg and others [1991]), a process quite distinct from the one discussed in this chapter.

necessary.[4] "Homes" hereafter means single-family, owner-occupied dwellings.

Precision in terminology is called for because each of the studies reviewed focuses on a particular sort of housing as a potential generator of externalities, so generalizations must be made rarely. Moreover, there is much less diversity in the types of housing analyzed in the extant literature than one would wish: most studies have focused on subsidized, multifamily housing that is occupied by special needs households or generic low-income households. There is little guidance about how the market may react to the same tenants housed in a subsidized single-family housing context or in a private rental context where the unit is "affordable" only because of weak neighborhood conditions or low structural quality. Unfortunately, the literature is not yet rich enough to permit us to disentangle precisely the degree to which externalities associated with affordable and multifamily dwellings may be emanating from the characteristics of the structures, management, or tenants. Thus it would not be wise, for example, to extend the findings reported here to how neighboring home prices are related to "affordable" housing consisting not of subsidized units but instead of unsubsidized units that are priced cheaply because of modest scale, amenities, and maintenance.

Methodological Challenges

The fundamental challenges facing investigators of the home price impacts of affordable and multifamily housing are twofold. First, the analyst must carefully identify the magnitude of the statistical relationship between proximity to an affordable or multifamily housing site and a single-family home's sales price, while controlling for other factors that may blur the precise measurement of this relationship. Second, the analyst's approach must establish a plausible case that the affordable or multifamily housing is the cause of any measured relationship with proximate prices, instead of such housing being sited systematically in neighborhoods with preexisting price idiosyncrasies that would attract these developments. This section describes how researchers have tried to meet these challenges and, unfortunately, typically fallen short. It is crucial to understand the comparative strengths and weak-

---

4. Single-family units include detached, attached, and planned-unit developments.

nesses of the different methods so the accuracy of their conclusions can be assessed.

Three Traditional Approaches

The three traditional approaches to measuring home price impacts from nearby activities or land uses can be called control area, pre/post, and cross sectional. Though each possesses unique weaknesses, they also share some in common.

The control area approach selects neighborhoods that are otherwise comparable to ones that have affordable or multifamily housing located within them and then compares home price levels or trends in both sets.[5] The fundamental challenge is identifying areas that are, indeed, identical in all respects save for the affordable or multifamily housing and that have no other forces or land developments that differentially affect them subsequent to the development of such housing. Indeed, this challenge may be insurmountable, given the myriad attributes composing the neighborhood environment. Moreover, developers or occupants of affordable and multifamily dwellings may choose certain neighborhoods precisely because they have attributes that are particularly attractive for their purposes.

The pre/post approach compares levels or trends in home prices in the same neighborhoods between periods preceding and then succeeding the introduction of an affordable or multifamily housing development.[6] The difficulty is ensuring that there are no additional forces that may affect home prices in the target neighborhood, such as macroeconomic or local housing submarket pressures, and are coincident with opening the development of interest. For example, the entire metropolitan area's housing market may be in an era of deflationary prices, whereupon there will be a tendency for any pre/post comparison of prices in any neighborhood to show a secular trend

5. For illustrations, see Nourse (1963); Schafer (1972); DeSalvo (1974); Dear (1977); Wolpert (1978); Boeckh, Dear, and Taylor (1980); Lauber (1986); Iglhaut (1988); William Berry and Company (1988); Boydell, Trainor and Pierri (1989).

6. The comparison often is accomplished with the aid of multivariate statistical procedures to control for differences in the properties being sold pre- and postannouncement of the site. For illustrations see Wagner and Mitchell (1980); Lindauer, Tungt, and O'Donnell (1980); Rabiega, Lin, and Robinson (1984); Ryan and Coyne (1985); District of Columbia Association for Retarded Citizens (1987); Iglhaut (1988); Puryear (1989); and Boydell, Trainor, and Pierri (1989).

of decline, regardless of the development of a nearby affordable or multi-family housing site.

The cross-sectional approach has many variants, but typically it tries to ascertain through multiple regression whether there is an independent, cross-sectional variation in home prices that can be associated with proximity to affordable or multifamily housing sites already in operation. Virtually all previous cross-sectional econometric studies have failed to control for the idiosyncratic characteristics of the neighborhood that immediately surrounds (say, within a radius of a quarter mile) but is unrelated to the housing site whose impact is of interest.[7] Instead, most settle for variables that measure characteristics of the encompassing census tract, which may be poor proxies for conditions in the area near the supportive site. Thus, if these omitted, nearby-neighborhood variables were correlated with the location of the housing of interest, apparently statistically significant proximity effects might erroneously be attributed to the latter instead of the former.

This criticism takes on additional importance when one considers a fundamental shortcoming of all three previous approaches: they do not convincingly provide evidence that can be used to distinguish the direction of causation between patterns of single-family home values and the siting of affordable or multifamily housing.[8] Put differently, they cannot ascertain whether the affordable or multifamily housing sites lead to home price declines in the proximate neighborhood or whether these sites are systematically located in areas having home prices that are already low, or expected to depreciate in the future, for reasons unrelated to the new housing.[9]

The latter causal pattern is likely because of the following selection biases related to numerous possible, not mutually exclusive, behaviors of the developers and occupants of the affordable or multifamily housing and the nature of the local real estate market:[10]

—The public authority or nonprofit organization developing affordable housing will be encouraged to conserve its scare resources by acquiring the

7. For example, one might specify a series of localized fixed-effect dummy variables.

8. Lyons and Loveridge (1993) also discuss this problem. Similar methodological critiques are provided by Freeman and Botein, though the emphasis and scope of criticisms are somewhat different (2002).

9. The econometric problems associated with selection bias can of course be viewed as equivalent to an omitted variables problem; Heckman (1979). Thus the two main criticisms levied here can be thought of as opposite sides of the same coin.

10. For a thorough discussion of selection biases associated with the measurement of neighborhood effects, see Haurin, Dietz and Weinberg (2003).

least expensive properties (vacant land for building or existing structures for rehab) available.

—The public authority developing affordable housing may wish to use land that it already owns through property tax reversion or otherwise target the "neediest" areas.[11]

—If new construction of affordable and multifamily housing is contemplated, the location of vacant, sufficiently scaled, appropriately zoned parcels will likely be constraining on choices; neighborhoods with mixed-use or higher-density zoning are likely to have lower home values.

—If rehabilitation of structures for use as affordable housing is contemplated, minimization of expected lifetime development costs of the structure implies choices of certain building types that likely are concentrated in certain types of lower-valued neighborhoods.[12]

—Developers of affordable and multifamily housing might search in lower-value areas because they expect less public opposition there.[13]

—In the case of the Housing Opportunity Program (formerly Section 8) of affordable housing through tenant subsidies in existing apartments, both landlords and participating households would disproportionately select lower-priced neighborhoods because, respectively, they cannot otherwise obtain fair market rents for their apartments, and they can free up more of their income for nonhousing consumption, inasmuch as the value of their voucher is fixed.[14]

All these reasons imply that the particular neighborhoods in which affordable and multifamily housing is developed are not likely to be representative ones, but rather will be biased toward ones with lower or declining property values, for whatever reasons. This implication has been supported by a host of empirical studies.[15] This means statistically that there will likely be a negative correlation between home prices and proximate affordable or multifamily housing, but the relationship may well be produced by reverse causation. The cross-sectional approach can measure this negative correlation but cannot be used reliably to support inferences about causation.

11. Ellen and others (2001).

12. Newman and others (1997).

13. Pendall (1999).

14. Goering and others (1995); Pollock and Rutkowski (1998); Turner, Popkin, and Cunningham (2000).

15. See Galster and others (1999, 2000); Galster, Tatian and Smith (1999); Santiago, Galster, and Tatian (2001); Johnson and Bednarz (2002); Ellen and others. (2001); Schill and others (2002); Schwartz and others (2002); Cummings, DiPasquale, and Kahn (2002), Galster, Tatian, and Pettit (2004).

The Difference in Differences Approach

In 1998 I developed a new empirical approach for measuring impacts on home prices from various sorts of affordable housing.[16] Subsequently, the basic approach was enhanced in several valuable ways by others.[17] This approach measures the level and trend in home prices in two sorts of neighborhoods during two periods: in neighborhoods surrounding affordable or multifamily housing before and after it was developed, and in otherwise similar neighborhoods where no affordable or multifamily housing was developed, for the same years as above. The approach then compares home prices after such housing of interest was developed to what they would have been had predevelopment trends in the neighborhood persisted, adjusting for any areawide changes in trends occurring during the postdevelopment period (as evinced by neighborhoods where no such housing was developed). Were actual home prices to differ from the counterfactual prices, impact would be deduced. Ellen and others equivalently framed this comparison in terms of "difference in differences": the difference between target and control neighborhoods' price differences in the predevelopment and postdevelopment periods.[18] Were these differences to vary between pre- and postdevelopment periods, impact would be deduced.

This difference in differences approach overcomes the shortcomings of prior approaches as follows. By measuring both level and trend of home prices in a small-scale surrounding area before an affordable or multifamily development is present, this method controls for the idiosyncratic local neighborhood characteristics that are reflected in these prices.[19] By relating postdevelopment home price trends and levels in the affected neighborhood nearby to those in larger, unaffected geographic areas, it controls for forces having areawide effects, such as metropolitanwide changes in the economy. By doing both, the model plausibly distinguishes the self-selection of affordable and multifamily housing into weak neighborhood submarkets from the

16. Galster and others (1999; 2000). The emergence of Geographic Information Systems (GIS) and longitudinal, geocoded information about home sales made it much easier to implement this new approach.

17. Johnson and Bednarz (2002); Ellen and others (2001); Schill and others (2002); Schwartz and others (2002).

18. Ellen and others (2001).

19. The studies reported typically measure potential impacts within several local neighborhood areas defined by concentric rings centered on the assisted housing site; the largest ring typically has a radius of 2,000 feet, the smallest, 500 feet. Other variants employ price gradients centered on the development of interest. Johnson and Bednarz (2002); Schwartz and others (2002).

ultimate consequences of such housing on these neighborhoods. In other words, by controlling what would have happened in the neighborhood had preaffordable housing development trends persisted (adjusting for areawide changes that would have altered all neighborhood home price trends), the method measures correlations that can be convincingly used to draw causal inferences of effects attributable to the new development.

Figure 5-1 illustrates several hypothetical alternatives, which should help one gain a better intuitive grasp of what this difference in differences approach does. The method essentially estimates home price trends and levels in two sorts of neighborhoods within the metro area under investigation: one in the vicinity of affordable or multifamily housing (variants of the dashed line) and other, control neighborhoods without such housing (solid line).

The approach argues that the correct test of whether the development had an effect is whether there is a pre/post break in the trend in the proximate-impact neighborhood, which is different than what was observed in the other, control areas of the metropolitan housing market. Thus were we to estimate line A-A'-A", this would signify no impact, because the price trend break after the housing of interest opened mirrored the trend break observed in control neighborhoods in the metro area (line C-C'-C").[20] However, if prices in the impact neighborhood after the housing of interest opened were to shift up to a higher level (A-A'-D'-D") or increase more rapidly than the control area trends (A-A'-D'''), this would signify a positive impact.[21] Conversely, if prices in the impact neighborhood after the housing of interest opened were to shift down to a lower level (A-A'-B'-B") or increase less rapidly (decrease more rapidly) than the control area trends (A-A'-B), this would signify a negative impact.[22]

Contrast these conclusions to those following from the three traditional approaches. Were price profiles A-A'-B or A-A'-A" to be observed, the pre/post approach would have erroneously deduced a positive impact because prices (trends or average levels) were higher after the development. Were any of the price profiles shown actually manifested, the cross-sectional approach would have erroneously deduced a negative impact because the observed prices were lower near areas where affordable or multifamily housing opened

20. Or, expressed equivalently, the postdevelopment difference C"-A" is unchanged from the predevelopment difference C'-A'.
21. Or, expressed equivalently, the postdevelopment difference C"-D" (or C"-D''') is smaller than the predevelopment difference C'-A'.
22. Or, expressed equivalently, the postdevelopment difference C"-B (or C"-B") is smaller than the predevelopment difference C'-A'.

Figure 5-1. *Potential Types of Home Price Impacts from Affordable and Multifamily Housing*

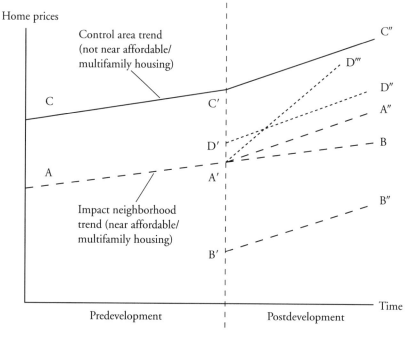

Note: Positive impact, absolute increase in trend: A-A'-D‴
       Positive impact, absolute upward shift in level: A-A'-D'-D″
       No impact, no relative change in trend from citywide trend: A-A'-A″
       Negative impact, relative decrease in trend: A-A'-B
       Negative impact, absolute downward shift in level: A-A'-B'-B″

than elsewhere. The traditional control area approach could not be operationalized in this scenario because of the inability to match impact areas having the developments of interest with otherwise identical (for example, same price) areas.

The foregoing presentation of the difference in differences approach notes the importance of measuring levels and trends in prices before and after a development of interest. This is more than a minor technicality. There are three examples in the literature of approaches similar to the one advocated here, but they only contrast the pre- and (area-adjusted) postdevelopment

Figure 5-2. *Potential Types of Home Price Impacts from Affordable and Multifamily Housing (Pre/Post Levels of Prices Method)*

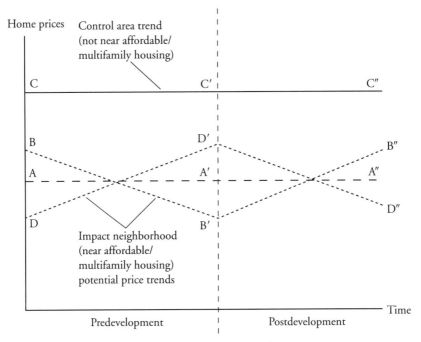

Note: Positive impact, absolute increase in trend: B-B'-B"
 Negative impact, absolute decrease in trend: D-D'-D"

average levels of home prices in the impact neighborhoods.[23] This approach offers a substantial improvement over the three traditional approaches in confronting the omitted variables and causation challenges, but nevertheless it falls short. Comparisons of price levels alone may obscure significantly different price trends pre- and postdevelopment, thereby leading to erroneous conclusions. The argument is illustrated in figure 5-2.

Assume for simplicity that during the period in question there is no change in home prices in control areas (line C-C'-C"). But suppose that we also observe no change in the average level of prices in target neighborhoods

23. Galster and Williams (1994); Briggs, Darden, and Aidala (1999); Cummings, DiPasquale, and Kahn (2002).

proximate to developments of interest (that is, average A-A′ identical to average A′-A″). One might be tempted to deduce no impact from the development, but such a conclusion might be seriously in error. As figure 5-2 illustrates, such a comparison might well overlook pre- and postdevelopment trend shifts suggesting either strong positive (B-B′-B″) or negative (D-D′-D″) impacts.

To conclude, the difference in differences method is not simply different from earlier approaches, it provides a more accurate and precise measure of what arguably can be claimed as the causal impact. The traditional approaches essentially produce a result such as, "Within X feet of an affordable housing development, home prices are $Y different (from other neighborhoods or from what they used to be here), though we can not be sure what other factors (areawide or within X feet) may also be affecting these prices or whether these differences were already present before the development occurred." The difference in differences approach produces a result such as, "Within X feet of an affordable housing development, home prices are $Y different from what they would have been had the development not occurred." As a consequence, the following review pays scant attention to studies employing the traditional approaches, instead placing most credence on those employing the difference in differences approach.

Early Research on Home Price Impacts

Through the 1980s, at least a dozen scholarly studies investigated whether various forms of subsidized housing for low-income households generate a negative impact on neighboring single-family home prices.[24] The preponderant conclusion reached by these studies was that there was no sizable or statistically significant impact, while a few studies even concluded that there was a positive impact. For example, Nourse found that prices rose faster in St. Louis neighborhoods surrounding newly built, large-scale public housing than in control neighborhoods. De Salvo concluded that developing Mitchell-Lama apartment complexes led to much faster rates of appreciation in the low-moderate quality submarkets in which they were located compared with control areas. Warren, Aduddell, and Tatalovich claimed that positive externalities associated with privately owned, federally subsidized apart-

---

24. See Matulef (1988); Martinez (1988); Puryear (1989) for reviews.

ment complexes resulted in higher median home prices in the Chicago census tracts where they were located.[25]

Only two studies of this period even hinted at dissension, and both could be convincingly discounted on methodological grounds. Warren, Aduddell, and Tatalovich found that in Chicago census tracts with more than one-third poor households and two-thirds minority households, the presence of 30 percent or more of the housing stock consisting of public housing units proved detrimental to home prices. Unfortunately, this study suffers from serious omitted variables bias and aggregation bias (inasmuch as census tract median home prices are employed as the dependent variable). Guy, Hysom, and Ruth found that new Fairfax County townhouse clusters' prices were directly related to distance from two privately owned, mixed-income apartment complexes subsidized by the federal Below-Market Interest Rate (BMIR) program. These conclusions can be challenged because there is no way to distinguish the effects of low-income neighbors from those of a large-scale apartment building nearby (since the two are perfectly collinear), and there is a strong association between distance from the BMIR developments and the median income of the census tract.[26]

During the 1990s, however, the conventional wisdom of no impact was shaken by several regression-based studies employing the cross-sectional approach, which emphasized the contextuality of impacts. These studies concluded that, depending on circumstances and kinds of developers and developments, subsidized housing for low-income households can create positive, negative, or minimal effects on nearby home prices.

Cummings and Landis studied six multifamily developments built by the San Francisco Bay-area nonprofit, BRIDGE. Although they found no impacts on home price from three developments and positive impacts from two, one was claimed to lower sales prices within a half mile by $49,519.[27]

Goetz, Lam, and Heitlinger studied home prices near several types of subsidized, multifamily rental housing developments in Minneapolis. They concluded that each 100 feet closer proximity to a Minneapolis Community Development Corporation's subsidized rental development was associated with higher prices of $86 per home, but each 100 feet closer to a subsidized rental development run by a private, for-profit owner (such as site-based Section 8) was associated with lower prices of $82 per home.[28]

25. Nourse (1963); De Salvo (1974); Warren, Aduddell, and Tatalovich (1983).
26. Warren, Aduddell, and Tatalovich (1983); Guy, Husom, and Ruth (1985).
27. Cummings and Landis (1993).
28. Goetz, Lam, and Heitlinger (1996).

Lyons and Loveridge investigated the impacts of 120 locations where tenants subsidized by a variety of federal programs resided in St. Paul, Minnesota. They found that each additional subsidized tenant residing within one-quarter mile of a single-family home was correlated with a reduction in the assessed value of that home by a statistically significant $21; within two miles the corresponding figure was $5. Adding an additional proximate site where one or more subsidized tenants lived was correlated with a reduction in the assessed property values of $1,585 if the sites were located within one-quarter mile. Moreover, this reduction in assessed value fell with distance from subsidized site until it reached $609 if the sites were within two miles.[29]

Lyons and Loveridge also disaggregated the number of subsidized units by program type at various distances from the home being assessed and found that the statistically significant relationships ranged from negative to positive. Specifically, within a quarter mile, each additional unit in a Section 8, site-based assisted complex was associated with a lower assessed value of $50 per home; the comparable figure for Section 202 complex units for the elderly was $200. Within a half mile, each unit in a Section 221d(3) subsidized apartment complex was associated with a higher assessed value of $603 per home and, surprisingly, the corresponding figure for public housing units was $19. The authors found no statistically significant relationship between the locations of Section 8 tenants holding certificates or vouchers in the sample and assessed values at any distance from them ranging from 300 feet to two miles. All the statistically significant coefficients for subsidized units or tenant-based assistance sites showed monotonically decreasing magnitudes at progressively larger radii measured from the given assessed value. Moreover, coefficients for the squared values of the number of subsidized units or sites consistently showed diminishing marginal impacts.

Lee, Culhane, and Wachter examined various kinds of assisted housing in Philadelphia and single-family homes sales occurring within one-eighth and one-fourth mile of them during the 1989–91 period. Results indicated a remarkable variation in correlation according to subsidized housing program. Home prices were 9.4 percent lower within one-eighth mile of any conventional public housing site, 0.8 percent lower for each additional scattered public housing unit, 0.2 percent higher for each additional FHA-assisted unit, 0.1 percent higher for each additional new or rehabilitated Section 8 site-assisted unit; 0.5 percent lower for each additional Section 8 certificate or voucher household, and 0.1 percent lower for each additional low-income

29. Lyons and Loveridge (1993).

housing tax credit unit. When proximity was measured at a quarter-mile distance, the magnitude of the foregoing coefficients consistently dropped by roughly half.[30]

Briggs, Darden, and Aidala examined the court-ordered construction of small-scale public housing complexes scattered in middle-class neighborhoods of Yonkers, New York. They employed a spatial fixed-effects regression specification wherein dummy variables denoted the idiosyncratic level of home prices associated with the neighborhood within a certain distance from a public housing site (future or current). A corresponding set of dummy variables denoted whether these price levels differed significantly after the public housing was announced or began operation. This second set provided their test for impact. They observed no price impacts at either stage. Though this approach offers advantages over the conventional cross-sectional approach, the veracity of conclusions produced must be questioned nevertheless, for reasons stated earlier, in the context of figure 5-2.[31]

Cummings, DiPasquale, and Kahn employed an econometric synthesis of both control area and pre/post approaches in their investigation of neighborhoodwide home price effects of single-family homes newly constructed through the Nehemiah program in inner city Philadelphia. They found that a quality-adjusted home increased in value in the Nehemiah tracts by 12 percent after the projects were completed, whereas it increased 12 percent in other poor tracts nearby and 23 percent in distant poor tracts during the comparable period. The authors concluded no tractwide impact from the Nehemiah new construction projects, though a reinterpretation of their findings produces a conclusion of positive impact.[32]

Supportive Housing for Special Needs Households

The intellectual history of research on home price impacts from supportive and special needs housing offers remarkable parallels to that related to subsidized housing for low-income households in general. Through the 1980s numerous studies had reached a common conclusion: there was no impact of

30. Lee, Culhane, and Wachter (1999).
31. Briggs, Darden, and Aidala (1999).
32. Cummings, DiPasquale, and Kahn (2002). A superior test of impact would have been to compare the pre/post difference in prices for the target tracts and the control tracts, as in Briggs, Darden, and Aidala (1999). Using Cummings, DiPasquale, and Kahn's own results (2002, table 12), such would have revealed that the Nehemiah project area prices began 13 (21) percentage points below nearby (distant) poor tracts', but after construction were only 10 percentage points lower than nearby tracts' prices and 2 percentage points higher than distant poor tracts' prices.

supportive housing on neighboring single-family home prices. After review-ing "every available study," the Mental Health Law Project concluded that "[they] conclusively establish that a group home as community residential facility for mentally disabled people does not adversely affect neighbors' property values or destabilize a neighborhood." Several studies even con-cluded that there was a positive property value impact, especially in lower-valued neighborhoods.[33]

Only one study of this period provided dissension, and it could be chal-lenged on methodological grounds. Gabriel and Wolch studied the relation-ship between the number of human service facilities per 1,000 residents of census tracts in Oakland and median home sales prices in the tract, using multiple regression analysis. When all tracts were included in the regression, larger numbers of residential facilities for adult and children proved inversely related to median prices. When regressions were disaggregated by predomi-nant race of occupancy, however, the only adverse impacts appeared to be from adult residential facilities located in predominantly black-occupied tracts. In any event, besides the criticisms associated with all variants of the cross-sectional approach, the lack of variables controlling for other aspects of census tracts that could affect prices besides human service facilities renders all conclusions from this study particularly suspect.[34]

Again in the 1990s, however, the conventional wisdom was shaken by several studies that concluded that, depending on circumstances, supportive housing may create negative effects on proximate home prices.

Lyons and Loveridge investigated the impacts of four locations where fed-erally assisted, multifamily buildings housed disabled tenants in St. Paul, Minnesota. The apartment complexes ranged in size from 10 to 103 units. Employing the cross-sectional approach, they found a general negative cor-relation between assessed home values and proximity to multifamily com-plexes for the disabled, but the size and sign of the relationship depended in a nonlinear fashion on the number of such units in the development. For example, an apartment with 10 units for the disabled located within one-half mile of a single-family home was associated with a statistically significant lower assessed value of $1,670 of that home; within one mile the figure was $682. But an apartment with 100 units for the disabled located within one-

---

33. Mental Health Law Project (1988, abstract); Dear (1977); Wagner and Mitchell (1980); Gabriel and Wolch (1984); Farber (1986); Boydell, Trainor, and Pierri (1989); Hargreaves, Callanan, and Maskell (1998).
34. Gabriel and Wolch (1984).

half mile of a single-family home was associated with a statistically significant higher value of $1,300 in the assessment of that home; although within one mile the corresponding figure was a lower value of $1,600. The authors offered no explanation for these results.[35]

Galster and Williams investigated the relationship between multifamily dwellings occupied exclusively by severely mentally disabled tenants and selling prices of nearby homes in two small Ohio towns. Like Briggs, Darden, and Aidala, they employ a series of dummy variables to measure average price levels before and after the developments of interest are in operation.[36] Controlling for features of the neighborhood and sold dwellings, seasonality, and areawide secular price trends, proximity within two blocks of two small, newly constructed apartment buildings for the mentally ill was associated with a 40 percent decrease in home prices over what they were before the opening of those buildings. However, proximity to three similar, new apartment complexes or to three rehabilitated apartment buildings for the mentally ill had no relationship with prices after their development. The authors interpreted the results as suggesting that siting, building scale, and tenant allocation procedures mattered more for potential neighborhood spillover effects than merely noting the fact that a multifamily building occupied by mentally ill tenants was nearby.

Colwell, Dehring, and Lash analyzed with a sophisticated model seven group homes that opened during the 1987–94 period in seven communities in suburban Chicago.[37] Each site housed between four and eight disabled tenants. They found evidence consistent with no postannouncement impact within 750 feet, but an apparent reduction in home sales prices of 13 percent if the sales were within sight of the group home.[38] Moreover, if a community protest were to arise after the announcement, an additional 7.7 percent price decline would occur, which the authors attributed to the negative "signaling" effect that such a protest had for the market evaluation of the area. The approach of Colwell, Dehring, and Lash is fundamentally similar to (and therefore is subject to the same criticisms noted as) that of Galster and Williams (and Briggs, Darden, and Aidala), inasmuch as their variables

35. Lyons and Loveridge (1993).

36. Galster and Williams (1994); Briggs, Darden, and Aidala (1999).

37. Colwell, Dehring, and Lash (2000).

38. They not only consider a proximity ring but also a gradient to measure distance between home sale and development of interest. Moreover, they identify whether the sale occurred within sight of the development of interest.

measuring postannouncement price levels provide the impact test, controlling for a predevelopment, neighborhood-specific fixed effect. These authors also control for the average rate of price appreciation in each individual impact neighborhood measured over pre- and postdevelopment periods combined, instead of using this as another measure of impact as in the difference in differences approach.[39] The potential shortcoming of this specification is demonstrated in a hypothetical situation portrayed in figure 5-2. An impact neighborhood evinces a sharp break in its home price trend at the time of announcement (or opening) of a multifamily or affordable housing complex, yet these two distinctive trends exactly offset each other. Thus, as measured over the analysis period as a whole, the average level of prices appears constant, and the average trend in prices appears as zero in the impact area. No impact would have been inferred from these findings when using the Colwell, Dehring, and Lash approach, whereas both intuition and the difference in differences method would clearly suggest otherwise.

Multifamily Housing for Market-Rate Households

There has been little research on this question, although a more substantial literature has examined the value of tenure composition (neighbors who rent versus own, controlling for structure type, on home prices). The only extant work comes from Moody and Nelson, who study home sales prices in Gwinnett County, Georgia, using a conventional, cross-sectional approach.[40] They explore variously specified proximity relationships between home price and different types of apartments categorized by expense and scale. They find the strongest positive relationships between home prices and distance from large, inexpensive apartment complexes and the smallest (though still positive) relationships for small, expensive complexes. The former relationships appear to extend roughly twice as far as the latter (4,000 versus 2,000 feet). Surprisingly, Moody and Nelson find census tractwide home price appreciation rates positively associated with the density of apartments in the tract. These authors employ a traditional cross-sectional econometric approach, so no inferences about causality can be drawn.

39. Galster and Williams (1994); Briggs, Darden, and Aidala (1999).
40. For work on the value of tenure composition, see, for example, Wang and others (1991); Coulson, Hwang, and Mai (2002); Haurin, Dietz, and Weinberg (2003); for a conventional cross-sectional approach, see Moody and Nelson (2002).

Concentration, Context, and Type of Development

Prior research just cited has rarely tested explicitly whether the reputed home price impacts of affordable or multifamily housing varied according to neighborhood context, concentration of the given development type in the neighborhood, and facility type. There are good reasons to believe that each aspect may shape the findings.[41] For example, adding a few low-income tenants to a neighborhood having low poverty rates, minimal household turnover, and home prices that are high and stable is not likely to generate the same impact as the same number added to a lower-valued, unstable neighborhood that is on the threshold of racial tipping or class succession.[42] Similarly, a few, small-scale affordable or multifamily developments that are widely scattered across a neighborhood would seem unlikely to produce the same results when they are clustered at higher concentrations. Indeed, such commonsense arguments led the Department of Housing and Urban Development to adopt "impaction standards" for its site-based assisted housing programs decades ago.[43]

Certainly some of the earlier work provides provocative hints that impacts may be contingent on one or more of the above factors. But, because of their methodological shortcomings, these hints should only be viewed as suggestive. For example, does the common claim of differential impacts from different sorts of affordable housing programs operating within the same metropolitan area provide conclusive evidence of contingent impacts, or rather that each program type is subject to a different sort of neighborhood selection bias?[44] Once again, the difference in differences approach offers the superior method for investigating concentration, context, and type of development.

Difference in Differences Research on Impacts on Home Prices

For reasons just articulated, more credence should be placed on studies that employ the difference in differences approach. Fortunately, in the last few

---

41. Freeman and Botein (2002).

42. For more on neighborhood threshold effects, see Quercia and Galster (2000); Galster, Quercia, and Cortes (2000).

43. Gray and Tursky (1986).

44. See, for example, Lyons and Loveridge (1993); Goetz, Lam, and Heitlinger (1996); Lee, Culhane, and Wachter (1999). The same challenge can be offered to the contingency of apartment type impacts concluded by Moody and Nelson (2002).

Table 5-1. *Typologies of Development and Corresponding Research on Home Price Impacts*[a]

| Clientele and development type | Ownership units | | Rental units |
	Single family	Multifamily	Multifamily
Market rate, new construction	Baseline price for comparison	No extant studies	No extant studies
Low income, new construction	Ellen and others (2001)	Ellen and others (2001)	Schwartz and others (2002)
	Schill and others (2002)	Schill and others (2002)	Johnson and Bednarz (2002)
	Schwartz and others (2002)		
Low income, rehabilitation	Schill and others (2002)	Schill and others (2002)	Galster and others (1999)
			Santiago, Galster, and Tatian (2001)
Low income, tenant subsidy	n.a.	n.a.	Galster and others (1999)
			Galster, Tatian, and Smith (1999)
Special needs, rehabilitation	n.a.	n.a.	Galster and others (2000)
			Galster, Tatian, and Pettit (2004)

n.a. Not applicable.
a. Studies cited employ the difference in differences approach; see text for rationale.

years the breadth and depth of such literature has grown substantially enough that some emerging consensual conclusions can be drawn. Table 5-1 helps organize the review of this section, by placing each difference in differences study in a category based on the building type, tenure, clientele, and development technique involved in the project being investigated. Unfortunately, so far there have been no studies using this approach that have investigated the home price impacts of market-rate multifamily developments, either owner or renter occupied.

Newly Constructed, Affordable, Single- and Multifamily Housing

Ellen and others investigated the neighborhood price impacts of two sorts of new construction efforts to supply affordable housing in New York City during the 1980s and 1990s: the Nehemiah program for large-scale development of single-family homeownership units, and the Housing Partnership program for small-scale, two- or three-family units with the owner occupying one.[45] Both these programs operated in distressed New York neighborhoods, so the generality of results must be assessed in this context. They identified what they interpreted as substantial positive home price impacts from both programs, with the size of the impact attenuating over distance from the developments: 11 percent within 500 feet, 6 percent at 1,000 feet, and 3 percent at 2,000 feet. Larger concentrations of new homes constructed by either program provided larger positive impacts, they claimed. Housing Partnership developments provided somewhat smaller positive spillovers than Nehemiah developments, at least in close proximity. A hundred units of Housing Partnership developments evinced an 8 percentage point smaller positive effect on home prices within 500 feet than a comparable concentration of Nehemiah developments, suggesting the market did not value the multiunit, partially renter-occupied developments supplied by the former as highly as the single-family, owner-occupied ones supplied by the latter. Unfortunately, there was no way to parse the apparent impacts of tenure and structure-type differences between these two programs.

Schill and others examined the impact of New York City's Ten-Year Plan, which built or rehabilitated more than 180,000 housing units in many of the city's distressed neighborhoods since the mid-1980s.[46] They found what they interpreted as substantial positive price effects, which were directly related to the concentrations of projects: within 500 feet prices were boosted 1.8 percentage points by developments of 50 units or fewer, but 7.4 percentage points by developments of more than 100 units. Though these concentration effects were manifested for rental and ownership developments, the positive impacts were a few percentage points smaller for rental developments under 100 units. These results proved robust to tests involving various aspects of the units developed, including structure-type characteristics and whether newly constructed or rehabilitated.

Schwartz and others continued the investigation of New York's Ten-Year Plan, focusing on new construction projects and employing various enhancements to the basic difference in differences approach. They also identified evidence consistent with substantial positive price impacts from these

---

45. Ellen and others (2001). The sales price sample not only included single-family homes and condominiums but also two-family homes and some smaller apartments.
46. Schill and others (2002).

developments, which decayed over distance up to 2,000 feet.[47] Sales within 500 feet of where a development was going to occur were 28 percent lower than identical homes in other neighborhoods in the zip code; immediately after construction they were only 13 percent lower and after five years they were only 11 percent lower. Higher concentrations of new units generated larger positive spillovers, but with diminishing returns, they claimed. Projects with a smaller percentage of their units in multifamily, rental configurations generated larger positive impacts. The effect of neighborhood context on measured impact varied according to the concentration of projects. Fifty new units produced twice as large a positive impact (14 percentage points) in areas with median incomes above 80 percent of the area's median as in areas of lower income. However, because the marginal impact of each new unit was greater in poorer neighborhoods, the average concentration of developments yielded a 2 percentage point higher benefit in poorer than in less-poor areas.

Johnson and Bednarz conducted a multicity impact study of newly constructed Low Income Housing Tax Credit (LIHTC) developments that came online 1995–97.[48] They modified the difference in differences approach slightly to estimate housing price trends not only during preannouncement and postopening periods, but during an interim period as well, inasmuch as at least two-thirds of the LIHTC sites investigated in each city involved new construction projects typically taking years to complete. All of the multifamily sites investigated had at least 95 percent of their units occupied by low-income tenants and, with one exception, involved 100 apartments or fewer. The putative property value impacts within 300 meters of LIHTC projects in all three cities proved to be positive, often commencing when the development was announced. But in Cleveland there was evidence that this impact weakened progressively as larger-scale projects were built and would become negative if it were to exceed a threshold of 456 units. Within 301 to 600 meters of LIHTC projects there was no property value impact in modestly valued neighborhoods of Portland and Seattle, unless (in Portland) the project exceeded a threshold concentration of 0.2 percent of all units. In the lower-valued, more distressed neighborhoods into which LIHTC sites were placed in Cleveland, however, evidence supported the conclusion of a clear negative impact, regardless of the scale of the facility.

47. Schwartz and others (2002).
48. Johnson and Bednarz (2002).

Rehabilitated, Affordable, Single- and Multifamily Housing

Galster and others and Santiago, Galster, and Tatian studied the price impacts of scattered-site public housing in Denver, Colorado, which typically was developed through the acquisition of single-family dwellings at foreclosure sales and their subsequent rehabilitation.[49] These public housing units were developed across the city and county of Denver, in an unusually wide range of neighborhood types. The general pattern during the late 1980s through the mid-1990s, however, was that this scattered-site public housing was developed in pockets that were systematically lower valued than the rest of the surrounding neighborhood, perhaps because they were generating negative externalities before they were acquired by the Denver Housing Authority. After rehabilitation and occupancy as public housing, however, proximity to such sites (at least in the range of 1,000 to 2,000 feet) generally resulted in higher home prices than would have been predicted otherwise. The authors interpreted this result as indicative of a positive impact, probably because of the rehabilitation of previously poorly maintained dwellings and subsequent high maintenance standards that this program involved. The magnitude and direction of implied impact clearly proved contingent, however, on the concentration of scattered-site facilities in the neighborhood and on the neighborhood's submarket position. There was a pattern of threshold effects, whereby home price impacts became negative when more than a critical mass of public housing sites or units were located in a neighborhood. This danger of "re-concentration" was most acute in lower-value neighborhoods, especially where homeowners perceived a vulnerability to their quality of life (as revealed by focus groups during the study). These results are summarized in more detail in the left column of table 5-2.

Affordable Housing Provided through Tenant-Based Subsidies

Galster and others and Galster, Tatian, and Smith investigated the home price impacts of the Section 8 tenant rental subsidy program in Baltimore County, Maryland, during the late 1980s through the mid-1990s.[50] There was clear evidence of adverse selection, as Section 8 households occupied

---

49. Galster and others (1999); Santiago, Galster, and Tatian (2001). To a minor degree this program also rehabilitated small-scale duplex or apartment buildings.

50. Galster and others (1999); Santiago, Galster, and Tatian (2001).

Table 5-2. *Summary of Statistical Estimates of Impacts on Residential Property Values: Scattered-Site Public Housing and Section 8 Tenant-Based Assistance (difference in differences methodology)*[a]

Neighborhood context	Dispersed public housing (Denver)	Section 8 subsidies (Baltimore County)
Higher value, less vulnerable	Positive impacts if there are not more than 5 sites within 1,000 to 2,000 feet	Positive impacts if there are not more than 3 sites within 500 feet
	Negative impacts if there is more than 1 site within 1,000 feet or more than 5 sites within 1,000 to 2,000 feet	Negative impacts if there are more than 3 sites within 500 feet (maximum number observed = 4)
Lower value, more vulnerable	Small positive impacts if there are not more than 4 sites within 1,000 to 2,000 feet	Negative impacts if any sites within 2,000 feet. Size of impact grows with number of sites.
	Negative impacts if there are more than 4 sites within 1,000 to 2,000 feet	Impacts slightly mitigated if the same number of Section 8 tenants are in fewer sites.

Sources: Galster and others (1999); Galster, Tatian, and Smith (1999); Santiago, Galster, and Tatian (2001).

a. The term "site" is an address with one or more dwelling units occupied by assisted tenants.

pockets within neighborhoods in Baltimore County that were systematically lower valued than the norm for the entire neighborhood. Their predominant finding was that in-moving Section 8 tenants were not related to subsequent single-family home prices within 2,000 feet in the average neighborhood in which they were located, contrary to conventional wisdom. Once more, however, the magnitude and direction of relationship was contingent on the interaction of neighborhood and Section 8 concentration. The presence of one Section 8 household in a higher-valued neighborhood apparently resulted in higher home prices nearby than otherwise predicted, arguably because of the structural rehabilitation that participation in the County's Section 8 program required. In lower-valued, higher-poverty neighborhoods where owners felt more vulnerable to forces of decline (as revealed by focus groups), any additional Section 8 households apparently had harmful impacts on home prices. These results are summarized in greater detail in table 5-2.

Rehabilitated, Affordable, Multifamily Supportive Housing for Special Needs Households

The only impact studies of supportive housing employing the difference in differences approach were conducted by Galster and others and Galster, Tatian, and Pettit.[51] They analyzed the proximate home price impacts of eleven small-scale supportive housing facilities announced in Denver during 1989–95, which comprised a wide range of supportive housing types but included no homeless shelters or community corrections facilities. They found that announcement (and subsequent development) of these facilities was associated with higher home prices in a range of 1,001 to 2,000 feet than would have been expected. After this announcement, areas near these facilities experienced an increase in level of prices and an upward trend in prices compared with those of similar homes in the same census tract not near such facilities. On average across all eleven supportive sites announced during the study period, home prices 3.5 years after announcement were about 3.5 percentage points higher within 1,001 to 2,000 feet of a supportive facility than they would have been in the facility's absence. This reversed a relative decline in prices (compared with elsewhere in the census tract) that existed in these areas before the announcement of the supportive housing facility.

Conclusion: The Contingent Nature of Home Price Impacts

In its totality, the body of home price impact literature employing the difference in differences approach provides a distinct theme. The impacts of affordable and multifamily housing on prices of nearby single-family homes will depend in an interactive way on concentration, context, and type of development.[52]

---

51. Galster and others (2000); Galster, Tatian, and Pettit (2004).

52. One might argue that the results reviewed above are subject to a censoring problem. Only those affordable housing units that were observed after being developed survived the scrutiny of local policymakers or neighborhood activists and thus must have been those having the greatest probability of generating positive externalities. By contrast, those prospectively generating the worst negative externalities may never have been observed because their development was successfully thwarted by NIMBY activists. Though this argument may have credence in some cases, it clearly does not in the cases of Denver scattered-site public housing and Baltimore County Section 8.

As for concentration, it appears that higher amounts of new construction or rehabilitation in a given area involving single- or multifamily affordable units will provide larger positive price impacts for nearby homes.[53] However, apparently there is a diminishing marginal positive impact that, at least in the case of affordable, multifamily rental complexes, can become a negative impact once concentrations exceed a threshold amount. This potentially negative "overconcentration" effect seems particularly apparent in the case of tenant-based subsidy programs.[54] Affordable housing seems least likely to generate negative impacts when it is inserted into high-value, low-poverty, stable neighborhoods.

Neighborhood context seemingly also affects the magnitude or even direction of concentration effects. There seems to be growing evidence, however, that neighborhoods with modest values, nontrivial poverty rates, and owner perceptions of vulnerability will experience smaller positive price impacts and have a greater risk of experiencing negative price impacts at lower concentrations of affordable or multifamily housing. (This is the case for tenant-based subsidy programs, scattered-site public housing developed through rehabilitation, or newly constructed LIHTC developments.) In depopulated, highly distressed neighborhoods, however, effects may be more positive. Schwartz and others find that the marginal positive impact of additional newly constructed subsidized units is higher in such New York City neighborhoods.[55]

Finally, it seems clear that the type of affordable or multifamily development will influence impacts. Owner-occupied affordable developments apparently generate more positive impacts than renter-occupied ones. Developments that remove (through rehabilitation or construction) a preexisting source of negative externalities likely generate more positive impacts than those developed on vacant land.[56]

All this is to say that predicting the consequences for single-family home prices of prospective "growth management" policies is not a straightforward exercise. Developing more affordable and multifamily housing in a metropolitan area—in the suburbs and in the core—clearly can be done in ways

53. Galster and others (1999); Santiago, Galster, and Tatian (2001); Ellen and others (2001); Schill and others (2002); Schwartz and others (2002).

54. See Schwartz and others (2002); Johnson and Bednarz (2002); Galster and others (1999); Galster, Tatian, and Smith (1999).

55. Galster and others (1999); Galster, Tatian, and Smith (1999); Galster and others (1999); Santiago, Galster, and Tatian (2001); Johnson and Bednarz (2002); Schwartz and others (2002).

56. Ellen and others (2001); Schill and others (2002); Schwartz and others (2002); Galster and others (1999); Santiago, Galster, and Tatian (2001); Schill and others (2002).

that enhance proximate property values. Just as clearly, it can be done in ways that, because of inappropriate concentrations and neighborhood contexts, erode those values. Thus the adjective "smart" should not only be applied as a descriptor of "growth policies" but also to a much wider range of policies related to the development of affordable and multifamily housing.[57]

COMMENT BY

Ingrid Gould Ellen

George Galster's chapter is a terrific literature review on a very important topic—what is the effect of affordable and multifamily housing on the value of nearby homes? As we all know, efforts to build such developments are often met by fierce opposition, driven by worries that these developments will inevitably lead to neighborhood decline and reductions in property values. This chapter reviews what we know about these impacts. As Galster points out, there has been virtually no research on the property value effects of developing higher-density, *market*-rate housing in low-density communities. So he has focused on the effects of affordable and special needs housing.

Literature reviews are always valuable, but they are particularly welcome in areas like this one, where strongly held assumptions and conventional beliefs are plentiful. And they are also especially welcome when they are as well executed as this one. Rather than just reporting that study "A" finds negative effects and that study "B" finds no effect, Galster reads these studies with care and attention and critically evaluates their methods.

He starts with the fundamental challenge of identifying the spillover effects of these housing developments. (For example, does the construction of affordable housing developments reduce surrounding property values, or are they simply sited in distressed locations to begin with?) He develops a clear and useful typology of empirical studies and persuasively, I think, explains why several past methods cannot be used to infer a causal link between the development of affordable housing and subsequent changes in property values.

Galster argues that the most credible studies are those that rely on a difference in differences methodology to identify these spillover effects. These studies compare the value of properties located within a certain distance of

57. Galster and others (2003).

affordable housing developments to comparable properties located in the same neighborhood but farther away from the affordable housing. The studies then compare the magnitude of this "difference" before and after the development of affordable housing—hence the difference in differences.

Although I agree with the priority given to the difference in differences studies, I would have placed greater emphasis on the importance of the data that permit these more sophisticated analyses. This methodology is only made possible by the availability of longitudinal, geocoded data on housing development and property transactions. These data were simply not available to previous authors, so they had no choice but to rely on less persuasive methodologies.

Galster shows that these new papers paint a fairly optimistic portrait of the effects of subsidized housing. Indeed, several studies identify a substantial increase in surrounding sales prices after the development of subsidized housing. And Galster, correctly I think, concludes that impacts are likely to depend on certain features of the affordable housing, such as local concentration, as well as neighborhood context.

Yet this conclusion leads to my main point of departure with the literature review internally. For although Galster rightly emphasizes the importance of context, I do not think the review adequately distinguishes among different neighborhood environments. The original title of the paper, "The Effects of Affordable and Multifamily Housing on Market Values of Nearby Single-Family Homes," would suggest a review of the effects of affordable housing development in low-density (and typically suburban) communities—the kind of housing development that Anthony Downs advocated in his 1973 book *Opening up the Suburbs*.[58] But, in fact, the various papers reviewed evaluate the effects of housing development in very different types of communities.

The literature review includes a discussion, for instance, of several of the papers that I have written on spillover effects with Michael Schill, Amy Schwartz, and Ioan Voicu. These papers study the impact of building new housing in distressed urban neighborhoods. These are dense, New York City neighborhoods that are not made up of single-family homes—indeed, they are higher density in some instances than the new affordable housing that is built. And these neighborhoods were typically quite distressed. Studying the development of affordable housing in this context, we find that it generates significant, positive spillovers on surrounding communities. But although I would love to infer from this result that building affordable, multifamily

58. Downs (1973).

housing will increase surrounding property values in suburban, single-family communities as well, this inference is not at all obvious to me.

For one thing, we believe that some of the external benefits we have found from the housing built in New York City neighborhoods occur because the creation of new housing in urban areas often requires the removal of an existing disamenity, for instance, a dilapidated, boarded-up building or a vacant lot. So one source of benefit is simply that the construction of new housing removes blight. This is typically not a benefit delivered by housing developed in suburban areas. And many distressed urban neighborhoods are likely to benefit from bringing more people back to the streets.

So I am pleased that "single-family homes" has been omitted from the title of the published paper, but I would have liked to see Galster divide the existing literature into papers that study the effects of building new housing in lower-density, suburban environments and those that study the effects of building infill housing in depopulated, urban neighborhoods. These are very different propositions, but I would argue that both are critical to sensible growth management. If we are to generate truly "smart" patterns of growth, after all, we need to focus not only on getting higher-density housing built in low-density, suburban communities but also on rebuilding our depopulated urban cores.

Indeed, in dividing the literature in this way, I think one would find mounting evidence that rebuilding the housing stock in blighted urban neighborhoods delivers significant, positive spillover effects, which at least suggests another reason to advocate smart growth.

As for the broader significance of this literature review and its relationship to this conference on growth management, I think the review could be clearer on the links. The chapter asserts that the higher-density, multifamily, and affordable residences set aside for low-income and special needs households are types of housing developments typically associated with growth management.

Clearly, higher-density housing is associated with growth management. Promoting compact, higher-density development is one of the five nearly universal elements of smart growth that Richard Voith and David Crawford identify in their chapter in this volume. Growth management and smart growth are both fundamentally about conserving land and space, especially at the periphery of our metropolitan areas. To do so, it is critical to introduce higher-density development into existing, low-density areas.

But, as mentioned, Galster's review focuses on the effects of affordable and special needs housing. And here, the link to growth management is less obvious. As the organizer of this conference has written, "Affordable housing is not high on the priority lists of the advocacy groups and is often omitted from their smart growth goals."[59] And surely, housing for special needs populations is even farther down on those priority lists.

So though I share George Galster's and Anthony Downs's view that smart growth plans *should* include affordable housing development, I think such plans may be the exception, and I think the literature review needs to make this point clear. In essence, Galster is making an implicit challenge to proponents of the smart growth movement to include affordable housing in their plans, pointing out that if they are designed effectively, such developments should not undermine surrounding property values.

That said, let me end by emphasizing that this is an excellent review—and one that offers clear and valuable lessons for policymakers, developers, and most important, perhaps, neighborhood residents themselves.

COMMENT BY
Jill Khadduri

In this well-constructed critical review of the literature, Galster has drawn out the most important points from a large number of studies on the effect of subsidized housing on nearby property values.

First, Galster points out almost all the studies completed so far, and all of those that pass his methodological screen, relate only to subsidized housing. That makes their relevance to the managed growth debate limited. Key to the managed growth debate is not how much subsidized housing to locate in particular areas but how much multifamily or other high-density development that, because of its lower per unit costs and rents or sales prices, can be affordable for low-income households (either at market prices or with a housing voucher).

However, there are two instances in which continued studies of the effect of *subsidized* housing can be relevant to managed growth. Those are, first, more sophisticated studies of the effect of multifamily rental housing produced with the Low-Income Housing Tax Credit and, second, additional studies of the effect of housing vouchers on nearby property values. Vouchers and the Low-Income Housing Tax Credit are the two largest programs that currently subsidize affordable housing—reason enough to study them.

59. Downs (2001, p. 22).

Furthermore, in most cases neither program suffers from the problem (cited by one of the participants in the symposium) that subsidized housing looks like subsidized housing. Therefore, they may be more relevant to the question of the effect of housing with affordable costs (but not necessarily subsidized housing) on the neighborhoods in which it is located.

The second important point Galster draws out of the literature, and the basic theme of his chapter, is that in the world of subsidized housing, the finding about impacts on property values is, "It depends." The difference in differences studies described by Galster—those that pass his screen for appropriately controlling for both the types of locations where subsidized housing gets placed and for overall housing market trends—show that the *direction* of the effect on house prices can depend on how much assisted housing is concentrated in one place and on the starting strength of the neighborhood. Higher concentrations are more likely to lead to a decline in property values, and weaker neighborhoods are more vulnerable to negative effects.

I agree with Galster's conclusion that the lessons from the studies conducted so far—to pay attention to scale and to the strength or fragility of neighborhoods when planning for the inclusion of subsidized housing—should be heeded.

Galster brings out a third point that he does not emphasize enough: almost all of the effects found, positive or negative, are small. The small size even of negative impacts means that homeowners need not rally against a subsidized housing program. This finding should be broadcast far and wide, even though the studies done so far have been restricted to certain locations and types of subsidized housing.

The only study that tries to discriminate among a number of different types of subsidized housing—Lee, Culhane, and Wachter—produces a mishmash of findings that make little sense, perhaps because of the methodological shortcomings Galster identifies and, perhaps, because the authors do a poor job of sorting subsidized housing into categories.[60]

The work done by Ellen, Schill, and their colleagues in New York City uses rigorous methodology and focuses on a very important question: whether concentrated subsidized housing can have a positive effect in distressed neighborhoods.[61] This is a central issue for housing policy, but it is not the same issue as the effect of higher-density, lower-cost housing on property values in other types of neighborhoods. In addition, findings from New York City may

60. Lee, Culhane, and Wachter (1999).
61. Ellen and others (2001).

or may not be relevant to other places. Despite the careful way in which these studies control for market trends in the neighborhoods and the city, we cannot know how much of what happens in New York is affected by the city's highly regulated housing market, where the uneven relationships between price and value may affect the expectations of housing consumers. People in New York may be used to the idea that they are buying houses near other people who are getting some sort of special deal. New Yorkers may be more indifferent to that fact regarding the price they are willing to pay for a housing unit than buyers in other cities would be.

Moreover, the studies of subsidized housing that lead to the "it depends" finding may not have controlled for everything on which the effect of subsidized housing depends. The study by Johnson and Bednarz that finds that Low-Income Housing Tax Credit developments had a negative effect on property values when they were located in distressed neighborhoods in Cleveland is not able to control for such potentially important factors as the type of tenants who occupy the tax credit developments and the way in which the developments are managed.[62] Some tax credit developments include many households with incomes close to the upper end of the tax credit limit, while others (particularly those that rehabilitate preexisting subsidized housing projects in low-end neighborhoods) are occupied entirely by the poor. The style of management of the property is also critical to whether it is perceived as a nuisance—or even a danger—by residents of the nearby neighborhood. The effect of subsidized housing on nearby property values may depend very much on these factors.

Another study of the tax credit, by Green, Malpezzi, and Seah (which may not pass Galster's methodological screen) finds that, in Wisconsin, tax credit developments had essentially no effect on property values in Madison and two suburban counties of Milwaukee but may have a slight negative effect in the Milwaukee central city. Once again, these authors were unable to control for any aspects of the tax credit developments other than location, size, and the year placed in service.[63]

There are several potentially useful directions for research to answer the question that is most relevant for growth management policies—that is, the effect of multifamily or other dense and low-cost development.

First, one could study the effects of density on nearby property values. For example, in the Washington metro area, it would be interesting to try the dif-

---

62. Johnson and Bednarz (2002).
63. Green, Malpezzi, and Kiat-Ying (2002).

ference in differences approach Galster recommends to studying the discrete patterns of development around suburban metro stations. Some political jurisdictions (for example, Arlington County) have encouraged density, while others have discouraged it. Holding constant the different starting points in house values and the overall boom in house prices in Washington, have the places that have encouraged high density around transportation nodes simply redistributed value to newcomers or also increased it for existing property owners?

It could also be useful to analyze different types of tax credit developments, because tax credit developments with occupants close to the tax credit limit of 60 percent of area median income may be very similar to market rate multifamily developments. Studies of such developments could be highly relevant to the effect of higher-density housing on property values generally. Studying tax credit developments with different occupancy patterns will require information from the state agencies that allocate the tax credit and monitor its use. As far as I know, no one has been able to do this, but I think it is important to try.

Another direction for further research that is relevant to growth management is replication of the study Galster and his colleagues did of tenant-based housing in Baltimore county. This question does not relate to density. However, it is relevant to growth management because it relates to the availability of housing with moderate or nonluxury rents.

Because of the importance of the voucher program, the most effective growth management policies may be those that produce or preserve some housing in many neighborhoods that can be rented by voucher holders within the program's Fair Market Rents. The Baltimore study found that vouchers had a negative effect only in fragile neighborhoods or when they were highly concentrated in a particular location.

The implication for growth management programs is that they should be coordinated closely with the housing authorities or other entities that administer the housing voucher program. Case studies that we conducted at Abt Associates show that the effect of vouchers on neighborhood perceptions is highly dependent on how vouchers are administered.[64]

Finally, whatever we decide to study next should be sensitive to the distinct growth patterns of different types of metropolitan areas and different portions of metropolitan areas. For example, policies that affect the size and shape of subdivisions on the growth perimeter of metropolitan areas may be more important for understanding overall housing affordability than studies

64. Churchill, Holin, and Khadduri (2001).

that focus on distressed areas of central cities—and need to be studied separately. Similarly, central city or inner suburban areas that are beginning to rise in value may have different market dynamics—and implications for policy—than growth perimeters or distressed neighborhoods.

References

Boeckh, John, Michael Dear, and S. Martin Taylor 1980. "Property-Values and Mental-Health Facilities in Metropolitan Toronto." *Canadian Geographer–Geographe Canadien* 24: 270–85.

Boydell, Katherine, John Trainor, and Anna Pierri. 1989. "The Effect of Group Homes for the Mentally-Ill on Residential Property-Values." *Hospital and Community Psychiatry* 40 (9): 957–58.

Briggs, Xavier de Souza, Joe Darden, and Angela Aidala. 1999. "In the Wake of Desegregation—Early Impacts of Scattered-Site Public Housing on Neighborhoods in Yonkers, New York." *Journal of the American Planning Association* 65(1): 27–49.

Churchill, Sarah, Mary Joel Holin, Jill Khadduri, and Jennifer Turnham. 2001. *Strategies That Enhance Community Relations in Tenant-Based Section 8 Programs.* Cambridge: Abt Associates.

Colwell, Peter, Carolyn Dehring, and Nicolas Lash. 2000. "The Effect of Group Homes on Neighborhood Property Values." *Land Economics* 76 (4): 615–37.

Coulson, N. Edward, Seok-Joon Hwang, and Susumu Imai. 2002. "The Value of Owner Occupation in Neighborhoods." *Journal of Housing Research* 13 (2): 153–74.

Cummings, Jean L., Denise DiPasquale, and Matthew E. Kahn. 2002. "Measuring the Consequences of Promoting Inner City Homeownership." *Journal of Housing Economics* 11: 330–59.

Cummings, Paul M., and John D. Landis. 1993. "Relationships between Affordable Housing Developments and Neighboring Property Values." Working Paper 599. Institute of Urban and Regional Development, University of California at Berkeley.

Dear, Michael. 1977. "Impact of Mental Health Facilities on Property Values." *Community Mental Health Journal* 13 (Summer): 150–59.

De Salvo, Joseph. 1974. "Neighborhood Upgrading Effects of Middle Income Housing Projects in New York City." *Journal of Urban Economics* 1 (3): 269–77.

District of Columbia Association for Retarded Citizens. 1987. *Group Homes for Persons with Mental Retardation in District of Columbia: Effects of Single-Family House Sales and Sales Prices.* Washington.

Downs, Anthony. 1973. *Opening Up the Suburbs.* Yale University Press.

———. 2001. "What Does Smart Growth Really Mean?" *Planning* 67 (April): 20–25.

Ellen, Ingrid Gould, Michael H. Schill, Scott Susin, and Amy Ellen Schwartz. 2001. "Building Homes, Reviving Neighborhoods: Spillovers from Subsidized Construction of Owner-Occupied Housing in New York City." *Journal of Housing Research* 12 (2): 185–216.

Farber, Stephen. 1986. "Market-Segmentation and the Effects of Group Homes for the Handicapped on Residential Property-Values." *Urban Studies* 23 (6): 519–25.

Freeman, Lance, and Hillary Botein. 2002. "Subsidized Housing and Neighborhood Impacts: A Theoretical Discussion and Review of the Evidence." *Journal of Planning Literature* 16 (3): 359–78.

Gabriel, Stuart, and Jennifer Wolch. 1984. "Spillover Effects of Human-Service Facilities in a Racially Segmented Housing-Market." *Journal of Urban Economics* 16 (3): 339–50.

Galster, George, Roberto Quercia, and Alvaro Cortes. 2000. "Identifying Neighborhood Thresholds: An Empirical Exploration." *Housing Policy Debate* 11 (3): 701–32.

Galster, George, and Yolanda Williams. 1994. "Dwellings for the Severely Mentally-Disabled and Neighborhood Property Values—The Details Matter." *Land Economics* 70 (4): 466–77.

Galster, George, Anna Santiago, Robin Smith, and Peter Tatian. 1999. *Assessing Property Value Impacts of Dispersed Housing Subsidy Programs*. Report to HUD. Washington: Urban Institute.

Galster, George, Peter Tatian, and Robin Smith. 1999. "The Impact of Neighbors Who Use Section 8 Certificates on Property Values." *Housing Policy Debate* 10 (4): 879–917.

Galster, George, Kathryn Pettit, Peter Tatian, Anna Santiago, and Sandra Newman. 2000. *The Impacts of Supportive Housing on Neighborhoods and Neighbors*. Report to HUD. Washington: Urban Institute.

Galster, George, Peter Tatian, and Kathryn Pettit. 2004. "Supportive Housing and Neighborhood Property Value Externalities." *Land Economics* 80 (1): 33–54.

Galster, George, Peter Tatian, Anna Santiago, Kathryn Pettit, and Robin Smith. 2003. *Why NOT In My Back Yard? Neighborhood Impacts of Assisted Housing*. CUPR/Rutgers University Press.

Goering, John, Helene Stebbins, and Michael Siewert. 1995. *Promoting Housing Choice in HUD's Rental Assistance Programs*. Report to Congress. Office of Policy Development and Research. Department of Housing and Urban Development.

Goetz, Edward G., Hin Kin Lam, and Anne Heitlinger. 1996. "There Goes the Neighborhood? The Impact of Subsidized Multi-Family Housing on Urban Neighborhoods." Center for Urban and Regional Affairs, University of Minnesota.

Gray, Robert and Stephen Tursky. 1986. "Location and Racial/Ethnic Occupancy Patterns for HUD Subsidized Family Housing in Ten Metropolitan Areas." In John M. Goering, ed., *Housing Desegregation and Federal Policy*. University of North Carolina Press.

Green, Richard K., Stephen Malpezzi, and Kiat-Ying Seah. 2002. "Low Income Housing Tax Credit Housing Developments and Property Values." University of Wisconsin. Center for Urban Land Economics Research. Working Paper (June).

Guy, Donald C., John L. Hysom, and Stephen R. Ruth. 1985. "The Effect of Subsidized Housing on Values of Adjacent Housing." *AREUEA Journal-Journal of the American Real Estate & Urban Economics Association* 13(4): 378–87.

Hargreaves, Bob, Judith Callanan, and Glenn Maskell. 1998. "Does Community Housing Reduce Neighborhood Property Values?" Presented at AREUEA annual meeting, Chicago.

Haurin, Donald, Robert D. Dietz, and Bruce A. Weinberg. 2003. "The Impact of Homeownership Rates: A Review of the Theoretical and Empirical Literature." *Journal of Housing Research* 13 (2): 119–51.

Heckman, James. 1979. "Sample Bias as a Specification Error." *Econometrica* 47 (January): 143–62.

Iglhaut, Daniel M. 1988. "The Impact of Group Homes on Residential Property Values." Marlboro, Md.: Prince George's County, Research and Public Facilities Planning Division.

Johnson, Jennifer, and Beata Bednarz. 2002. "Neighborhood Effects of the Low Income Housing Tax Credit Program: Final Report." Department of Housing and Urban Development.

Lauber, Daniel. 1986. *Impacts on the Surrounding Neighborhood of Group Homes for Persons with Disabilities.* Report to the Governor's Planning Council on Developmental Disabilities. Springfield, Ill.

Lee, Chang-Moo, Dennis Culhane, and Susan Wachter. 1999. "The Differential Impacts of Federally Assisted Housing Programs on Nearby Property Values: A Philadelphia Case Study." *Housing Policy Debate* 10 (1): 75–93.

Lindauer, Martin, Pauline Tungt, and Frank O'Donnell. 1980. "The Effect of Community Residences for the Mentally Retarded on Real Estate in the Neighborhoods in Which They Are Located." State University of New York at Brockport.

Lyons, Robert F., and Scott Loveridge. 1993. "An Hedonic Estimation of the Effect of Federally Subsidized Housing on Nearby Residential Property Values." Staff Paper. Department of Agriculture and Applied Economics, University of Minnesota.

Martinez, Marco. 1988. "The Effects of Supportive and Affordable Housing on Property Values: A Survey of Research." Department of Housing and Community Development. Sacramento.

Matulef, Mark. 1988. "The Effects of Subsidized Housing on Property Values." *Journal of Housing* 45: 286–87.

Mental Health Law Project. 1988. "The Effects of Group Homes on Neighboring Property: An Annotated Bibliography." Washington.

Moody, Mitch, and Arthur C. Nelson. 2002. "Price Effects of Apartments on Nearby Single-Family Detached Residential Homes." Report for the National Association of Realtors. Washington.

Newman, Sandra, Joe Harkness, George Galster, and James Reschovsky. 1997. "Life-Cycle Costs of Housing for the Mentally Ill." *Journal of Housing Economics* 6 (3): 223–47.

Nourse, Hugh. 1963. "The Effect of Public Housing on Property Values in St. Louis." *Land Economics* 39 (4): 433–41.

Pendall, Rolf. 1999. "Opposition to Housing: NIMBY and Beyond." *Urban Affairs Review* 31(1): 112–36.

Pollock, Marcus, and Ed Rutkowski. 1988. *The Urban Transition Zone: A Place Worth a Fight.* Baltimore, Md.: Patterson Park Community Development Association.

Quercia, Roberto, and George Galster. 1997. "Threshold Effects and the Expected Benefits of Attracting Middle-Income Households to the Central City." *Housing Policy Debate* 8 (2): 409–35.

———. 2000. "Threshold Effects and Neighborhood Change." *Journal of Planning Education and Research* 20 (2): 146–62.

Puryear, Vivian. 1989. "The Effects of Scattered-Site Public Housing on Residential Property Values." Master's thesis. University of North Carolina at Charlotte.

Rabiega, William A., Ta-Win Lin, and Linda M. Robinson. 1984. "The Property Value Impacts of Public-Housing Projects in Low and Moderate Density Residential Neighborhoods." *Land Economics* 60 (2): 174–79.

Rothenberg, Jerome, George Galster, Richard Butler, and John Pitkin. 1991. *The Maze of Urban Housing Markets*. University of Chicago Press.

Ryan, Carey S., and Anne Coyne. 1985. "Effects of Group Homes on Neighborhood Property-Values." *Mental Retardation* 23 (5): 241–45.

Santiago, Anna, George Galster, and Peter Tatian. 2001. "Assessing the Property Value Impacts of the Dispersed Housing Subsidy Program in Denver." *Journal of Policy Analysis and Management* 20 (1): 65–88.

Schafer, Robert. 1972. "The Effect of BMIR Housing on Property Values." *Land Economics* 42 (1): 282–86.

Schill, Michael H., Ingrid Gould Ellen, Amy Ellen Schwartz, and Ioan Voicu. 2002. "Revitalizing Inner-City Neighborhoods: New York City's Ten Year Plan." *Housing Policy Debate* 13 (3): 529–66.

Schwartz, Amy Ellen, Ingrid Gould Ellen, and Ioan Voicu. 2002. "Estimating the External Effects of Subsidized Housing Investment on Property Values." Report Presented to National Bureau of Economic Research Universities Research Conference. Cambridge.

Turner, Margery Austin, Susan Popkin, and Mary Cunningham. 2000. *Section 8 Mobility and Neighborhood Health: Emerging Issues and Policy Challenges*. Washington: Urban Institute.

Wagner, Christopher, and Christine Mitchell. 1980. *Group Homes and Property Values: A Second Look*. Columbus, Ohio: Metropolitan Services Commission.

Wang, Ko, Terry V. Grissom, James R. Webb, and Lewis Spellman. 1991. "The Impact of Rental Properties on the Value of Single-Family Residences." *Journal of Urban Economics* 30 (2): 152–66.

Warren, Elizabeth, R. M. Aduddell, and Raymond Tatalovich. 1983. "The Impact of Subsidized Housing on Property Values: A Two-Pronged Analysis of Chicago and Cook County Suburbs." Center for Urban Policy, Loyola University of Chicago.

William L. Berry and Co. 1988. *A Comparison of the Appreciation Rates of Homes in Montgomery County Communities with and without Moderately Priced Dwelling Units (MPDUs)*. Bethesda, Md.

Wolpert, Julian. 1978. "Group Homes for the Mentally Retarded: An Investigation of Neighborhood Property Impacts." State Office of Mental Retardation and Development Disabilities. Albany, N.Y.

6

DOUGLAS R. PORTER

The Promise and Practice of Inclusionary Zoning

IN TWENTY-FIVE years of surveying growth management programs, I have
found affordable housing to be a concern that generally arises well after
initial growth regulations are put in place. Only following growth controls'
successful enhancement of community quality, and consequent increases in
housing prices, does affordability begin to surface as a community issue. Now
smart growth principles are reminding us that affordable housing is an essential ingredient of livable communities. Formulations of smart growth generally cite the importance of widening housing choices to satisfy the increasingly diverse demands of our changing society. Soaring housing prices across
the nation underscore the importance of this aspect of smart growth and
have stimulated actions by federal, state, and local government to expand the
supply of affordable housing. To attain that goal requires skillful use of
growth management techniques.

One measure for achieving this goal is *inclusionary zoning* (sometimes
called *inclusionary housing*).[1] It is gaining renewed interest by leveraging

1. Inclusionary zoning, inclusionary housing, and "fair-share" housing requirements are
sometimes confused in relation to requirements for affordable housing. Inclusionary zoning provides requirements in a zoning ordinance for setting aside a proportion of housing units in a residential development for lower-income households. Inclusionary housing attempts to accomplish
the same end but may include case-by-case negotiated agreements and other "informal" under-
standings promoted through policy determinations rather than adopted ordinances. Fair-share

strong private residential markets in many metropolitan areas to induce developers to incorporate affordable housing in their projects.

The Promise of Inclusionary Zoning

The concept of inclusionary zoning arose during the late 1960s and early 1970s from the convergence of three trends: pressures by housing advocates to overcome what they viewed as suburban zoning practices that excluded racial minorities and the poor; waning federal support for producing housing for low- and moderate-income households; and local governments' growing use of regulatory exactions to require developers' contributions to project qualities formerly viewed as public responsibilities. What might be called the "first generation" of inclusionary laws stemmed primarily from these concerns—opening up the suburbs to minority residents and boosting production of affordable units. Then, in the 1980s and 1990s, the rapid appreciation of housing prices focused builders' attention on producing expensive housing and left more and more households unable to afford new or existing units. These circumstances have energized state and local governments and housing advocates to broaden their efforts to stimulate production of affordable housing, a movement that has resulted in a new wave of inclusionary zoning programs.

The plain fact is that the supply of housing affordable to many Americans has not kept up with needs. Indeed, a recent study of housing trends in twenty-eight metropolitan statistical areas determined that, from 1981 to 2000, jobs had increased by 12 million while housing completions added up to only 7 million units. Using a jobs-housing balance of 0.7, the study found a shortfall in housing production of 1.7 million units, or an average of 88,000 units per year.[2] The shortfall is worse for rental units. Tenants constitute one-third of American households, but rental units constitute only 21 percent of residential units built in between 1997 and 2003. Since 1997, rental costs have risen faster than the consumer price index. The Department of Housing and Urban Development estimates that housing affordable by very low-income renters dropped by 7 percent—1.14 million units—in just two years (1997–99). Clearly, in many areas, construction of new housing has not kept

---

housing refers to requirements in some states for communities to provide for a fair share of regional housing needs, which may be implemented through a variety of programs including inclusionary zoning.

2. Gruen (2001).

pace with job growth and household formation, and the pace of multifamily construction suitable for lower-income households is far below that of single-family homes.

Inclusionary zoning aims to respond to these trends by requiring or encouraging developers to incorporate some proportion of housing for low- and moderate-income households in market-rate residential projects. The concept is based on the economic premise that developers' interest in building residential projects in strong housing markets offers an opportunity to exact contributions from the development industry to the stock of affordable housing.

The political acceptability of inclusionary programs stems from altruistic concerns of housing advocates for providing decent, safe, and sanitary housing for all community residents and from the recognition by local public officials that high or escalating housing prices exclude some classes of residents who might be of economic and social value to the community. A few states—most prominently California, Massachusetts, and New Jersey—have accepted these arguments seriously enough to require that local governments address affordable housing needs in development policies and regulations. Frequently, local governments respond to these requirements by employing forms of inclusionary zoning that use private rather than public financing to accomplish this goal.

However, in most communities inclusionary zoning is but one component of more comprehensive affordable housing programs administered by public and nonprofit agencies, which offer a wide variety of assistance to a broad range of needy families and individuals.

The inclusionary zoning approaches examined in this chapter focus on demands made on developers of residential projects. So-called linkage programs that exact contributions for affordable housing from developers of nonresidential projects or from employers, although significant in a few cities and areas, are not part of this evaluation.

Inclusionary Zoning as a Tool for Smart Growth

Besides expanding the supply of affordable housing, a goal generally identified as smart growth, inclusionary zoning contributes to achieving other smart growth goals. By encouraging or requiring developers to incorporate affordable units in market-rate residential developments, usually with compensatory incentives, inclusionary zoning does the following:

—Distributes affordable housing—and the people that go with it—throughout the community—a social benefit often unrecognized in smart growth conceptions.

—Promotes more compact development by raising allowable density in most inclusionary projects, thereby reducing conversion of open space and lessening dependence on automobile travel.

—Helps to provide a positive political climate for preserving existing affordable housing and for redevelopment and infill in appreciating inner-city housing markets.

—Spurs collaboration among the private, public, and nonprofit sectors engaged in housing development.

These claims may be seen as exaggerated, considering that inclusionary zoning is a single program focused only on housing. It must also be admitted that inclusionary zoning works to produce affordable housing only in strong markets that can absorb the costs associated with program requirements. Inclusionary zoning programs were initially conceived as a tool to overcome the exclusionary effects of much suburban zoning and are mostly found in relatively wealthy suburban jurisdictions. In those circumstances they may contribute to meeting smart growth goals. And in recent years some forms of inclusionary zoning have been found useful in flourishing inner city neighborhoods where new or renovated dwellings are fetching top prices. Inclusionary policies or requirements can help to reduce displacement of existing residents unable to afford rising home prices and rents. But inclusionary zoning cannot function where the housing market is flat or declining, and it will not serve the lowest range of household incomes without substantial public subsidies. Furthermore, inclusionary programs raise significant issues that frequently impede their adoption.

Economic and Legal Obstacles

Obstacles to the adoption of inclusionary programs may be economic, legal, or both.

Legal Issues

The legal standing of inclusionary zoning is rather murky. Solinski comments in her review of affordable housing laws in three states that "despite the often heard claim by housing advocates that all persons have a fundamental right to decent housing no matter what their income, a constitutional right to be housed, running to each citizen of the Republic, has never been established." Furthermore, the author states, "neither federal nor state governments are under a statutory duty to construct low and moderate income housing."[3] Court cases that bear directly on the legal standing of inclusionary zoning are few and far between.

In 1971, Norman Williams Jr., one of the most notable land use attorneys of the day, succinctly summarized the legal arguments that could be put forth to oppose exclusionary practices:

> A constitutional decision based upon the equal protection clause; that is, a judicial declaration of equality of rights in access to housing and good residential land . . . based on either the federal or state constitutions; . . .
>
> A new interpretation of the "general welfare" as including housing needs . . . together with the notion that promotion of the "general welfare" is an affirmative criterion to which zoning laws must conform. . . .
>
> A further interpretation of the evolving constitutional doctrine of the right to travel and to settle in different parts of the country.[4]

These findings are illustrated in the decision in *Oakwood at Madison* v. *Township of Madison,* in which the court determined that "in pursuing the valid zoning purpose of a balanced community, a municipality must not ignore housing needs, that is, its fair proportion of the obligation to meet the housing needs of its own population and of the region." The same court reaffirmed the ruling in 1974.[5]

And in 1975, in *Berenson* v. *Town of New Castle,* the New York Court of Appeals ruled that "in enacting a zoning ordinance, consideration must be given to regional needs and requirements."[6] The decision was later reaffirmed and expanded by the same court: "a municipality may not legitimately exercise its zoning power to effectuate socioeconomic or racial discrimination."[7]

---

3. For both quotations see Solinski (1998, p. 1).
4. Williams, Dought, and Potter (1972).
5. 117 N. J. Super, 11, 283 A. 2d 353 (1971).
6. 38 N.Y.2d 102, 110, 341 N.E. 2d 236, 242, 38 N.Y.S.2 672, 681 (1975).
7. *Suffolk Housing Services* v. *Town of Brookhaven,* 70 N.Y.2d 122, 129, 511 N.E. 2d 67, 69, 519 N.Y.S.2d 924, 926 (1987).

The famous *Mount Laurel I* and *Mount Laurel II* cases in 1975 and 1983 in New Jersey amplified these principles. In these decisions the court found that municipalities could not use the delegated power of zoning—power that derives from the state and that must be implemented pursuant to the "regional general welfare"—to exclude needed housing. As a precedent cited repeatedly in other cases, the decisions have had wide effect. The regional general welfare approach was adopted also by California and Washington courts.[8]

But now the legal ground has shifted to emphasize the "takings" issue, turning on whether inclusionary requirements might constitute a taking of property without just compensation. According to Kayden, the courts have yet to subject inclusionary zoning to an intensive and comprehensive constitutional review, but because it affects one class of property owners, such zoning "does not enjoy as solid a constitutional grounding as some land use regulations."[9] "Although the federal constitution's due process, equal protection, and just compensation clauses each have relevance for examining inclusionary zoning," he says, "recent United States Supreme Court decisions have effectively rendered the just compensation clause the first among constitutional equals." Accordingly, the takings issue has prompted many of the most controversial land use cases in recent years.

But Kayden concludes that if inclusionary ordinances allow density bonuses and other compensatory incentives for developers affected by inclusionary requirements, a takings decision is unlikely.[10]

---

8. For an overview of these cases, see Brower (1979).

9. Kayden (2002, pp. 10, 12). For a more detailed discussion of how the takings issue affects inclusionary zoning see Kautz (2002). For an exhaustive list of articles concerning "who pays" see Kautz (2002, note 91).

10. Kayden (2002). Numerous Supreme Court opinions, Kayden says, have allowed landowners to claim that regulations have been so restrictive as to constitute a taking and require compensation. But the rulings generally have established that a taking occurs when regulations deny owners all economically viable, beneficial, productive, or feasible use of their land, although regulations that have a significant impact on an owner's investment-backed expectations for use will be scrutinized on a case by case basis. However, the regulation involved must also substantially advance legitimate state interests. Kayden says the specific meaning of this requirement is uncertain but where a government makes approval of development on the owner's agreement contingent on dedicating part of the property to public use, the Court has required an "essential nexus" between the condition and the legitimate state interest as well as a "rough proportionality" between the impact of the proposed development and the condition demanded. (The phrases "essential nexus" and "rough proportionality" come respectively from *Nollan* v. *California Coastal Commission*, 483 U.S. at 837 and *Dolan* v. *City of Tigard*, 512 U.S. 374, 391 [1994].)

To reduce the risk of negative finding by courts, inclusionary zoning ordinances should allow property owners to make a reasonable return on a proposed project and receive some form of regulatory relief such as density bonuses that partially or wholly compensate for the affordable unit subsidies. Voluntary programs with incentives to encourage developer participation, Kayden says, raise no constitutional issue.

However, Kayden suggests that cities adopting mandatory programs, especially those without compensatory incentives, should prepare a compelling case that construction of private, market-rate housing units affects specific community interests addressed by the inclusionary requirements. An example would be that new market-rate housing creates a need for workers who can only afford lower-cost housing, or that it displaces low-cost housing needed for existing residents.[11]

The lack of extensive litigation and the positive rulings in favor of inclusionary zoning suggest that proper caution in drawing up inclusionary provisions can avoid legal troubles.

Economic Incidence: The "Who Pays" Issue

Who bears the cost of incorporating below-market units in residential projects otherwise priced at market rates is a highly controversial issue. Many developers and builders of residential projects believe inclusionary require-

---

11. Astonishing as it may seem, only four cases challenging the constitutionality of inclusionary ordinances have been decided. According to Kautz (2002), none was based on the takings issue. One involved the Fairfax County ordinance, the first in the nation. In *Fairfax County* v. *DeGroff Enterprises* (198 S.E. 2d 600 [Va. 1973]), the Virginia court found that the county's zoning inclusionary provisions related to socioeconomic concerns rather than the traditional physical character of development and thus exceeded the authority given by the state. Two New Jersey cases were *Mount Laurel II* and *Holmdel Builders Association* v. *Township of Holmdel*, 583 A.2d 277 (N.J. 1990). In the *Mount Laurel* case the court specifically rejected the Virginia decision, noting that all zoning had inherent socioeconomic characteristics, and found that communities in New Jersey must provide realistic opportunities to construct lower-income housing and that inclusionary zoning was an appropriate means of achieving that goal. The *Holmdel* decision supported the notion that inclusionary requirements are land use regulations meant to improve the capacity of municipalities to meet needs for lower-income residential development rather than exactions subject to the rational nexus test. The most recent case, in 2001, is *Home Builders Association* v. *City of Napa* (108 *California Reporter* 2d 60), which determined that an inclusionary zoning ordinance in California is not subject to the essential nexus or rough proportionality tests required of exactions but rather should be considered a land use regulation.

ments are forcing them to take on a community-wide responsibility for creating decent, safe, and sanitary housing for all residents. They often claim that local governments have largely created the problem of unaffordable housing by regulatory restrictions and excessive requirements. Builders sometimes claim that buyers and renters of market-rate units also complain their housing costs are higher than necessary in order to subsidize housing for lower-income households.

The classic economic argument is that, in the long run, developers of projects subject to special development costs (such as impact fees and inclusionary requirements) will drive down prices for developable land, since housing must be produced at prices and rents the market will bear. However, many communities with inclusionary requirements are located in maturing urban areas in appreciating markets. Their supply of developable land may be decreasing as housing demands increase, putting land prices under inflationary pressures.

Ellickson, in an early and influential analysis of the economic effects of inclusionary zoning, claimed that the cost impacts of inclusionary zoning would depend on the relative desirability of the community.[12] In a highly desirable community, where housing prices are relatively inelastic, developers could raise prices of market-rate units to provide at least part of the subsidy for low-priced units. However, in less desirable communities with fewer options to raise housing prices, developers would be forced to absorb the cost of affordable units. Ellickson concluded that inclusionary zoning generally would be enacted in highly desirable housing markets in which subsidy costs would likely be passed along to market-rate homebuyers and renters. Although this effect relieves developers of most of the subsidy cost, he said, the increased cost of market-rate housing would in turn affect housing development in an exclusionary fashion—the ironic result of inclusionary requirements.

Ellickson's analysis has been challenged by many other studies that claim he overstates the downsides of the price effects of inclusionary zoning.[13] Smith, Delaney, and Liou, in a 1996 article, point out that Ellickson takes no account of three factors: the existence of alternative regional locales that could provide substitute sites for developments unduly affected by inclusionary requirements; the special attributes of desirable communities that attract certain types of households; and the degree to which neighboring

12. Ellickson (1981).
13. Kautz (2002).

communities may adopt similar requirements, leveling competition for land.[14] All these factors affect housing price elasticity and therefore the effects of inclusionary subsidy requirements.

The significance of the subsidy costs of inclusionary units becomes almost moot, however, if the inclusionary zoning program provides incentives that largely offset these costs. Most ordinances allow for such incentives as density bonuses, fee reductions or waivers, reductions in code standards for subsidized units, waivers of growth limits, and expedited approval processes. Such contributions to reducing development costs can make enough of a difference to allow developers and builders to make sufficient profit to continue housing production. Density bonuses are quite common, although difficult to calculate given the number of site, development cost, and other variables that must be taken into account. According to Smart, a real estate economist who has computed density bonuses for a number of Washington jurisdictions, differentials in site and development cost conditions virtually preclude creation of a set formula to determine such bonuses.[15]

Dietderich also counters Ellickson's conclusions, claiming that market forces operating under inclusionary programs actually create more affordable housing than if market forces are left to operate under rules applicable in most regions now. "In fact," he says, "a switch to inclusionary zoning rules is likely to expand the aggregate supply of housing available across income strata, while leaving regional housing markets no less (and possibly more) 'efficient' than they are today."[16]

Dietderich concludes that the choice between voluntary and mandatory programs depends on how much affordable housing the community needs and desires and whether its residents can afford to purchase the higher-priced units that can allow developers to internalize subsidies for lower-priced units. This puts in a nutshell the two major conditions for effective inclusionary zoning: a prospering, affluent housing market and the political will to promote affordable housing.

The proof that inclusionary programs can make economic sense for developers is that existing programs have not shut down housing development and that developers continue to plan and construct projects that include affordable housing within affordable and mixed-income projects.

14. Smith, Delaney, and Liou (1996).
15. Author's interview with Eric Smart, March 11, 2003.
16. Dietderich (1996).

Components of Inclusionary Zoning

In lieu of state enabling statutes, which rarely discuss the elements of inclusionary zoning, most communities' ordinances incorporate a fairly common list of provisions first laid out in the ordinances of the two earliest jurisdictions to adopt ordinances—Montgomery County, Maryland, and Fairfax County, Virginia. However, the specific requirements vary widely from one community to another, as demonstrated in the summary of examples shown in table 6-1.

Program Incidence

Many communities adopt sections within the zoning ordinance that contain inclusionary requirements applicable in certain zoning districts or for specific types of residential development. In some cases, such requirements become applicable only upon requests for rezoning or annexation, as in the ordinance of Longmont, Colorado. Some communities incorporate inclusionary provisions within ordinance sections pertaining to specific types of development, such as planned unit development or multifamily development. And some inclusionary provisions, primarily pertaining to voluntary programs, are simply adopted as policies to guide public actions on proposed developments, either in zoning actions or subdivision review. Montgomery County's Moderately Priced Dwelling Unit (MPDU) program is unique in being adopted as a separate law and administered by the Department of Housing and Community Affairs rather than the zoning office. Boston's program was instituted through an Executive Order, subsequently backed up by administrative guidelines. However, almost always inclusionary programs are integrated within comprehensive programs for assisting development and financing of affordable housing.

Strength of Requirements

Inclusionary zoning requirements may be mandatory, mandatory with incentives, voluntary under prescribed conditions, or voluntary through ad hoc negotiated agreements. Most programs, including Montgomery and Fairfax counties, require developers of residential projects of certain sizes to provide a share of affordable units in return for density bonuses or other compensatory incentives. A few communities with extraordinarily strong housing markets, such as Boulder, Colorado, and Carlsbad, California, impose

Table 6-1. *Local Examples of Inclusionary Zoning*

Location	Afford-able units produced	Type	Threshold size	Afford-able units
Boston	184	Mandatory	>10 units for projects using zoning variance or city financing	10%
Boulder	300	Mandatory	All residential development	20%
Burlington	97	Mandatory	>5 units new construction or rehab; >10 units nonresidential conversion	15-25% based on price of market-rate units
Cambridge	131	Mandatory	10 units or projects >10,000 sq. ft.	15% of units if >10 units or 15% of sq. ft.
Carlsbad	935	Mandatory	7 units except smaller projects subject to in-lieu fee	15%
Chula Vista	1,200	Voluntary	50 units	10%
Denver	766 + ca. 300 negotiated prior to ordinance	Mandatory	30 for-sale homes or multi-family units	10%
Fairfax County	1,655	Mandatory	50 units for projects with lots less than one acre and excluding elevator buildings	Sliding scale, from 12.5% for single-family units and 6.25% for multifamily units

Household eligibility	Bonuses and incentives	Fee/site options	Control period
Half of units for <80% AMI; remaining 80–120% AMI; average 100% AMI	Increase in height or FAR; tax abatement	Off-site if 15% affordable units; in-lieu payments	99 years
Average of HUD definition of low-income households	No bonus; development excise tax (impact fee) waived	Off-site allowed for half of for-sale units, flexible for rental units; in-lieu fee for <5-unit projects	Permanent for for-sale units, 50 years for rental units
<80% AMI adjusted for family size	15–25% density bonus based on zoning district, reduced parking, impact fee waivers, lot coverage bonus	Off-site at 1.25 of required affordable units, no in-lieu fee	30 years for home-ownership units; 55 years for rental units
Average 65% AMI	30% density bonus; increased FAR, decreased lot area, no variances required for affordable units	Off-site prohibited and in-lieu fee allowed only under special circumstances	"Maximum allowed by law"
<80% AMI for for-sale units; <70% AMI for rental units	No density bonus but alternatives allowed, for example, rehab or conversion of market-rate units	Alternatives to on-site construction of new units allowed	Single-family re-sales allowed but rental units may not be resold
1/2 50–80% AMI 1/2 80–120% AMI	25–40% density bonus, deferred fees	No in-lieu fees	Negotiated
<80% AMI	No density bonus but payments of $5,000 to $10,000 per affordable unit up to 50% of total units, plus parking reductions and expedited permit process	Off-site units if increased over minimum requirement, and in-lieu fee allowed	For-sale units 10 years; rental units 20 years
<70% AMI	Density bonus up to 20% for single-family units and up to 10% for multifamily units	No off-site units, in-lieu fee for hardship	For-sale units 10 years; rental units 20 years

(continued)

Table 6-1. *Local Examples of Inclusionary Zoning (Continued)*

Location	Afford-able units produced	Type	Threshold size	Afford-able units
Fort Collins	2,441 mostly subsidized by public funds	Voluntary	No minimum	10%
Longmont	627	Mandatory	For-sale residential develop-ment except in annexation areas where rental units are allowed	10%
Montgomery County	11,000	Mandatory	35 units for projects with lots less than half acre	Sliding scale based on requested density from 12.5%–15%
Palo Alto	253	Mandatory	Projects of three or more owner units or five or more rental units	15% except projects of 5 or more acres 20%
Princeton Borough	16	Borough nonprofit agency	Any size	50%
Princeton Township	216	Mandatory: township-administered development	Any size	50% in one project, 20% in another
San Diego	New program 6/2003	Mandatory	2 or more units (current requirements in North City Future Urbanizing Area continue to apply)	10%; 20% in NCFUA
Somerville	25	Voluntary ex-cept for projects re-quiring special permits	8 or more units	12.5%, half for low-income

Note: AMI is the area median income as established by the Department of Housing and Urban Development.

Household eligibility	Bonuses and incentives	Fee/site options	Control period
<80% AMI	Land bank, fee waivers or deferral; expedited review, negotiated density bonuses	None	No requirements
<80% for for-sale units: <60% for rental units	Negotiated density bonus up to 20%; expedited review, relaxed standards, fee waivers	Off-site negotiated case-by-case, in-lieu fee allowed	40 years
<60% AMI	Density bonus up to 22%; fee waivers, decreased lot area; 10% compatibility price increase allowed	Off-site allowed in contiguous areas and in-lieu fees allowed, both in exceptional cases	10 years for home-ownership units; 20 years for rental units
<80–100% AMI for for-sale units; <60–80% AMI for rental units	None stated	Off-site and in-lieu payments allowed in exceptional circumstances	59 years with re-sale restarting control period
State requires half of affordable units at 40–50% AMI and half at 50-80% AMI	None stated	Not applicable	Perpetuity
State requires half of affordable units at 40–50% AMI and half at 50-80% AMI	None stated	No options	Perpetuity
<100% for for-sale units; <65% AMI for rental units	Expedited permitting	Off-site allowed in same planning area and in-lieu fees allowed	Financial recapture for for-sale units, 55 years for rentals
Low-moderate income <80% AMI; moderate income 81–110% AMI	Density bonus, fast-track permitting, fee waivers for more affordable units	Off-site locations and in-lieu payments by exception only	Perpetuity

requirements with no compensatory incentives (except cooperative assistance from city staff). Some communities, including Irvine, California, and Somerville, Massachusetts, have adopted voluntary programs that provide incentives for developers willing to participate. Several communities, including the city of Chicago, negotiate voluntary contributions of affordable housing during rezoning procedures without adopting formal policies. And some jurisdictions with mandatory requirements allow developers of projects under the threshold size to voluntarily participate in the program to obtain density bonuses and other incentives.

Affected Projects

The size threshold for application of inclusionary requirements within proposed residential projects varies from one unit in Boulder, Colorado (affordable housing requirements are imposed on all residential development) to fifty units or more in Fairfax County. The typical minimum project size in California communities is ten units within a range of one unit (Irvine) to projects of fifty units or more.[17] Denver's law applies to projects of thirty units or more. But details count. In Fairfax County, the requirement is limited to properties zoned for less than one-acre lots and exempts high-rise multifamily buildings with elevators. In Montgomery County the law affects property zoned for lots of a half acre or less, and in 2002 the project threshold was lowered to thirty-five units as sites for large developments have become more and more difficult to find. Many communities impose requirements on only certain types of projects, such as the following:

—Redevelopment areas (required by California state redevelopment law);

—All housing on land approved for annexation (Longmont, Colorado);

—Projects of ten units or more requiring rezoning, on city-owned property, or using city financing (Boston, Mass.);

—Multifamily development (Arlington, Virginia); and

—Mandated only for for-sale units (Denver).

Only a handful of the ordinances require affordable units in rehabilitation of existing housing or allow credit toward new unit requirements for rehabilitating units or converting nonresidential buildings. (In part, this is because of the likelihood that such renovation projects would produce fewer than the threshold number of units.) Carlsbad, California, allows the require-

17. Calavita and Grimes (1998).

ment for new units to be satisfied by rehabilitation of affordable units, conversion of existing market units to affordable units, construction of special-needs housing, and construction of accessory units.

Proportion of Affordable Units

The general share of affordable units required in a project varies from 6 to 35 percent, with most communities (and the state of California) requesting that at least 15 percent of the project units be affordable. The high mark is in Placer County, California, where multifamily projects are required to set aside 50 percent of the units for affordable housing. The bottom is 6 percent in Vista, California.[18] Fairfax County requests set-asides of 6.5 percent in multifamily developments. Montgomery County, after initiating its program with a 15.0 percent requirement, reduced it to 12.5 percent in 1981 but in 1989 instituted a sliding scale from 12.5 to 15.0 percent depending on the size of the density bonus desired. In general, communities appear to determine the level of the requirement depending on the value of compensations offered by density bonuses and other incentives.

Incentives

The most common compensatory offering is density bonuses, which generally allow about a 20 percent increase in on-site units. Montgomery County's top bonus on its sliding scale depending on the proportion of MPDUs is 22 percent; Davis, California, allows up to a 25 percent density increase; Denver allows a 10 percent density increase but tempers it by requiring the same proportion of affordable units in the added units as in the project as a whole. Computing a feasible and fair bonus is more of an art than a science, since so many variables enter into the formula (see the previous section on Economic Incidence), but workable bonuses must rest on a rational foundation.

Many communities provide additional incentives, such as the following:

—Waiver of some or all development and building fees;

—Expedited processing for project approvals;

—Parking reductions (based on the assumption that lower-priced units will require less parking);

18. Calavita and Grimes (1998).

—Variances to lot and street standards;

—Exemptions from growth limits; and

—Reductions in unit size and equipment to lower development costs.

Typically the level of these incentives is administratively determined during the site design process. Denver is perhaps unique in offering developers cash awards of $5,000 per MPDU priced for households below 80 percent of average median income (AMI) and $10,000 per MPDU priced for households below 60 percent of AMI, both capped at half the total project units. The cash awards were requested by developers in lieu of rebates of processing and impact fees.

Types of Households Served

Most programs apply to for-sale and rental projects, although Denver and other Colorado communities confine their programs to for-sale projects owing to a state law prohibiting rent controls. Some communities, especially in California, concentrate on rental projects assisted by federal and state subsidy programs. Obviously, the mix of for-sale and rental projects depends completely on market conditions that vary over time. In Montgomery County, for example, for-sale housing developments are declining in size while the number of rental projects achieving the threshold for the MPDU program is increasing. Most of the units produced in Burlington, Vermont, have been for-sale units, but new developer interest in the Low-Income Housing Tax Credit program is suggesting a shift to more rental units.

Household Income Eligibility

Communities tend to set eligibility levels that reflect local housing market conditions and determine priorities for eligibility for inclusionary units by such factors as household size and existing residence in the community. Most programs translate "affordable" housing as units affordable to households with low- to moderate-income levels based on the area's or city's AMI. Montgomery County aims at households with incomes no higher than 65 percent of the AMI. Longmont's program is targeted for households with incomes no greater than 80 percent of AMI for ownership or 60 percent of AMI for rental units. California's state law requires that at least 6 percent of the units have prices or rents suitable for households earning between 80 and 120 percent of AMI; 3 percent for low-income households earning between 50 and 80 percent of AMI, and 6 percent for very low-income households earning at or below 50 percent of AMI.

Options for Off-Site Construction or In-Lieu Fees

Many developers would prefer to construct required affordable units on less expensive sites elsewhere or simply pay a fee into a trust fund that can be used by public or nonprofit agencies to construct affordable units. Their motivations range from anxieties about the marketing effects of mixing poorer folks with wealthier ones, to reducing development costs for low-income units, to avoiding the design and administrative headaches of building affordable units in a market-rate development. Though building elsewhere or paying fees may add units to the stock of affordable housing, it tends to defeat the goal of distributing affordable housing throughout the community and increasing neighborhood housing diversity. Paying fees also means that responsibility for actual production of affordable units passes from the private sector to the public or nonprofit sector, usually slowing the production process.

Nevertheless, sometimes site or development conditions are such that options make sense. For example, small projects on tight sites or larger ones with substantial amounts of undevelopable land may not be able to take advantage of on-site density bonuses. Projects isolated from commercial and transit services or employment nodes might better produce affordable units in more accessible areas. Density bonuses and other incentives cannot begin to compensate for the high unit construction costs of high-rise buildings; fees or off-site options can produce substantially more units than could be incorporated in high-rise residential buildings.

Most inclusionary programs acknowledge these possibilities and allow relief in the form of off-site construction and in-lieu fees. Boulder, for example, allows up to one-half of for-sale units and a "flexible" proportion of rental units to be built off-site. Davis, California, permits an in-lieu payment for developments under thirty units or for projects with "unique hardship" for on-site inclusion of affordable units. Fees must be calculated on a rational basis, and some ordinances detail methods for calculating fees. Calavita and Grimes cite a range of in-lieu fees in California communities from $600 per unit in Pleasanton to a high of more than $36,000 per unit in Oceanside. Carlsbad, California, requires a fee of $4,515 per market-rate unit for developments under the seven-unit threshold for inclusionary projects.[19] In-lieu fees are usually paid into a city-established housing trust fund that will construct affordable units on other sites. In return for fee and off-site development options,

19. Calavita and Grimes (1998).

developers are often required to fund or produce a greater number of affordable units.

Unit Dispersal, Appearance, and Size

Program requirements and administrators take care to ensure that affordable
units in market-rate developments are physically unified—and often visually
blended—within the development. Developers are required to design projects to avoid isolating affordable units in out-of-the-way portions of the site
and to present an appearance comparable to and compatible with market-
rate units. Site plans are carefully reviewed to achieve that end. However,
most inclusionary provisions allow affordable units to be smaller and less
well equipped than market-rate units. Minimum standards are usually established administratively, but in Burlington, Vermont, an ordinance requires
minimum gross floor areas of inclusionary units (750 square feet for one-
bedroom units up to 1,250 square feet for four-bedroom units). Some jurisdictions provide for design compatibility with adjoining development,
requiring, for example, that townhouse or apartment projects incorporate
single-family dwellings on borders with subdivisions of single-family housing
subdivisions.

Duration of Affordability

Inclusionary programs usually require that units remain affordable for a specific length of time, rather than allowing them to be resold at market-rate
prices and thus lost from the inventory of affordable housing. The "control
period" set forth in the owner or renter agreement varies from none at all (as
for for-sale units in Longmont, Colorado, and Davis, California) to permanent protection (as in Boulder, Colorado, and Somerville, Massachusetts).
Most common are control periods of ten to thirty years. Some jurisdictions
control resales of rental buildings for longer periods than for-sale units. And
in the event of resale, many ordinances or agreements provide for the jurisdiction's right of first refusal for purchasing the unit. Montgomery County,
Maryland, controls resales of for-sale housing over a ten-year period. But
because of many units being lost to the affordable housing inventory after
passing the ten-year period, Montgomery County has set up a revolving fund
to purchase units as they come on the market, thereby retaining at least a portion of them at affordable levels.

Ownership agreements for affordable units usually require that the increase in sales price be shared by the owner and the agency administering the program. The unit value is computed to allow for inflation and costs of owner improvements. If the agency chooses not to exercise its right of first refusal, its share generally flows into a funding pool such as a housing trust fund to be used for construction or acquisition of additional affordable units.

Owner/Renter Selection and Unit Management

Most inclusionary programs are administered by an agency of local government, usually a housing department or commission or the department that administers the zoning ordinance. Typically the administering agency advertises for and screens applicants for eligibility based on specified criteria and unit availability, selects purchasers and renters (often by lottery), writes agreements that are recorded with deeds, and monitors or manages resales.

Underlining that inclusionary ordinances are just one approach to enlarging the stock of affordable housing, some jurisdictions allow a certain proportion of new units to be acquired by public housing agencies or nonprofit housing groups. These organizations may tap into a trust fund fed by fees and resale proceeds from the inclusionary requirements. Such organizations can then employ federal, state, and local subsidies to lower prices and rents to serve households not otherwise eligible for the units. Montgomery County's Housing Opportunity Commission, for example, commonly acquires almost a third of new MPDU units to make them available to households with incomes normally allowing only access to public housing. Such an organization may also provide counseling and other services to retain occupants.

Inclusionary Zoning in Practice

From various and sundry sources, including recent reports on three major state programs, it seems that more than 600 communities have adopted policies or regulations that encourage or mandate inclusion of affordable units in residential developments. The difficulty in pinning down better data stems from the ambiguities of local policies and their implementation through regulations and program administration. For example, Herr cites Lexington, Massachusetts, as a jurisdiction whose zoning bylaw provides only that affordable housing is a "significant public benefit" to be weighed in considering cluster or special residential development.[20] But, as Herr states, "those simple words of intention have translated into an effective program for achieving affordability, largely because of the Town's firm policy support." To re-coin an old phrase, "The proof is in the practice."

The "Big Three" State Laws

Most jurisdictions administering inclusionary policies and regulations are located in California, New Jersey, and, to a lesser extent, Massachusetts. All three states require local governments to promote production of affordable housing in the exercise of planning and regulating development. Many housing planners and public officials believe that state programs have been quite successful in generating affordable housing, but experience in these states demonstrates the difficulties in prodding reluctant local governments to meet such needs.

Chapter 40B of the General Laws of Massachusetts, enacted in 1969 and usually referred to as the "antisnob" law, allows developers to skirt local zoning restrictions on development of subsidized housing by appealing to the local zoning board of appeals. To impose the so-called builder's remedy, the board is required only to decide that low- and moderate-income housing needs outweigh any valid planning objections (such as health, design, or open space protection) to override the local zoning. Furthermore, the state law declared that any jurisdiction that had less than 10 percent of its year-round housing stock subsidized was in need of affordable housing. Following that instruction, Newton's ordinance adopted in 1972 mandated virtually all new multifamily housing to make 10 percent of its units affordable (two years, incidentally, before Montgomery County, Maryland's, law became effective). The effect of the law was strengthened by Executive Order 215, issued in 1982 by Governor Edward J. King, which directed state agencies to withhold discretionary funding from communities that unreasonably restricted new residential development.

Herr, in his survey for the Massachusetts Housing Partnership Fund, determined that from 1990 to 1997, more than 20,000 subsidized units were added to the inventory of affordable housing. Taking into account rehabilitated units and other affordable units created through nonsubsidy programs, Herr reckons that the increase statewide "has more than equaled the policy objective of 10 percent of overall housing production" in those seven years.[21]

20. Herr (2000).
21. Herr (2000, p. 4).

Herr found, however, that inclusionary zoning played only a minor role in this achievement, as most affordable units were financed by governmental housing subsidies rather than through developer financing. Communities exercise great latitude in implementing what Herr calls "affordability zoning." On one hand, the town of Lincoln, like Lexington, is one of many communities that determined years ago to negotiate with developers to obtain a share of affordable housing rather than by adopting specific zoning requirements.[22] On the other hand, many communities "provide" for affordable housing simply by adopting policies or goals, rather than binding provisions, and enacting regulations that pertain only to certain types of development in a few zoning districts. Herr concludes from his survey that "the modest impact of the [40B] provisions was . . . surprising and disappointing. . . . These affordability zoning efforts, although widely adopted, have produced relatively little housing."[23] Herr estimates that only a little more than 1,000 units were produced as a result of inclusionary zoning from 1990 to 1997, motivated mostly by positive efforts in communities with strong or rising land values.

The state of California strengthened its requirements for the housing element in local general plans in 1975 to require that communities "make adequate provision for the existing and projected needs of all segments of the community." It added a string of further requirements in later years in response to a continuing crisis in the supply of affordable housing. Between 1970 and 1993, gross rent levels in California rose 436 percent, and home prices increased 723 percent, while median household income grew by only 316 percent.[24] By 1992 the median resale housing price in California was almost double the median price level for the United States.[25] The surge in housing prices was fueled by rapid growth from in-migration, growth limitation measures that limit supply in some areas, and high development impact fees required as a result of property tax revenue limits imposed by Proposition 13 in 1978.

The 1975 amendments relating to general plan housing elements gave the Department of Housing and Community Development responsibility for identifying any not meeting state law enforcement powers. In 1980, however, the legislature enacted a requirement for local governments to create policies and programs to meet a "fair share" of regional needs for affordable housing.

22. Porter (1996).
23. Herr (2000, p. 5).
24. California Department of Housing and Community Development (1993, 1996).
25. Center for Continuing Study of the California Economy (1993).

The Department of Housing and Community Development published a model inclusionary zoning ordinance to guide local governments, but no cost offsets or incentives were included other than those provided by the 1979 Density Bonus Law. It required a 25 percent density bonus for any development that contained 25 percent or more of affordable units. But by 1997, Calavita, Grimes, and Mallach observe that the housing agency had changed its position, cautioning that without cost offsets or incentives the inclusionary requirement became a constraint on new development.[26]

Yet by 1992, only 19 percent of local governments had complied with the law. After strenuous efforts by the Department of Housing and Community Development, by 1995, 58 percent of the 527 counties and cities had complied.[27] However, according to Calavita and Grimes, "even when a locality's housing element meets state requirements, there are no mechanisms to ensure that it is implemented." Nevertheless, Calavita and Grimes were able to identify 75 inclusionary zoning programs in California cities and counties at the beginning of 1996, mostly in jurisdictions clustered around San Francisco and the coastal counties in Southern California. More recently, the Nonprofit Housing Association of Northern California reported the results of a 2002 survey that identifies twelve counties and ninety-five local governments that had produced 34,000 units through inclusionary programs. Most recently, state legislators have indicated interest in prodding cities to improve adherence to the housing element law and the fair share requirement.[28]

Two other California programs promoted inclusionary housing production as well, including the California Coastal Commission and the Community Redevelopment law. Between 1976 and 1981, the commission pushed local governments to implement a goal of 25 percent of affordable units in residential developments within the coastal zone, a requirement that state and local officials abolished in 1981. The California Community Redevelopment law has been somewhat more effective, requiring 20 percent of tax increment revenues from redevelopment areas to be spent on low- and moderate-income housing; 30 percent of all units developed or rehabilitated by a redevelopment agency to be affordable; and 15 percent of all private and public units built in a redevelopment area to be affordable. The law succeeded in producing about 5,300 units in 1995, the first year the state assembled and published the data.

26. Calavita, Grimes, and Mallach (1998).
27. California Department of Housing and Community Development (1993, 1996).
28. Calavita and Grimes (1998, p. 154); Nonprofit Housing Association of Northern California (2003); Shigley (2002).

Like Massachusetts, New Jersey also provides for a builder's remedy to meet needs for affordable housing. The famous case of *Southern Burlington County NAACP* v. *Township of Mount Laurel*, also known as *Mount Laurel I*, determined that "developing communities must make realistically possible the opportunity for an appropriate variety and choice of housing for all categories of people who may wish to live there"—a fair share of regional needs.[29] In 1983, after massive resistance by New Jersey's local governments to the court's proclamation, *Mount Laurel II* reaffirmed the first decision and added a list of remedies to force communities to take action.[30]

After specially assigned judges began ordering changes in local land use plans according to the court-ordered mandate, the New Jersey legislature adopted the New Jersey Fair Housing Act of 1985.[31] The law created a Council on Affordable Housing (COAH) that relieved municipalities of further litigation over builder's remedies if COAH certified their affordable housing plans. COAH also administers "regional contribution agreements" by which suburban municipalities can satisfy up to half of their fair share obligations by funding production of affordable housing in urban municipalities elsewhere in the state. According to the latest (2001) COAH figures, since 1985 approximately 29,000 units of affordable housing have been built or are under construction as a result of these programs.

The Fair Housing Act compels every municipality to prepare a housing element of its master plan that describes how the municipality will provide a "realistic" opportunity for achieving the fair share obligation. The act identified inclusionary zoning, including mandatory set-asides and density bonuses, as a technique municipalities could use. Other suggested measures are rezoning for higher densities, policies to retain affordability of existing housing, an infrastructure plan to support development of affordable housing, donations of municipal land, tax abatements, use of state and federal subsidy programs, and use of municipal funds. But Solinski points out that the act also stipulates that "nothing in this Act shall require a municipality to raise or expend municipal revenues in order to provide low and moderate income housing."[32]

Calavita, Grimes, and Mallach found that although half of below-market units in New Jersey were required to be for low-income households (with incomes 50 percent or less of AMI), few were available to households earning

29. 336 A.2d 713 (N.J. 1975).
30. *Southern Burlington County NAACP* v. *Township of Mount Laurel*, 456 A.2d 390 (N.J. 1983).
31. N. J. Statutes Annotated, Art 52-27D-301 to –329.
32. N. J. Statutes Annotated, 52:27D-311b.

less than 45 percent. Lamar, Mallach, and Payne determined that 87 percent of affordable units in inclusionary developments were offered for sale rather than rent, which effectively excluded much of the demand by lower-income households.[33]

According to Calavita, Grimes, and Mallach, in the late 1980s more developers began including rental units as they discovered the value of low-income tax credits and as COAH gave municipalities extra credit for producing rental units toward their fair share requirement. But in the 1990s, the character of residential development changed. Much residential development in the housing boom of the 1990s into the twenty-first century has emphasized large, upscale houses, which stimulated developers to avoid inclusionary requirements whenever possible.

To escape or reduce the obligation to place affordable units in the newly planned subdivisions, developers seek waivers, offer payments for municipalities to use in executing regional contribution agreements, or request significant reductions in requirements for affordable units. Many New Jersey municipalities now depend on negotiating inclusionary agreements with developers rather than imposing mandatory requirements.

Other State Programs

Connecticut and Rhode Island adopted state laws similar in many respects to those of Massachusetts. Oregon and Florida, two states with lengthy experience in state growth management, require local governments to adopt and implement housing goals that could prompt local governments to consider inclusionary zoning. Oregon's housing goal requires local plans to "encourage the availability of adequate numbers of housing units at price ranges and rent levels which are commensurate with the financial capabilities of Oregon households."[34] The state Land Conservation and Development Commission worked with Portland's metro regional organization to formulate a Metropolitan Housing Rule for the Portland metropolitan area.[35] Adopted in 1981, the policy statement required cities and counties to designate enough land so that at least half of new residential development would be in the form of attached and multifamily housing and to prescribe density targets for central and outlying jurisdictions to promote lower-cost housing. An evaluation conducted in 1991 found that the proportion of multifamily and attached

33. Calavita, Grimes, and Mallach (1997); Lamar, Mallach, and Payne (1988).
34. Oregon Land Conservation and Development Commission (1973).
35. Metropolitan Service District (1991).

single-family housing and smaller single-family lots had increased dramatically.[36] In 2000, Portland's metro adopted a regional housing strategy that called on local governments to adopt voluntary affordable housing production goals and land-use strategies to implement them. The strategy is only advisory, however, and local jurisdictions have been slow to adopt it. Furthermore, the Oregon Building Industry Association successfully lobbied the state legislature to adopt a law forbidding local jurisdictions and metro from requiring mandatory set-asides of for-sale affordable housing in market-rate developments.[37] Even Portland, it seems, has problems in spurring regional attention to affordable housing needs.

Florida, combining aspects of Oregon's and California's approaches, requires local governments to prepare, as part of required comprehensive plans, a housing element consistent with the state housing goal and to adopt innovative techniques such as inclusionary zoning to advance the affordable housing goal. This law has assisted affordable housing developers to obtain incentives such as impact fee waivers and state and local housing funds to build thousands of affordable units in almost every area of Florida. However, Florida has no direct administrative control to enforce implementation of affordable housing goals. Ross, housing director for the 1,000 Friends of Florida, reports that except for negotiated agreements with developers of projects considered "Development of Regional Interest," no local governments have adopted inclusionary requirements that require developers of market-rate housing to incorporate affordable units.[38]

Other state growth management laws also contain language supporting production of affordable housing, but the gap between goal and implementation remains. For example, McGee Jr. conducted a recent analysis of Washington state's requirement for "provision of affordable housing for all economic segments of the community" and a fair share approach to accommodating regional needs. He concludes that the goal "remains a destination without the barest directions to achieve its objective" and that the affordable housing goal "is inefficient and ineffective."[39]

Maryland helped boost the term "smart growth" to the status of a political icon but has accomplished little in promoting inclusionary zoning. Maryland's state planning acts are rather passive in the area of affordable housing,

36. 1,000 Friends of Oregon and the Home Builders Association of Metropolitan Portland (1991).
37. Meck, Retzlaff, and Schwab (2003, pp. 70–72).
38. Ross (2003).
39. McGee Jr. (2000).

calling for local governments to enact ordinances "providing for or requiring affordable housing" and empowering local governments to adopt inclusionary zoning. Long after Montgomery County's program became effective, the city of Rockville in Montgomery County adopted an ordinance in 1990, and Howard and Frederick counties adopted inclusionary programs in 2002 and 2003, respectively. But the vaunted state smart growth program is based on seven "vision" statements that fail to even mention housing.[40]

Local Examples

Table 6-2 provides basic data about a number of local jurisdictions that have adopted inclusionary housing programs. They demonstrate the variety of approaches that have been found politically acceptable in communities concerned with creating a mix of households. All are growing communities with active housing markets, and many would be considered upscale in terms of wealth and desirable living conditions.

A comparison of Montgomery County's MPDU program with those shown in table 6-2 shows that it has outproduced inclusionary programs in every state except California and New Jersey and any single jurisdiction anywhere. Of course, Montgomery County's program started early—its 11,000 units have been produced over a period of twenty-eight years and benefited from a continuously strong housing market during most of those years. Unfortunately, after ten years the units pass out of the control period, increasing their value for resale. According to Larsen, less than 10 percent of units eligible for resale have been offered to the market, but unit values have increased above affordability levels.[41] A revolving fund established in 2000 provides funds for county buyback, but many units have become too expensive to retain in this manner.

Four central cities—Boston, Denver, New York, and San Diego—have recently adopted programs that are already producing inclusionary units. Other central cities, such as Chicago, Washington, D.C., and Buffalo, have negotiated agreements with developers during rezoning processes to obtain affordable units. Although central cities welcome new and wealthier migrants from the suburbs, they must come to terms with displacement of existing, often poorer, residents. Inclusionary zoning that requires a mixed-income

40. Sec. 3.06, 10.01, and 12.01, Article 66B, Annotated Code of Maryland.
41. Author's interview with Eric Larsen, February 13, 2003.

Table 6-2. *Inclusionary Housing Programs and Housing Production in Selected States*

State	Local jurisdictions	Units produced
California[a]	107	34,000
Massachusetts[b]	105	1,200
New Jersey[c]	283	29,000
Rhode Island[d]	16	n.a.
Connecticut	74	1,600
Florida[e]	0	n.a.
Total	585	65,800

n.a. Not available.

a. Nonprofit Housing Association of Northern California (2003).

b. Herr (2000). Of the 18,000 subsidized units produced under various programs from 1990 to 1997, only about 1,200 were attributed directly to inclusionary zoning—equaling about 1 percent of statewide housing production.

c. COAH (2001). This estimate includes affordable units produced through various approaches, but a substantial share are thought to have been produced through inclusionary programs.

d. Herr (2000).

e. The number of units produced through DRI agreements has not been estimated.

approach to housing redevelopment and renovation is one answer to that conundrum. Another is adding inclusionary requirements (such as fees) for tear-downs, substantial rehabilitation, and conversion of existing affordable units.

Regional Programs

It seems almost impossible for most or all suburban jurisdictions to agree with a central city on a development policy that will affect all of them to some degree. Nevertheless, some regional initiatives suggest a glimmer of hope.

One is the agreement worked out by Chicago's Metropolitan Planning Council with the Metropolitan Mayors Caucus to publish a list of "housing endorsement criteria." One of the seven principles is to "encourage an array of quality housing options throughout the region," including developments with housing units priced to be "accessible to a wide range of income levels."[42] Armed with the housing criteria, the Metropolitan Planning Council

42. Metropolitan Mayors Caucus (2002).

is facilitating community discussions of inclusionary zoning and other measures to stimulate work force housing production, initially with the suburban jurisdictions of Highland Park, Oak Park, and Evanston.

In Massachusetts, regional commissions in Cape Cod and Martha's Vineyard have imposed inclusionary requirements for large-scale developments. The Cape Cod law offers incentives for communities to prepare comprehensive plans that incorporate responsibilities for promoting housing affordability. Herr credits these regional mandates, and serious housing affordability issues owing to high land values, for persuading four of the six towns on Martha's Vineyard and nine of the fifteen towns on the Cape to adopt affordability provisions.[43]

Westchester County, New York, initiated an attempt to stimulate region-wide inclusionary housing requirements through facilitating rather than mandating local action.[44] Westchester's board of legislators set up a Housing Implementation Commission in 1990 to determine a fair share of affordable units for each of the county's forty-three municipalities. Yet it acknowledges that the county lacked authority to build affordable housing and would not assist such housing development against the will of local governments. A successor organization, the Housing Opportunity Commission, was established in 1993 to achieve municipal consensus on allocations, ultimately succeeding in having nineteen municipalities adopt resolutions supporting the allocations and agreeing to pursue efforts to produce affordable units. As a result, such municipalities as the city of Yonkers, the towns of Bedford, Greenburgh, Lewisboro, and the villages of Briarcliff Manor and Tarrytown, among others, have adopted inclusionary zoning.

To these regional efforts one might add the more-or-less serendipitous clustering of inclusionary housing programs in certain metropolitan areas, no doubt generated by similar economic circumstances that are blocking construction of affordable housing. In the Washington, D.C., area, for example, the populous counties of Montgomery, Howard, and Frederick in Maryland and Fairfax, Arlington, and Loudoun in northern Virginia have adopted some form of inclusionary zoning.

Similar clusters of jurisdictions with inclusionary programs exist around San Francisco, Los Angeles, and San Diego in California, Denver, and Boston. Undoubtedly there are other regional coalitions working to promote affordable housing and promoting, as one approach, the concept of inclusionary zoning.

43. Herr (2000).
44. Westchester County Housing Opportunity Commission (1997).

Assessment of the Promise and Practice of Inclusionary Zoning

As only one weapon in the arsenal of affordable housing programs promoted by federal, state, and local agencies and nonprofit organizations, inclusionary zoning is unique in its requirements for developers to fund and construct affordable housing. Have such programs worked to significantly increase production of affordable housing? Have they truly benefited low- and moderate-income families and individuals? And, returning to the origin of the concept, have they succeeded in relocating lower-income households from poverty-stricken inner-city areas to pleasant suburban surroundings?

Affordable Housing Production

From state reports, research studies, and anecdotal and news reports across the nation, it appears that from 350 to 400 suburban jurisdictions have adopted and applied some form of inclusionary zoning. However, the unknown number of jurisdictions lacking specific regulations but whose public officials wheedle developers to incorporate some affordable units in projects awaiting approval could be significant—perhaps greater than those that have officially instituted inclusionary programs. Thus a definitive count is impossible and, similarly, so is an estimate of the number of units produced through inclusionary programs.

Still, after thirty years of experience, while inclusionary programs have certainly added to the stock of affordable housing, the production record is underwhelming. The total of units known or estimated to have been produced across the nation reaches 80,000 to 90,000 units—about 65,000 units in states that mandate production of affordable housing and perhaps 15,000 to 25,000 units from individual jurisdictions in other states. Admittedly, without a nationwide survey, this is a rough estimate. Despite the ripple of new inclusionary housing initiatives indicated by recent research and news reports, many suburban programs have produced only a few units to date—some less than a dozen, others a few dozen. Santa Fe's program, while widely reported, had produced exactly one unit by 2002. Calavita and Grimes's report on California communities from 1998 showed that 19 had generated no units several years after adoption of inclusionary programs. Herr's analysis of Massachusetts's progress, which included interviews with local planners, demonstrated that many communities were trying to meet the state-mandated 10 percent subsidized housing requirement by means other than inclusionary zoning, although creating almost 18 percent of total year-round housing built from 1990 to 1997.[45] Production by New Jersey communities is especially difficult to pin down, because they employ a bewildering variety of stratagems to meet—or avoid meeting—their allocation goals, including simply adding an affordable housing district to their zoning ordinance but never mapping it. Many New Jersey communities adopted inclusionary zoning requirements soon after the *Mount Laurel* decisions but tend to negotiate inclusionary agreements with developers rather than impose across-the-board requirements. Even Montgomery County's highly rated program has developed numbers of affordable units averaging about 8 percent of the county's total annual housing permits.[46]

The range of affordable units created by inclusionary programs over a thirty-year period amounts to a fraction of units produced under HUD subsidy programs. In Massachusetts, which managed to generate 20,340 subsidized units from 1990 to 1997 (in a state with about 100,000 low-income families on waiting lists), only 1,200 were created through inclusionary zoning.[47] William Fischel, in testimony before a subcommittee of the House of Representatives Committee on Banking, Finance, and Urban Affairs, prognosticated that even under the best circumstances, inclusionary housing can provide only about 10 percent of community affordable housing needs, an estimate borne out by experience in Montgomery County's program.[48]

With this record, some may view inclusionary zoning programs as ineffective in meeting affordable housing needs in all but a few jurisdictions such as Orange County, Irvine, and Montgomery County. There is hope, however. More programs are now in place and more are under serious consideration as the national housing market remains strong, housing prices continue to rise, and the affordable housing crisis deepens. Agencies and organizations in many metropolitan areas are promoting inclusionary approaches. Models of effective programs are now well known, and developers are beginning to understand that density bonuses and other incentives can do much to offset the costs of inclusionary requirements. Combined with subsidy programs, inclusionary zoning may yet make a difference.

Beneficiaries of Inclusionary Zoning

Housing advocates initially pressed for suburban inclusionary housing programs to allow inner city poor and especially minority households to escape

45. Herr (2000).
46. Larsen (2003).
47. Roisman (2001).
48. See Smith, Delaney, and Liou (1996, note 30).

miserable living conditions and improve housing opportunities. More recently, inclusionary programs tend to be sold to suburban officials on the basis that affordable units are needed to provide housing for local teachers, police officers, and other public servants whose salaries are insufficient to afford living in the suburban communities in which they are employed. Both are significant objectives, but neither is necessarily well served by inclusionary programs.

Data on occupants of units produced through inclusionary programs are meager. Fortunately, Montgomery County offers a glimpse of occupant characteristics in its records on occupants of MPDU units.[49]

—Household incomes averaged $33,076, about 63 percent of AMI household income in 1997. Incomes ranged from $16,000 to just over $39,000 in 1997.

—Average sales price of 129 units was $106,508 in 1999.

—In 1999, 12 percent of occupants were Caucasian, 16 percent black, 57 percent Asian, and 15 percent Hispanic, compared with the years from 1990 to 1994 when about 46 percent were Caucasian, 20 percent black, 26 percent Asian, 9 percent Hispanic, and 2 percent unknown.

—Of eighty-nine certified households in 1999, 2 percent were one person; 17 percent, two persons; 29 percent, three persons; 30 percent, four persons; and 22 percent five or more persons.

—In terms of units occupied in 1999, none had one or two bedrooms, 81 percent had three bedrooms, and 19 percent had four bedrooms. (Unit sizes also vary significantly from year to year.)

—95 percent were Montgomery County residents, and only one purchaser neither lived nor worked in the county.

Ethnic origins and household sizes of MPDU occupants vary significantly from year to year. Based on statistics from 1990 to 1999, it appears that the proportion of Caucasians is declining while the percentages of Asians and Hispanics are rising.

Although the Montgomery County program draws 95 percent of its occupants from the county, the ethnic mix of MPDC occupants reflects the increasing diversity of the more than 800,000 county residents. But evaluations of inclusionary programs in New Jersey and Massachusetts communities, which tend to draw most occupants from a much smaller and less diverse population pool, show that inclusionary programs serve mostly white suburban households. For example, Wish and Eisdorfer sampled New Jersey inclusionary projects and found that 88 percent of the occupants had previously

49. Montgomery County Department of Housing and Community Development (2000).

been suburbanites and less than a quarter of the remainder (or about 3 percent of the total) were African American. Calavita, Grimes, and Mallach concluded that the beneficiaries of inclusionary zoning have been mostly white
suburban residents.[50]

Krefetz, who studied the 40B program in Massachusetts in 1990 and
again in 2001, found that most of the units built in the 1970s were intended
for elderly people. In the 2001 study, she found a "marked shift" to housing
built mostly for families—75 percent of the total units. But in her more
recent study of the impact of the 40B program, Krefetz indicates that Massachusetts communities continue to favor existing community residents,
many of them white, as occupants of subsidized housing.[51]

Suburban inclusionary projects may also favor moderate-income households and homeownership (in keeping with the character of many suburban
neighborhoods) over rental units for low-income households. Calavita and
Grimes state, "In the absence of organized pressure, local decision-makers
usually favor home ownership programs for middle-income groups over
rental housing for lower-income groups."[52] In Montgomery County's program, one-third of affordable units created by the inclusionary program are
purchased by the county's Housing Opportunity Commission (plus a few
acquired by nonprofit housing groups) for rental purposes. The other two-
thirds are for-sale housing.[53]

This picture of occupants of units produced through inclusionary zoning
does indicate a positive result: increased economic integration within the
jurisdictions. The dispersal of lower-priced units within market-rate projects
and areas would be unlikely without the inclusionary requirement. And all
accounts to date indicate that once in place, the income variety of households
is accommodated by local residents.

Regional Integration of Minority Households

An important initial premise of inclusionary zoning—that it would offer
opportunities for relocating inner city poor and minority households to
desirable suburban environments—appears to have failed in practice. For
example, Steinberg, in evaluating New Jersey's program, notes the early and

---

50. Wish and Eisdorfer (1996); Calavita, Grimes, and Mallach (1997, p. 129).
51. Krefetz (2001, n. 135).
52. Calavita and Grimes (1998, p. 165).
53. Calavita and Grimes (1998, p. 165); Larsen (2003).

continuing resistance of local governments to the *Mount Laurel* court decisions and COAH requirements and points out "the travails of achieving social equity in the face of widespread public dissent."[54] Indeed, the COAH amendment enacted in 1993 that allows communities to pay fees to export half of allocated affordable housing units works to increase segregation, since most unit transfers are made to cities whose residents are largely poor and minorities. The analysis by Wish and Eisdorfer of New Jersey applicants and occupants of housing created under the *Mount Laurel* requirements determined that the program "has not enabled previously urban residents to move to suburban municipalities and has not enabled Blacks and Latinos to move from heavily minority urban areas to the suburbs." Calavita, Grimes, and Mallach concluded that "if the underlying social goals of the *Mount Laurel* decision are held to be reducing urban-suburban disparities and fostering racial and economic integration with metropolitan regions [inclusionary housing] has not substantially succeeded."[55]

Krefetz concluded that Massachusetts's 40B statute "has not, for the most part, resulted in any significant 'opening up' of the suburbs to lower income, central city, minority populations." Roisman, surveying experience with inclusionary zoning in promoting racial integration, concludes that "except for the Montgomery County ordinance, the impact of the [inclusionary] initiatives has been to decrease economic segregation only. The initiatives have not ameliorated and indeed may have exacerbated racial inequality and segregation."[56]

Some help in redressing regional racial imbalances may stem from the recent fascination of former suburbanites and young professionals with inner city living. Mixed-income housing programs of all kinds, including inclusionary zoning programs such as those in Boston, Denver, and San Diego, can draw more whites into the cities. The population increment is small, however, and may displace current minority residents while offering little stimulation for greater integration in the suburbs.

Another perspective is offered by Pyatok, who works with indigenous minority groups to revitalize neighborhoods. Inclusionary policies applied to communities where there is a long tradition of racially and culturally cohesive living arrangements, he says, can undermine these efforts.[57] Rather than depending on private developers to improve housing conditions in such

54. Steinberg (1989, p. 31).
55. Wish and Eisdorfer (1996, p. 186); Calavita, Grimes, and Mallach (1997, p. 129).
56. Krefetz (2001); Roisman (2001, p. 180).
57. See the comment on this chapter by Michael Pyatok.

areas, he says, housing advocates should take advantage of opportunities for engaging community-based, self-help organizations in improving their circumstances. In the absence of special waivers to allow this approach, a blanket requirement for inclusionary applications in all new residential developments could prevent nonprofit minority groups from retaining their indigenous community environment.

Contributions to Smart Growth

To return to the question prompting preparation of this paper: do inclusionary zoning programs contribute significantly to achieving smart growth? Potential contributions were spelled out in the opening pages: creating needed affordable housing, distributing it throughout the community, using density bonuses to promote more compact development, affording opportunities for infill and redevelopment, and spurring collaborative efforts. Several community inclusionary programs have made great progress toward realizing these goals. They have produced substantial numbers of affordable housing units within desirable market-rate residential developments and have boosted housing densities in those areas. But to date the contributions of inclusionary zoning have been far less dramatic than originators of the concept had hoped. Except in a few communities, inclusionary programs have produced only a small proportion of needed units. Most programs have served existing community residents rather than increasing housing opportunities for poor and/or minority residents from central cities and declining suburbs. The so-called gentrification of many inner city neighborhoods is proceeding apace, replacing or renovating affordable units to create upscale housing. Experience with state mandates demonstrates the fallibility of expectations that reluctant local governments can be coaxed or coerced to do the right thing, and few states even try.

Where to Go from Here?

There are opportunities for broadening inclusionary zoning programs that would improve production. Most programs focus on mid- to large-scale new developments of medium density in suburban jurisdictions. Few have experimented with applying inclusionary requirements to other kinds of development, especially projects germane to older cities. Examples are the following:

—Conversions and adaptable reuse of existing buildings (which have been successful in Denver, for example). Perhaps communities wish to avoid burdening an already difficult development process in adapting existing buildings, but that would be overcome by a cooperative administrative approach.

—Rehabilitation of existing units, especially rental units, which is taking place in many cities without the benefit of including affordable units, which are perceived as a problem in luxury-priced buildings.

—Construction of high-rise units, which are significantly more expensive to build and perhaps provide a price premium incapable of supporting many subsidized units. However, this concern could be addressed by requirements for in-lieu payments sufficient to build affordable units elsewhere in the vicinity.

—Low-density, high-end subdivisions on the outskirts of the developing area (which are excluded from Montgomery County's program, for example) but which represent high-priced homes that could easily afford in-lieu payments for affordable housing construction. Some argue that these are locations inadequately served by facilities benefiting lower-income households, such as transit and social services, but use of in-lieu payments would allow a more suitable location to be found.

Examples of all these applications can be found in communities today. What is needed is greater resolve of local officials to seek out and fashion inclusionary approaches that will be most productive over the long term.

Can states stimulate greater attention to inclusionary zoning by local governments? In evaluating the four New England states' "override" statutes, Stonefield finds that the "state override tool has only limited ability to increase the supply of suburban affordable housing and to enhance opportunities for mobility." The builder's remedy in the New England statutes, he says, "creates only a private right, not a public (state and local) obligation" to produce affordable housing. Instead of imposing and/or financing construction requirements, states "chose an indirect, non-directive, and non-financial tool that has been . . . limited in its effectiveness."[58] According to Stonefield, states took this route because public support for integrated and affordable housing was thin and divided, too weak to overcome opposition to a more effective program.

Instead, he advocates a stronger state requirement: to direct every local government to plan and zone for a fair share of affordable housing—the

58. Stonefield (2001, pp. 24, 21).

approach taken by New Jersey and California. And yet the majority of New Jersey's and California's suburban governments have continued to erect road blocks to adequate construction of affordable housing. State mandates can go only so far in persuading local governments to establish a positive context for production of affordable housing. And direct state efforts to intervene in local housing markets by building affordable housing are an unrealizable dream. (Stonefield cites the efforts in the 1960s by New York State's Urban Development Corporation to build affordable housing without local approval in suburban Westchester County. The effort failed in the first instance and helped to ensure the demise of the corporation soon after.) But Stonefield suggests that states could assert power by imposing financial sanctions (that is, loss of certain state program funds) for communities not meeting fair share production goals or offering program incentives for communities that do—an approach in which many states have expressed interest for other aspects of growth management.

Inclusionary zoning provides one kind of remedy for the great need for affordable housing, especially if it is aggressively supported by state and regional agencies. But only a greater top-to-bottom—federal to local—commitment to energizing a battery of affordable housing programs, many already in force, will truly begin to meet needs for decent, safe, and sanitary housing for all Americans.

It is hoped that the increasing number of communities adopting inclusionary zoning programs, added to almost three decades of experience with what works and what does not, will prove more productive in coming years. Past experience can inform future community programs. Three lessons learned are

—The value of packaging inclusionary programs with an array of complementary affordable housing programs to make significant advances toward meeting demands for affordable units;

—The benefits of even partially effective state requirements for local attention to affordable housing needs; and

—The underlying vulnerability of inclusionary programs to economic cycles that cut housing production, thereby reducing creation of affordable units. Public officials should understand that inclusionary zoning provides a unique opportunity to produce affordable units during a robust housing market but cannot stand alone as "the answer" to a community's or the nation's increasing needs for affordable housing.

COMMENT BY
Karen Destorel Brown

Douglas R. Porter's chapter details the many inclusionary programs that exist, mentions many of the major programs in the country, and highlights key research on this topic. The chapter is full of useful and relevant information.

The three major issues I have with it are as follows:

One, the terminology used is confusing because the terms *fair share, inclusionary housing,* and *inclusionary zoning* are used interchangeably, though there are notable differences among them. Comparing these different programs to one another seems to mask the benefits, or in some cases, the disadvantages, of each one. The definitions I prefer come from "The Link between Growth Management and Affordable Housing," by Arthur C. Nelson, Rolf Pendall, Casey Dawkins, and Gerrit Knaap, in this volume. I think they are clear and concise as follows:

—Fair share plans. Plans for meeting each jurisdiction's "fair share" of a region's or state's affordable housing needs.

—Inclusionary housing. Various strategies that link the creation of affordable housing to market-rate units. These include linkage fees, below-market-rate programs, and so on.

—Inclusionary zoning. A form of inclusionary housing that modifies zoning and land use law to tie the creation of affordable housing to the larger developmental process.

Two, I would have liked a lengthier discussion of growth management and its possible links to inclusionary zoning. Providing affordable housing is not always one of growth management's explicit goals, but this chapter could show how these two policies can come together if affordable housing programs are planned more thoughtfully. Porter lists several ways that inclusionary zoning can help to meet smart growth objectives. They include creating needed affordable housing, distributing it throughout the community, using density bonuses to promote more compact development, affording opportunities for in-fill and redevelopment, and spurring collaborative efforts. But he does not present any comprehensive definition of smart growth. It would be helpful to have more background on the goals of smart growth in the chapter.

Finally, and most important, more information on the *potential* of inclusionary zoning programs and how they can be more effective would be valuable. The chapter offers a great deal on the history of these programs, how they are administered, and their different components, but the promise mentioned in the title is not as fully explored.

In the original draft, the author used only two measures to assess inclusionary zoning programs. The first is the number of affordable units created, which is fine. The second measure is the regional integration of minority households. Although the provision of affordable units for low- and moderate-income *minority* households is sometimes an added program benefit, as is the case in Montgomery County, economic integration may be a more useful goal to highlight, besides several others. I think racial integration and moving inner city households to suburban locations are goals better suited to state and regional fair share programs or to broader inclusionary housing programs. Local inclusionary zoning programs are more interested in creating mixed-income communities and ensuring that local residents have the ability to live throughout the jurisdiction. The author's statement that most of the beneficiaries of inclusionary zoning programs have been white suburbanites seems strange. What were their incomes? If there are income requirements (and all inclusionary zoning programs are aimed at people making some percentage below the median income), shouldn't these have been lower-income households, which is the goal of the program? Whether they are white or not is another issue.

In expanding the discussion of goals, I think a look at the goals provided by the Montgomery County Department of Housing and Community Affairs would be helpful. They are as follows:

—To produce moderately priced housing so that county residents and persons working in the county can afford to purchase or rent decent housing;

—To help distribute low- and moderate-income households throughout the growth areas of the county;

—To expand and retain an inventory of low-income housing in the county by permitting the Housing Opportunities Commission (HOC) and recognized nonprofit housing sponsors to purchase affordable units; and

—To provide funds for future affordable housing projects by sharing the windfall appreciation when moderately priced dwelling units (MPDUs) are first sold at the market price after expiration of the resale price controls.

Clearly, not every program has been as successful as Montgomery County's program. But by highlighting this program, the author shows more clearly what could be accomplished if inclusionary zoning programs were thoughtfully designed and implemented. I think one of the major lessons from this chapter could be that inclusionary zoning will be as successful as the framers allow it to be. Those jurisdictions with programs that are carefully crafted will find that this tool can help to meet an area's housing needs. Some programs, however, will only see minor success because they are limited in scope from the beginning. The author should assess mandatory versus voluntary programs, programs that do and do not provide incentives, and so on. Most of the downsides of the program and shortcomings are dependent on these factors.

Suggestions for corrections to these programs are as follows:

—What are some inner city examples of inclusionary zoning? And how do these programs work? This information would be helpful to more urban places, like Washington, D.C., that are trying to implement inclusionary housing requirements.

—In inclusionary zoning programs, developers are compensated by increased density. They are able to build more market-rate units on the same amount of land, thus decreasing the cost of units. So it is not necessarily the higher-cost units that subsidize the lower-cost ones. And it seems unlikely that developers would be able to raise the rent of the market-rate units because they are now on smaller sites.

—According to the "Promise and Practice of Inclusionary Zoning," developers are of mixed opinions on the profitability of MPDUs. At the very least, developers can break even because of the density bonus. At best, the affordable units are a dependable source of money because there is always a market for them, regardless of the current climate in the housing market. Basically, when designed properly, density bonuses keep the developers who include affordable units from reducing their profits.

—In Montgomery County's program rental and for-sale units are price controlled for twenty and ten years, respectively. In Fairfax County, there is a bottom level for the income requirements, which limits the program's ability to reach lower-income households. And the program only applies to those developments that seek a special action—such as a rezoning, special exemption, and so on. This means that developments allowed as of right are not subject to the inclusionary zoning requirements, thus severely limiting the program's reach. At least that was the case as of 2001. There has been a recent change to the program—the ordinance now applies to midrise buildings. As the law is written, developers are to be held "harmless," and the density bonus in these developments is 17 percent in exchange for 6.25 percent affordable dwelling units. Coupled with recent changes made in Montgomery County (lowering the percentage of MPDUs required in central business districts and lowering the threshold from fifty to thirty-five units), the area's programs are taking steps to be more effective. I do not think the chapter stresses this point strongly enough. If designed correctly, these programs can be effective, and over time they can be amended to be more responsive to changing development patterns.

—Porter says that the level of requirement seems to depend on the compensation offered by density bonuses and other incentives. At least for Montgomery County, a more accurate description would be that the percentage of affordable units required depends on the amount of the density bonus a developer can achieve on the site, hence the sliding scale. The more density the developer can achieve, the greater the number of affordable units he or she must provide.

—Fees exacted from developers are usually not enough to build a unit. In Fairfax County, for example, the formula for paying fees only amounts to 25 percent of the actual price of constructing an affordable unit; obviously this is not enough to build a comparable number of units elsewhere.

—The chapter states that on an annual basis, the MPDU program in Montgomery County only accounts for 8 percent of total housing permits. This is not necessarily a shortcoming of the program but rather a reflection of how it was designed. Until recently, the program only applied to developments with fifty or more units, and some developers are allowed to opt out. So it is clear that there will be limits on the overall impact of the program.

The real issue, however, is how many of the county's affordable units are created through this program. In my 2001 study, I found that over the lifetime of the program, affordable units created through inclusionary zoning account for more than 50 percent of newly created affordable units in the county.[59] So compared with other affordable housing tools, at least in Montgomery County, inclusionary zoning has been successful.

—The author states that inclusionary projects may favor moderate-income households and homeownership, but he does not explain why. If the production of affordable units is tied to market-rate development and the market is creating for-sale units, then those are the affordable units that will be created. This is not necessarily a defect of the inclusionary program. Rather, it results from the nature of the market in a particular jurisdiction. Some ordinances (for example, the one in Fairfax County, before the recent amendment) mostly exempted rental developments. In such cases, the program falls short, but that was because of the intent of the framers.

59. Destorel Brown (2001, p. 13).

—The chapter implies that Montgomery County purchases *all* the units it can under the law, and that these units represent all of the rentals created by the program. The Housing Opportunities Commission and nonprofits can purchase both rentals and for-sale units. Additional subsidies are used to make these units affordable as rentals to very low and low-income renters. One-third of the units created have been rentals, but they have not all been purchased by the county.

—Finally, Porter states that inclusionary programs have only created a small number and percentage of needed affordable housing units. But how does that compare with what other programs have produced? I believe inclusionary zoning has created a significant number of affordable units compared with other affordable housing programs.

COMMENT BY
Michael Pyatok

Before commenting on Douglas R. Porter's chapter, I want to explain my rather different perspective on inclusionary zoning. As an architect, I have worked with many nonprofit corporations, some community based and some regional in scale. I have designed about 10,000 affordable units in all. In the process of coauthoring the book, *Good Neighbors: Affordable Family Housing*, I examined hundreds of affordable housing projects across the country that had been developed by nonprofits, for-profit firms, and public housing authorities.[60] I believe there are many strategies for achieving affordable results, and each has its place. My approach aims at strengthening the roles and capabilities of community development organizations as much as possible, especially in low-income neighborhoods. From that perspective, inclusionary zoning is appropriate in some circumstances, but in others it can be quite harmful.

As Porter points out, "inclusionary zoning" arose as a strategy in suburban communities and small towns where there was a long history of de facto segregation by class and race, and where there was a limited, if any, network of nonprofit affordable housing producers, except perhaps for a local housing authority. Encouraging private developers to assume some of these

60. Jones, Pettus, and Pyatok (1998).

responsibilities seemed like a good way to get communities to bear their fair share, since they were the only producers of housing in any significant numbers. Porter also notes that market-rate projects could not always achieve the desired results through internal subsidies but often required some form of public assistance as well.

But when inclusionary policies are applied to older communities, where there is a long tradition of racially and culturally cohesive lower-income neighborhoods with their own community-based development corporations, shifting some of the limited local pool of public subsidies to private developers to achieve inclusionary goals can undermine indigenous efforts. Focusing on private developers to fill this need, even in newer communities where markets are strong, can undermine the potential for community-based, self-help organizations to learn how to solve the same problems in better ways. Inclusionary zoning may set the stage for promoting affordable housing, but who implements it is a critical decision for how well participating families will be served in the long run.

Nonprofit corporations can often accomplish the same goals in a superior fashion for the following reasons:

—The term of affordability is usually much longer since there is no intention to cash out or refinance in the future. Private developers, however, seek to make the term of affordability as short as possible.

—The housing is often "service enriched," providing child care, counseling, and other social services that meet the needs of lower-income households, unlike market-rate housing where everyone is expected to blend into the majority population as though they have no special needs.

—The housing is managed by nonprofit corporations or for-profit corporations with special experience in serving the needs of lower-income households.

—The process for designing the housing is often inclusive and participatory and can be an opportunity for political and community organizing. In contrast, market-rate housing is often undertaken behind closed doors, restricting community input to the minimum public hearings required by EIRs.

—The housing is often designed to express the culture and pride of the peoples it is intended to serve, unlike market-rate housing, which often must project a bland homogeneous image to lure the broadest population.

The following five examples of projects, which I designed for community-based nonprofits, demonstrate solutions that are more sensitive to the needs of lower-income households than what private developers could produce. One is located in southern California, one in the Seattle area, and three in Oakland.

Southern California

In a predominantly white upper-middle-class town in southern California, a Latino neighborhood, with help from an attorney, successfully sued the town for not producing its "fair share" of affordable housing as required by state law, a form of inclusionary housing as noted by Porter. Rather than demand that the municipality force private developers to undertake the task in other neighborhoods, the neighborhood formed its own development corporation to use the newly created funds to revitalize its community.

The Latino community chose this avenue for development because it wanted its constituents to live together in a cohesive community in which they could maintain their cultural traditions; the people wanted the political clout in town gained by remaining geographically cohesive; they wanted to form their own development corporation and develop their own housing so they could build their economic capacity and real estate development savvy; they wanted to sponsor participatory design workshops to incorporate neighborhood input into the project's design. In short, they wanted to determine their destinies.

None of this would have been possible if private developers did it all for them and in the process damaged their community by luring away some of their higher paid lower-income families, the "working poor," into inclusionary housing. In the community's opinion, if that happened, those who chose to leave the neighborhood would be, at best, a 20 percent minority in someone else's culture and economy. In fewer than three years after getting the money from the city and hiring a consultant and me, the community had a rental townhouse development with 88 units, all for large families (three to five bedrooms, which a private developer would never have done), with a child care center and community center. They involved more than eighty people from the neighborhood in participatory workshops to design the project. The project has won four regional and national design awards.

Since then, the community has produced hundreds more affordable units, some for homeownership, a teen recreation center, another child care center, and so on. All of these efforts would have been subverted, and may never have happened, had the "fair share" inclusionary solution relied on private developers using 80-20 models.

Seattle

In Seattle, Washington, four different language groups of Southeast Asian immigrants were organized by a nonprofit corporation to secure affordable housing to meet their needs. They were offered an inclusionary opportunity within a suburban subdivision, but they agreed to the offer on one condition: they would coexist within the predominantly white suburb only if their housing were developed by the nonprofit organization that serves Asian immigrants and not by the private developer of the rest of the subdivision.

They wanted this concession for several reasons. The codes, covenants, and restrictions that accompanied the largely white, middle-class subdivision disallowed many behaviors that typify the cultures of the four language groups. Prohibited were such activities as publicly exposed laundry drying in the sun, hanging foodstuffs from porches to dry in the sun, unkempt community vegetable gardens in public view, and the combining of houses to accommodate large, family clans. They also wanted the architectural character of their development to reflect their cultural tradition, not like the typical suburban subdivision that surrounded them. Finally, they wanted the nonprofit corporation serving the Asian community to gain more expertise in developing this type of housing.

The Asian nonprofit chose to associate with a church-based nonprofit housing developer operating in the suburban community. They worked within their separate language groups to develop ideas for what they wanted in several participatory design workshops. They now have a fifty-one-unit rental development for large, low-income families, including a 6,000-square-foot vegetable garden, community center, front and back porches designed to allow for hanging clothes and food, and a pig-roasting area. The housing is designed so that these activities do not face the surrounding white suburban condo owners. The surrounding community exerted control only over the colors of the buildings, limiting their palette to a bland combination of beiges. And the larger subdivision's homeowners' association, which diligently monitors the design of all additions to their community, disallowed ethnically inspired mural panels that were to be integrated into the architecture. The projects have won three regional and national design awards.

Oakland

In Oakland, California, a national, for-profit development corporation currently wants to build 800 units of housing in a downtown neighborhood. It has voluntarily offered to include 20 percent as "affordable" to households between 60 and 100 percent of the average median income. Mayor Jerry Brown, who believes that Oakland has too much affordable housing, has actively discouraged the corporation from including any affordable units. But the developer recognizes that it not only makes political sense to help win over local advocates, it also makes economic sense for two reasons. First, since this area of downtown Oakland shows the signs of long-term disinvestment, well-designed subsidized housing in the project will quickly attract "colonizers" from among the "working poor," activating what is perceived as an abandoned area of town and gracing it with handsome architecture. An all-market-rate housing development of 800 units, however, would pose too high a risk, filling up too slowly, given the surrounding conditions. Second, by voluntarily including affordable housing, the corporation was hoping to have a better chance of seeking subsidies not just for the affordable component but for all of the infrastructure costs associated with the entire development. It is seeking $64 million in local public assistance. Yet it is including only 160 affordable units, none of which serves very low-income households, and no special services for lower-income households are contemplated.

The local coalition of affordable housing activists is demanding even more units at more affordable rates and with less dependence on public subsidy. This activism stems from a long tradition of Oakland's community-based nonprofits successfully completing thousands of affordable units in Oakland. They see this form of inclusionary housing executed by a private developer as an incomplete solution if it is produced without services, and a drain on the local subsidies, which fuel their efforts in revitalizing lower-income neighborhoods outside of the downtown area. The following three case studies exemplify past successes.

A nonprofit corporation, primarily serving the Asian community in Oakland's downtown, recognized that many new Southeast Asian refugees were settling in East Oakland, where the African American and Hispanic American communities had settled in during the past five decades. To achieve harmony among the racial groups, the Asian-serving nonprofit elected to joint venture with a neighborhood-based nonprofit that had primarily been serving the African American and Hispanic American households in that neighborhood. Together they sponsored participatory design workshops to include local participation in the project's planning and design. The site was an abandoned supermarket, in an area long ignored by the private market.

The resulting project includes 92 affordable units with a child care center, a community center, and 12,000 square feet for local, small, incubating retail businesses. The latter ingredient was included as an economic development strategy, helping to spawn local small businesses that could also serve the community. The clients and design team applied for and won $50,000 from the National Endowment for the Arts to hire local artists from each of the racial groups living in the community. They embellished the development in a way that represented their histories and traditions. The project has won six regional and national design awards.

This project required ten different funding sources, an important one being the city of Oakland. Had there been in place at the time an "inclusionary zoning" requirement placed on private developers, this nonprofit joint venture partnership would have been forced to compete with private developers for these local funds. Such developers typically contribute to local city council and mayoral campaigns. Had a for-profit developer been awarded the city funds to make just 20 percent of a market-rate project affordable, the income levels served would have been higher. The housing would not have been built in a low-income neighborhood, filling a vacant lot. There would have been no social services or child care; there would have been no economic development component. There would have been no expression of a neighborhood's cultural diversity and local self-help pride.

A Hispanic American neighborhood in East Oakland, surrounded by freeways, railroads and industrial uses, was about to receive in their neighborhood a storage yard for semitrailer trucks on a five-acre parcel. The neighborhood wanted to stop the trucking company because of the danger and pollution it would bring to their streets with no gain in local jobs. They came to me to seek advice about how to change the zoning to disallow this use, replacing it with one that would allow affordable homes for first-time buyers like themselves, whose incomes were around 60 percent of the AMI. They succeeded in changing the zoning to industrial or housing. They made it very clear they would continue to protest the arrival of the trucking company; at the same time they solicited a nonprofit housing developer to purchase the land for housing.

They designed a fifty-three-unit, first-time homeowner project in a series of design workshops that utilized several funding sources, including a large contribution from the city's housing fund. In fewer than three years from the time they changed the zoning, the project was completed and occupied. The homes are expandable to permit the growth of families so they would not have to leave the neighborhood as their families and incomes grow. Some homes have the potential for accessory units for grandparents or in-laws. Some have the option to allow home-based businesses, which could be classified as light industrial because of the flexible zoning. The density of the development is three times that prevalent in the neighborhood, but the local residents who participated in the design workshops devised a site plan and dwelling types that shaped the open space to be useful for children. It also cleverly disguised the density so the development would fit into its early twentieth-century neighborhood. The project has won four regional and national design awards. Had this organization been required to compete with well-connected developers for the limited local housing funds, it may not have been able to achieve such success.

The homeless in downtown Oakland were angry that so many new office buildings were being built in an area where there had once been housing. Organized by a Unitarian church and a community organizer paid by the American Friends Service Committee, the homeless staged a series of well-publicized sit-ins in vacant buildings downtown. After about six months of embarrassing publicity, the city council gave the organization $1 million to purchase a parcel four blocks from City Hall to build affordable housing for the formerly homeless.

After several participatory design workshops, the coalition had designed twenty-six units for families and singles around a central courtyard with a child care center on a site that was only slightly larger than one-third of an acre. Within two and one-half years of the sit-in protests, the coalition celebrated the opening of this housing. With money from an arts foundation, the project was decorated with tiles designed by an African American artist who was inspired by the colors and patterns of West African houses. It included icons of frogs, which in some West African communities are considered signs of hope, since good rains bring many frogs, which in turn announce an upcoming season of lush crops. The building is also graced with three "spirit houses" to provide homes for the earth spirits whom the Buddhist community believes live on a property before a building is built. Spirit houses ensure that a new edifice will not displace such spirits. In light of their recent plight, members of the homeless coalition deemed this an appropriate addition to their new home. No private developer using inclusionary housing monies would have addressed the needs of the homeless, and certainly not in a way that would include their involvement in design, development, and execution.

Conclusion

Oakland is one example of many cities with very proud and capable minority- and lower-income neighborhoods. Up to now, the available subsidies have spawned a network of nonprofits, both neighborhood based and city-wide. They are not all perfect, but they have been responsible for nearly all of the affordable housing and other neighborhood-related projects produced in Oakland in the past twenty-five years, many receiving national attention for the quality of their programs and designs. This local self-determination is undermined when the limited supply of subsidies is funneled into the hands of for-profit developers.

Except for a few, private housing developers use the quantity of units produced and the bottom line as a measure of annual success, while the non-profits work to rebuild people and their communities. The for-profit development community in Oakland consistently fought to undermine these grass-roots efforts. They resisted public pressure to produce housing in the downtown when office buildings were all the rage. They fought against the introduction of rent control even when new construction was exempt, and they fought against protections against unjust evictions. They are now working with the mayor to buy out and shut down the few remaining single-room occupancy hotels in the downtown. Their version of inclusionary housing does not serve very low-income households and does not include the special services that low- and even moderate-income families need, such as child care, family counseling, and English-as-a-second-language classes. Finally, inclusionary housing by definition does not celebrate the special cultural origins of the minorities it is obligated to incorporate but seeks to achieve a blended homogeneity with the majority.

For all these reasons, this financial fuel for self-determination and capacity building in the nonprofit sector, whether from local or state sources, should not be siphoned off to assist the for-profit sector. If there is to be inclusionary zoning, private developers should pay for such housing primarily from their own profits or pay in-lieu fees to local affordable housing trust funds and at sufficient levels to accomplish the task. Such funding pools are an important assistance to the local nonprofit sector, which is far more capable of meeting the needs of lower incomes in a comprehensive way.

Inclusionary zoning policies, whether local or statewide, can be helpful, but they merely set the stage. Much more effort should be invested in increasing the overall government subsidy pool so that all developers, private and nonprofit, can meet the need, not just for housing but for the full array of social and educational services that lower-income families need to improve their lives.

References

Anderson, Mary. 2003. *Opening the Door to Inclusionary Housing.* Chicago: Business and Professional People for the Public Interest.

Bipartisan Millennial Housing Commission. 2002. *Meeting Our Nation's Housing Challenges.* Government Printing Office.

Brower, David J. 1979. "Courts Move toward Redefinition of General Welfare." *Land Use Law and Zoning Digest* 31. Chicago: American Planning Association.

Brown, Karen Destorel. 2001. *Expanding Affordable Housing through Inclusionary Zoning.* Brookings Center on Urban and Metropolitan Housing.

California Department of Housing and Urban Development. 1993. *Comprehensive Housing Affordability Strategy.* Sacramento.

———. 1996. *Status of Housing Elements in California: 1995 Report to the Legislature.* Sacramento.

Center for Continuing Study of the California Economy. 1993. *California Economic Growth.* Palo Alto.

Calavita, Nico, and Kenneth Grimes. 1998. "Inclusionary Housing in California: The Experience of Two Decades." *Journal of the American Planning Association* 64 (2): 150–69.

Calavita, Nico, Kenneth Grimes, and Alan Mallach. 1997. "Inclusionary Housing in California and New Jersey. A Comparative Analysis." *Housing Policy Debate* 8 (1): 109–42.

Davidoff, Paul, and Linda Davidoff. 1971. "Opening the Suburbs: Toward Inclusionary Controls." *Syracuse Law Review* 22: 509.

Daye, Charles E. 2000. "Whither 'Fair' Housing: Meditations on Wrong Paradigms, Ambivalent Answers, and a Legislative Proposal." *Washington University Journal of Law and Policy* 3: 243.

Dietderich, Andrew G. 1996. "An Egalitarian's Market: The Economics of Inclusionary Zoning Reclaimed." *Fordham Urban Law Journal* 23: 24–104.

Downs, Anthony. 1973. *Opening Up the Suburbs.* Yale University Press.

Ellickson, Robert C. 1981. "The Irony of 'Inclusionary Zoning.'" *Southern California Law Review* 54: 1167.

Fischel, William A. 1990. Testimony before the Subcommittee on Policy Research and Insurance of the House Committee on Banking, Finance, and Urban Affairs (cited in Smith, Delaney, and Liou [1996, n. 3]).

Franklin, Herbert M., David Falk, and Arthur J. Levin. 1974. *Inzoning: A Guide for Policy-Makers on Inclusionary Land Use Programs.* Washington: Potomac Institute.

Gruen, Aron. 2001. Presentation at the Urban Land Institute national conference, Boston (October).

Harvard Law Review Association. 1995. "State-Sponsored Growth Management as a Remedy for Exclusionary Zoning." *Harvard Law Review* 1:1136.

Herr, Philip B., and Associates, 2000. *Zoning for Housing Affordability, A Study Prepared for the Massachusetts Housing Partnership Fund.* Newton, Mass.: Philip B. Herr and Associates.

Higgins, Bill, ed. 2003. *The California Inclusionary Housing Reader.* Sacramento: Institute for Local Self-Government.

Jones, Tom, William Pettus, and Michael Pyatok. 1998. *Good Neighbors: Affordable Family Housing.* McGraw-Hill.

Kautz, Barbara Ehrlich. 2002. *University of San Francisco Law Review* 36: 971.

Kayden, Jerold S. 2002. "Inclusionary Zoning and the Constitution." *NHC Affordable Housing Policy Review* 2 (January): 10–13.

Kleit, Rachel Garshick. 1998. "Housing Mobility and Healthy Communities: Montgomery County, Maryland's Moderately Priced Dwelling Unit Program." Paper presented at the 1998 Tri-County Conference on Housing and Urban Issues. Washington: Fannie Mae Foundation.

Krefetz, Sharon Perlman. 2001. "The Impact and Evolution of the Massachusetts Comprehensive Permit and Zoning Appeals Act: Thirty Years of Experience with a State Legislative Effort to Overcome Exclusionary Zoning." *Western New England Law Review* 23: 61–110.

Lamar, Martha, Alan Mallach, and John Payne. 1998. "Mount Laurel at Work: Affordable Housing in New Jersey, 1983–88." *Rutgers Law Review* 41(4): 1199–277.

Larsen, Eric. 2003. Author's interview, February 13.

Lauber, Daniel 1973. *Recent Cases in Exclusionary Zoning.* ASPO Planning Advisory Service Report 2929. Chicago: American Society of Planning Officials.

McGee, Henry W., Jr. 2000. "Equity and Efficacy in Washington State's GMA Affordable Housing Goal." *Washington University Journal of Law and Policy* 3: 546.

Meck, Stuart, Rebecca Retzlaff, and James Schwab. 2003. *Regional Approaches to Affordable Housing.* Chicago: American Planning Association.

Merriam, Dwight, David J. Brower, and Philip D. Tegeler, eds. 1985. *Inclusionary Zoning Moves Downtown.* Chicago: American Planning Association.

Metropolitan Mayors Caucus. 2002. "Northeastern Illinois Housing Endorsement Criteria." Chicago: Metropolitan Planning Council.

Metropolitan Service District (Portland Metro). 1991. *Housing Issues Report.* Prepared by the Planning and Development Department. The Rule is incorporated in Chapter 660, Division 7, of the Oregon Administrative Rules.

Montgomery County Department of Housing and Community Development. 2000. "The Moderately Priced Dwelling Unit Program: Profile of MPDU Purchasers, 1997–1999."

Nonprofit Housing Association of Northern California and California Coalition for Rural Housing. 2003. *Inclusionary Housing in California: Thirty Years of Innovation.* Sacramento and San Francisco.

1,000 Friends of Oregon and the Home Builders Association of Metropolitan Portland. 1991. *Managing Growth to Promote Affordable Housing: Revisiting Oregon's Goal 10* (Executive Summary). Portland.

Oregon Land Conservation and Development Commission. Undated. *Statewide Planning Goals and Guidelines.*

Porter, Douglas, and others. 1996. *Profiles in Growth Management.* Washington: Urban Land Institute.

President's Commission on Urban Housing. 1969. *A Decent Home.* Government Printing Office.

Report of the National Advisory Commission on Civil Disorders. 1968. Government Printing Office.

Roisman, Florence Wagman. 2001. "Opening the Suburbs to Racial Integration: Lessons for the 21st Century." *Western New England Law Review* 23: 173–222.

Ross, Jaimie. 2003. (Director of Affordable Housing for 1,000 Friends of Florida). Interviews by author February 25 and March 13.

Scott, Randall. 1975. "Exclusion and Land Use: A Comment and a Research Bibliography." *Management and Control of Growth* 1: 47. Washington: Urban Land Institute.

Shigley, Paul. 2002. "Lawmaker Vows to Reform Housing Element Law." *California Planning and Development Report* (November): 1. Ventura.

Smith, Marc T., Charles J. Delaney, and Thomas Liou. 1996. "Inclusionary Housing Programs: Issues and Outcomes." *Real Estate Law Journal* 25 (2): 155.

Solinski, Julie M.1998. "Affordable Housing Law in New York, New Jersey and Connecticut." *Pace Law Review* (Fall 1996–Spring 1997).

Steinberg, Marcia K. 1989. *Adaptations to an Activist Court Ruling: Aftermath of the Mount Laurel II Decision for Lower-Income Housing.* Cambridge, Mass.: Lincoln Institute of Land Policy.

Stonefield, Sam. 2001. "Affordable Housing in Suburbia: The Importance but Limited Power and Effectiveness of the State Override Tool." *Western New England Law Review* 23: 3–34.

Tondro, Terry J. 2001. "Connecticut's Affordable Housing Appeals Statute: After Ten Years of Hope, Why Only Middling Results?" *Western New England Law Review* 23: 223–72

Westchester County Housing Opportunity Commission. 1997. *Housing Opportunities for West Chester, A Guide to Affordable Housing Development.* White Plains, N.Y. (Cited in Solinski [1998]).

Williams, Norman, Jr., Tatyana Dought, and R. William Potter. 1972. "The Strategy on Exclusionary Zoning: Towards What Rationale and What Remedy?" *Land Use Controls Annual 1972.* American Society of Planning Officials. (Abstracted in "Exclusionary Zoning Strategies: Effective Lawsuit Goals and Criteria." *Management and Control of Growth 1.* Washington: Urban Land Institute: 477–91.)

Wish, Naomi Bailin, and Stephen Eisdorfer. 1996. *The Impact of the Mt. Laurel Initiatives: An Analysis of the Characteristics of Applicants and Occupants.* Seton Hall University Center for Public Service.

7

ANTHONY DOWNS

Growth Management, Smart Growth, and Affordable Housing

T HE OBJECTIVE OF this chapter is to create a politically realistic overall perspective on the relationships among smart growth, growth
management, and affordable housing. It also advocates greater emphasis
on affordable housing in future growth management and smart growth
efforts.

Key Definitions

The terms *growth management, smart growth,* and *affordable housing* have
no standard, universally accepted definitions. As currently used, they
denote many different sets of policies espoused by diverse groups under
varying circumstances. Nevertheless, I propose specific definitions for them
in this chapter. Growth management means specific regulatory policies
aimed at influencing future growth so that it occurs in a more rational
manner than would occur without any overall planning. Growth management strategies are usually applied mainly in individual localities, since
there are few regional bodies with any powers over land uses. However,
several states have also adopted general growth management strategies; they
include Oregon, Florida, Washington, and New Jersey. Growth manage-

ment policies affect density, availability of land, mixtures of uses, and timing of development. Growth management seeks to accommodate growth sensibly, not to limit or prevent it.

Growth control means regulatory practices aimed at deliberately slowing or halting growth in a locality or region. This strategy encompasses building moratoriums, building permit caps, population growth caps, and severe down-zoning of densities that prevents significant additional growth. It is much more restrictive in intent than growth management. But like growth management, growth control strategies are usually applied in individual localities because of the absence of regional bodies with powers over land use.

Smart growth refers to an overall set of broad goals and policies designed to counteract sprawl. These usually include limiting outward expansion, encouraging higher-density development, encouraging mixed-use zoning as distinct from fully segregating land uses, reducing travel by private vehicles, revitalizing older areas, and preserving open space. Promoting more affordable housing can be a goal of smart growth programs, but usually it is not.

Since sprawl is a regional phenomenon, many smart growth goals cannot succeed without regionwide application. For example, limiting outward growth requires both regional growth boundaries and prohibitions against any urban development beyond those boundaries. Only state governments can do that. So smart growth must be applied simultaneously at different government levels by different authorities.

As a result, the smart growth elements *least likely* to be adopted are those needing large public subsidies, such as revitalizing old areas, or regional action, such as building major public transit systems. Smart growth tactics most likely to be adopted are ones that can be done locally and cheaply with wide popular support, such as preserving open space and limiting outward growth in certain localities.

Adoption of a consistent set of policies likely to achieve many smart growth goals is rare because few acceptable mechanisms exist for coordinating all these actions regionally. Thus smart growth as a coherent strategy is much more often talked about than achieved.

Defining Affordable Housing

There are different types of affordable housing, depending on to whom the housing is affordable, but they are not often clearly distinguished from one another. This analysis tries to differentiate between type one and type two versions of affordability.

The Department of Housing and Urban Development defines housing as "affordable" to any household if that household can pay for occupying a unit of "decent quality" (as determined by middle-class standards) without spending more than a certain fraction of its income for housing, usually 30 percent. Presumably, therefore, most households spending more than 30 percent of their incomes for housing are suffering from affordability problems. True, some may be doing so voluntarily to obtain higher-quality amenities. But most households spending more than this share are doing so by necessity. By this definition, a lot of households have affordability problems. In 2001, one-third of all U.S. households, including one-half of all renter households, paid 30 percent or more of their incomes for housing. One-sixth of all households, including one-fourth of all renters, paid 50 percent or more. Hence they all could be considered in need of affordable housing.

However, the people with the greatest housing needs are very low-income households who cannot afford to pay for decent-quality units. Most of these households are renters, but U.S. government housing policies are mainly designed to encourage ownership. So there is very little housing, especially newly built housing, affordable to the poor, who need housing assistance most. I define housing affordable to the poor as "type one affordable housing."

The basic problem for such poor households is an affordability gap between 30 percent of their incomes and the minimum cost of occupying a decent-quality home as defined by middle-class standards. In 2000, among households with incomes below the poverty level, 85 percent, or 11.7 million, paid 30 percent or more for housing, and two-thirds paid 50 percent or more.[1]

However, most housing being built today called affordable by smart growth and other planners is too costly for low-income households. But such housing is affordable to many working-class or moderate-income households—those with incomes from 50 to 80 percent of their area's median income. This category of housing will be referred to as "type two affordable housing." An affordability gap still exists for many such households, but it is smaller than that experienced by the poor and therefore can be bridged in various ways that do not require large public subsidies per unit. Many federal,

1. U.S. Census Bureau, "American Housing Survey for the United States: 2001," table 2-13 (www.census.gov/hhes/www/housing/ahs/ahs01/ahs01.html).

state, or local housing assistance programs define households in this group as qualifying for affordable housing units. Using 2001 national income data, that group included 16.8 million households with annual incomes of $20,000 to $32,000; they composed 15.8 percent of all households. Almost all had incomes above the poverty level, which for a four-person household in 2001 was $18,000. If they devoted 30 percent of their incomes to housing, they could afford to spend from $500 to $800 a month without exceeding the limits of affordability. One-fourth of all U.S. households were spending within that range on housing in 2001. Thus a large number of households are eligible to occupy type two affordable housing units defined in this manner, even though many are not spending more than 30 percent of their incomes on housing.

How to Close Affordability Gaps

There are only two basic strategies to make housing affordable for those who suffer from affordability problems. One is *raising their incomes*, directly as with the Earned Income Tax Credit, or indirectly through housing subsidies like Section 8. To do this for all very low-income households would be very costly, so American society does not aim at that broad goal.

The second strategy is reducing the cost of housing to the occupants. There are four tactics for doing this. One is making the financing of housing more available or cheaper. That is done through lower-down-payment mortgages, easier credit, and low interest rates. But these arrangements do not help low-income renters, who need help most. A second tactic is reducing the costs of producing housing units meeting middle-class quality standards. That involves modifying building codes, speeding up the development process, and raising residential densities.

The third tactic for lowering housing costs is reducing the size and quality standards required for new housing. This can be done by using manufactured housing, allowing creation of accessory apartments, constructing small "cottage" housing units like many homes built after World War II, and building more multifamily units. These arrangements can be carried out with mainly private financing. Yet most suburbs have made manufactured housing, accessory apartments, and smaller homes illegal. They have also blocked more multifamily units by limiting land zoned for them. Ironically, these forbidden tactics are all consistent with smart growth goals.

Political Obstacles

Almost all the households who have affordability problems live in older existing units, not brand new ones. Without major public subsidies, few such
households will ever be able to afford to occupy brand new units. So why not
make existing housing units more affordable? That is the fourth tactic for
reducing the cost of housing for low- and moderate-income households. It
could be done by expanding the total supply of housing through new construction much faster than growth in the number of households. Even if
most of the newly built units were expensive, the overall rise in supply relative to demand would cause housing prices in general to decline, including
prices of the older existing units used by low-income households.

However, in reality, making existing housing more affordable has almost no
political support in America. In fact, just the opposite is the case. Almost all
groups interested in existing housing want its market values to rise, not fall.

Existing housing could be made more affordable by reducing its price across
the board in relation to incomes. But all the institutions related to housing—
builders, mortgage lenders, Fannie Mae and Freddie Mac, bondholders, realtors, insurers, and all homeowners—have invested trillions in existing housing,
so they want their assets to rise in value. That goal is certainly understandable,
and there is nothing wrong with it. But it has an unfortunate impact on prevailing attitudes toward creating new low-cost housing. In the suburbs, local
governments are politically dominated by homeowners, who constitute a
majority of residents and are the most vocal citizens. For most homeowners,
their major assets are their homes. So they have strong incentives to want the
market values of homes to rise. Hence they oppose any policies they believe
might reduce home values.[2] They think letting more affordable units into their
communities would do that, and it might also lower the quality of local schools
and raise property taxes. So very few suburban homeowners want to permit
new low-cost housing near them or to accept low-income neighbors.

As a result, a key goal of most suburban governments is to prevent actions
that might reduce home values. They pass laws that require high standards of
quality for new units, limit multifamily housing, prohibit manufactured
housing, and so on. As long as full power over what housing can be built in
a community resides with its local government, not much additional affordable housing will be created in the suburbs. Yet that is where most growth of

2. See Fischel (2002) for a full development of this argument.

jobs and population is occurring. So that is where society most needs additional affordable units.

For the same reasons, most suburban homeowners want to keep their property taxes from rising. So they pressure their governments to block local development of added land uses that require public services more costly than the property taxes those uses pay. Such uses include most multifamily housing (except that restricted to senior citizens) and most single-family housing (except the very costliest). In contrast, local governments encourage development of land uses that pay more in taxes than they cost in local public services, such as shopping centers, office buildings, and industrial parks. This widespread strategy of local fiscal zoning in effect discourages creation of suburban housing that most low-wage workers can afford—even though every suburb needs such workers to operate its economy. Moreover, fiscal zoning is strongly biased against families with children, since they add to local school costs.

Consequently, making new or existing housing more affordable to those who need help most is a cause without powerful supporters in our society. Only a few housing-oriented trade associations and nonprofits, academics, and homebuilders who use low-income tax credits, care about this cause. True, broader homeownership has many promoters who would gain financially. But that does not help those most in need of more affordable housing.

Breaking this impasse will require shifting some of the decisionmaking power over where housing is built to other levels besides suburban local governments. Alternative stakeholders include developers, state governments, regional agencies, and possible public-private partnerships created to develop more widespread affordable housing. But well-entrenched resistance to reducing local autonomy over housing is intense. Why? Because it involves the social issues of who is going to live near me and who is going to attend school with my children. Most people accept regional approaches to infrastructures, such as sewage and transportation systems. But they reject regionalism on social decisions, such as those that pertain to schools and who lives where. Almost all attempts to create suburban affordable housing have been thwarted by such local NIMBYism (not in my backyard).

Even in the one state that has adopted a statewide affordable housing policy—New Jersey—resistance to locating affordable housing in suburbs has been fierce. And when such units were built there, occupants have usually been white households already residing in the suburbs. This is also true in

Massachusetts, which has passed laws helping developers build affordable units in the suburbs. So there has been very little movement of any households out of central city poverty areas into suburban affordable housing—one of the basic purposes of locating affordable housing in the suburbs.

Smart Growth Advocates and Affordable Housing

Many proponents of smart growth have not emphasized creating affordable housing because doing so would arouse strong opposition from suburban residents. Getting smart growth accepted by itself is hard enough. Why take on the even more controversial burden of promoting affordable housing too? Yet without affordable housing, the other main smart growth policies restrict the supply of land usable for development. That normally places upward pressure on prices of both new and existing units, making housing less affordable than it would otherwise be. If land-restricting policies are adopted only locally, housing prices are very likely to rise. Only if such policies are adopted regionally, along with other policies that raise densities, can smart growth avoid making housing less affordable. True, New Jersey's approach has caused construction or rehabilitation of quite a few low-cost housing units in older cities. Those units were paid for by suburbs "buying out" of their requirement to create affordable housing within their own boundaries. That is a definite benefit to central city households needing better quality housing. But in most regions, smart growth advocates do not strongly promote affordable housing in localities in which they want to pass land-limiting policies. Thus they are often making housing less affordable to those who need it most.

If smart growth advocates are to avoid this unjust and undesirable outcome, they must make strong efforts to promote building of affordable housing in localities and regions where they are promoting smart growth. Their reason for assuming this extra political burden is that doing so is necessary to make smart growth socially just and responsible. Policies that leave out, or harm, the interests of low-income households cannot be truly smart and just.

The Importance of Leadership

A crucial ingredient in getting more affordable housing built is responsible leadership from state governments, especially governors. Only states have the legal power to modify the current autonomy of local governments over where, and what kind, of housing can be built. The few state governments that have supported workable affordable housing policies have done so mainly in response to crises. In New Jersey, the crisis was imposed by state courts that began to take zoning powers away from local governments unless those governments provided for low-cost housing. This threat prompted action by the state legislature.

In the few other states that have started to promote more affordable housing, the crisis has been acute shortages of affordable housing also affecting middle-income households with greater political influence than the poor. This is most evident in California. Before the high-tech bubble burst there, housing prices were so high that many teachers, police, firefighters, and other city workers could not live near where they worked. That hurt employers trying to hire people from other regions and citizens trying to operate schools and governments. So California required every locality to adopt an affordable housing target. But the state did not provide funding or any means of enforcing those targets.

The Expanding Role of Slums

Consequently, thousands of poor immigrants entering California are forced to double and triple up in overcrowded, often deteriorated, units. Insofar as such slums are temporary way stations while these newcomers get established, this strategy can be perhaps be defended as the only feasible way to shelter very poor immigrants. In fact, it is the same strategy America has always used to house such people since colonial days.

But people forced to live in substandard, overcrowded units now include many households other than poor immigrants in temporary quarters. We are generating a whole new set of slums as de facto affordable housing for the poor and many working-class households. Since the housing is mainly in older urban areas out of sight of the middle-class majority, it is politically acceptable. Other cost-lowering tactics are seen as too costly or too upsetting to nearby middle-class households.

Further Causes of the Reluctance to Promote Affordable Housing

Achieving more affordable housing or smart growth requires strong support from state governments, which would permit regionwide implementation of policies now blocked by local governments. Advocates of both affordable housing and smart growth need to persuade state governments to support regional approaches. Such persuasion will be successful only if state leaders believe crisis conditions now exist.

However, most smart growth advocates, in my view, have until now not put much stress on improving housing affordability, for reasons I have stated. They have focused on reducing traffic congestion, loss of open space, school overcrowding, higher taxes, and slowing the spatial expansion of settlements into green fields. Some of these targets are in part inescapable results of rapid population growth.

But no region can control its own population growth. That is determined by the region's basic traits, such as location in the nation, climate, economic strength, demography, past investments, and topography. Insofar as the undesirable conditions associated with sprawl are caused by growth, they cannot be eliminated through regional or any policies. Thus, even if widely implemented, smart growth probably could not fully overcome the conditions it was created to change. Some sprawl will be with us for a long time.

Moreover, implementing smart growth would have two impacts that tend to raise strong citizen opposition, as noted earlier. Many smart growth ideas will not really work unless they are carried out regionally. So some authority must be shifted to a regional focus, which local governments oppose. Second, raising densities generally means raising them in many suburban neighborhoods too. But almost all suburbanites oppose higher densities in their own areas. Local NIMBYism limits smart growth's acceptability.

Implementing smart growth ideas without creating type one affordable housing is also likely to raise housing prices for the poor, even if some type two affordable housing is built for a few working-class and moderate-income households. Since most residents of growth areas do not want poor people living near them, they fight against type one affordable housing measures. Many such measures require sizable public funding, so they are kept small in scale.

As a result, the main tactics advocated by smart growth proponents that have attained widespread public support are those that can be done locally without much new public spending, tax increases, or social engineering. Those are local growth boundaries or other limits to developable land, mixed-use zoning, and permitting very limited higher densities for a few housing units. These tactics do not make much housing more affordable and may make a lot of it less affordable.

Conclusion

Smart growth goals would be furthered by much more widespread creation of affordable housing of both types because that would lead to higher densities, since the most affordable housing consists of multifamily or attached units; reduce traffic congestion, since low-wage workers would have to travel less to reach their jobs; promote more mixed-use development, since multifamily units can more easily be colocated with retail uses; and require a shift of some land-use regulation away from local governments, which is vital to effective smart growth. From this viewpoint, smart growth proponents ought to strongly promote affordable housing in the suburbs.

But trying to create more affordable housing in the suburbs where we need it most is vehemently opposed by a big majority of suburban residents and governments. So making widespread creation of more affordable housing a key goal of smart growth proponents might reduce their chance of getting any of their goals put into practice.

Yet several of smart growth's major goals cannot be attained without region-wide implementation or increased public spending or both. But these two actions are also unpopular. Consequently, in most U.S. regions, attempts to carry out smart growth have ended up with only local growth management policies. Those policies cannot stop sprawl and often reduce housing affordability.

Continuing the status quo is not likely to achieve smart growth or more affordable suburban housing in most metropolitan areas. What is needed is greater receptivity to regionwide tactics. That must be grounded in widespread citizen dissatisfaction with existing sprawl development and existing shortages of local housing affordable to those workers who are necessary to run suburbs efficiently. The best way to create such dissatisfaction is for advocates of both smart growth and affordable housing in the suburbs to work together to promote regional tactics aimed at their combined goals. Such coalitions could include churches and nonprofits interested in social justice, businesses seeking housing for their workers, and developers who want to build low-cost housing. All these groups could then realize they were working for socially just outcomes for all income groups.

There is no guarantee that such combined forces will prevail soon, if at all. But chances of attaining effective smart growth or more affordable housing without such coalitions are slim to none. Instead regions will wind up with more purely local growth management that pushes growth out farther, thus worsening sprawl and raising housing prices more than ever.

In truth, smart growth cannot be really socially just and responsible unless it includes a significant element of affordable housing. That would make it truly smart.

Reference

Fischel, William. 2002. *The Homevoter Hypothesis*. Harvard University Press.

Contributors

Karen Destorel Brown
Brookings Institution

Robert W. Burchell
Rutgers University

Daniel Carlson
University of Washington

David Crawford
Econsult Corporation

Casey J. Dawkins
Georgia Institute of Technology

Anthony Downs
Brookings Institution

Ingrid Gould Ellen
New York University

William A. Fischel
Dartmouth College

George C. Galster
Wayne State University

Jill Khadduri
Abt Associates

Gerrit J. Knaap
University of Maryland

Robert Lang
*Virginia Polytechnic Institute
and State University*

Shashir Mathur
University of Washington

Sahan Mukherji
Rutgers University

Arthur C. Nelson
*Virginia Polytechnic Institute
and State University*

Rolf Pendall
Cornell University

Douglas Porter
Growth Management Institute

Michael Pyatok
University of Washington

Michael H. Schill
New York University

Samuel R. Staley
Reason Public Policy Institute

Richard P. Voith
Econsult Corporation

Index

Abt Associates, 207

Accessory dwelling units (ADUs): advantages of, 31; for elderly residents, 56; in King County (Wash.), 36; opposition to, 31, 168–69; policies permitting, 30, 36, 86; proponents of, 31; restrictions on, 51, 150

Adequate public facilities ordinances (APFOs), 131, 155

Aduddell, R. M., 186–87

ADUs. *See* Accessory dwelling units

Affordability indicators, 27–29; affordability gap, 27, 266; in Fairfax County (Va.), 54–56, 62; house-value-to-income ratio, 27–28, 68; Housing Opportunity Index, 120; income thresholds, 72; in King County (Wash.), 33–36; median housing prices, 90; in Montgomery County (Md.), 39–41; in New Jersey, 46–50; proportion of income spent on housing, 2, 27, 28–29, 68, 106–08, 110, 120, 266; rent-to-income ratio, 27–28, 68; shelter poverty measure, 120; value of, 63; weaknesses, 68

Affordable Dwelling Unit Program (Fairfax County, Va.), 54, 56

Affordable housing: as a concern of growth management advocates, 68; definitions, 3, 24, 90–91, 106–10, 114–15, 119–21, 177, 265–67; design processes, 254; deteriorated housing, 108, 109, 271; duration of affordability, 30, 42, 51, 56–58, 65, 230–31; economic development integrated with, 257–59; effects of transportation costs, 63–64; existing units, 76–77, 268; history, 76; lack of attention by growth management and smart growth advocates, 1–2, 86–87, 204, 212, 270, 272; location, 180–81, 215; for low-income households, 72, 186–89; for moderate-income households, 72; need for, 77, 108–10, 115, 266;